Web Publishing with Adobe™ Acrobat™ and PDF

Bruce Page

Diana Holm

WILEY COMPUTER PUBLISHING

John Wiley & Sons, Inc.

New York • Chichester • Brisbane • Toronto • Singapore

To my family, and to Sanford and Bruce for making this possible.

D. H.

For my father, Chauncey Owen Page, who is a constant inspiration, and also for my late mother, Mary Cooper Page, whose sagacity and wit I'll remember always.

B. P.

Publisher: Katherine Schowalter
Editor: Philip Sutherland
Managing Editor: Angela Murphy
Electronic Products, Associate Editor: Mike Green
Text Design & Composition: Benchmark Productions, Inc.

Designations used by companies to distinguish their products are often claimed as trademarks. In all instances where John Wiley & Sons, Inc. is aware of a claim, the product names appear in initial capital or all capital letters. Readers, however, should contact the appropriate companies for more complete information regarding trademarks and registration.

Adobe, Acrobat, and Adobe Type Manager are trademarks of Adobe Systems, Inc., and may be registered in certain jurisdictions.

This text is printed on acid-free paper.

This publication is designed to provide accurate and authoritative information in regard to the subject matter covered. It is sold with the understanding that the publisher is not engaged in rendering legal, accounting, or other professional service. If legal advice or other expert assistance is required, the services of a competent professional person should be sought.

Library of Congress Cataloging-in-Publication Data:
ISBN 0-471-14948-9

Printed in the United States of America

10 9 8 7 6 5 4 3 2 1

Contents

Part One:
Acrobat, PDF, and the Internet:
Why Publish with PDF on the Web?   1

Part Two: Designing and Creating PDF Documents   77

Part Three:
Serving PDF from Your Web Server   235

Part Four:
Beyond the Web   287

Acknowledgments

I would like to thank Phil Sutherland, editor of this book, for his faith in such a "green" writer and encouragement throughout the writing process. Thank you, Otto Timmons, for making it all happen that day at the Soho Kitchen. Special thanks to the following Adobe people for giving their time, software, and advance information to make this book current when it is published: Rick Brown, Gary Cosimini, Pam Deziel, Judy Kirkpatrick, and Kevin Wandryk. Thanks also to Nick Arnett at Verity, to John Monahan of the Associated Press, and to Kendall Whitehouse of the Wharton School for your perspectives on Acrobat publishing.

Thanks to everybody at Magnetic Press for your support, especially to Sanford Bingham for the freedom to pursue this book and do nothing else, for telling me everything I needed to know, and for your contributions to the introduction and the chapter on encryption. Thanks to Barry Kaplan for your Acrobat production expertise, and also for your constant help with the ever-gnarled but always-working MPI network. Thanks to Jim Rile for your tips on Capture, and to Sam Dushkin and Malcolm Ellis for your artistic contributions.

DIANA HOLM

About the Authors

Diana Holm is Vice President of Marketing and Communications at Magnetic Press Inc., a research, consulting, and electronic publishing company specializing in the technologies, service architectures, and end-user applications of computer-based publishing media. She is also editor of *Acropolis,* the World Wide Web magazine of Acrobat publishing, which features news of the electronic publishing industry, in-depth analyses of trends in Acrobat publishing, and evaluations of new Acrobat-related products. The Acropolis Web site can be reached at http://www.acropolis.com/ acropolis. Ms. Holm hails from San Francisco and is a recent graduate of Columbia University, holding an honors degree in art history.

Bruce Page is Chairman and a founder of Magnetic Press Inc. Mr. Page is an expert in the electronic publishing industry, with an emphasis on the business models that will permit existing publishing operations to make the transition into interactive formats. Mr. Page pursued graduate business studies at New York University, and holds an honors degree in Science, Technology, and Society from Vassar College. He has authored research reports on dozens of topics in telecommunications and information services, and has published articles in *TIME, Newsweek,* the *International Herald Tribune, CommunicationsWeek,* and *PC Week,* among others. Mr. Page is currently working in France to extend electronic publishing with Acrobat to the European publishing market.

Introduction

Welcome to *Web Publishing with Adobe Acrobat and PDF.* This book is born of the recent convergence of communications and electronic publishing technologies that have formed the World Wide Web (WWW). It is a fortuitous convergence, not just because of the great optimism and growth it has engendered in the technology marketplace, but because of a sudden widespread interest in this new form of communicating, spanning divergent industries, nations, ages, and genders.

We are glad that in writing this book we were not exactly sure who our readers might be, because whoever you are and whatever you want to accomplish on the Web we are sure that this book will help you achieve it. Unable to pin you down as User, Hacker, Neophyte, Prodigy, or "Dummy," we have decided that for the purposes of our time together you will have the distinguished title of Publisher. No matter what your line of work, you will be a *bona fide*, not to mention *cutting-edge*, publisher once you master the art of Web publishing with Acrobat. But first, let's explore how it is you have come to be reading this book, and why you are so right in doing so.

Why You Want to Get on the Web

Before the Web, publishing on the Internet was attractive only to organizations, like libraries, which needed to make large volumes of raw information available to the public. In those days, text was transmitted as ASCII, and the software to access the information was a most unfriendly DOS or UNIX interface. There was no support for visual distinctiveness among documents, and there were no viable means for expanding the audience for your information. The Web changed all that, making it possible to link together remote documents with hypertext, and supporting a level of visual distinctiveness with the ability to transmit color images to client Web browsers. Now, publishers can establish a meaningful identity for themselves on the Internet, making their site a tangible "place" that visitors can remember and return to again. By linking your site to directories and sites that are related to yours, you can expand your audience and become part of a virtual community of sites. Concurrently, the number of users on the Web has exploded, with sales of home computers topping television sets and a widespread perception of the Web as the newest, greatest thing ever to happen to the computer world, to communications, to entertainment, to education. . . .You name the field, and it could probably benefit from the Web in some way.

The technological improvements to the Web, which have made the Internet so much more compelling and accessible to a great variety of people, combined with the general frenzy over its possibilities, have led to a "gold rush" mentality among would-be Web publishers. In just the three-year history of the Web, tens of thousands of sites have been established, many of which serve only a home page. But in this case the rewards for staking a place in this new territory are by no means instant and are difficult to grasp even in the long term. Vaguely speaking, you want to get on the Web to establish an identity in cyberspace, to experiment with different kinds of communication without a significant investment or risks, and to reach new audiences. Ultimately, many organizations hope to use the Web to replace outdated or costly aspects of their operations. What the Web will do for us is still unknown. We are in a transitional stage right now, as software companies intervene to mitigate the limitations of the Web's publishing and interactive capabilities. In the next few years, the Web could emerge to be an über-medium, bringing business, entertainment, education, and politics to great technological heights, all in the same space. Getting on board now with some of the second-stage technologies like Acrobat will position you well to establish and keep a meaningful presence on the Web.

If your primary business is publishing, getting on the Web is not just encouraged but crucial to the survival of your enterprise. There is little doubt today that all successful products and technologies for electronic publishing will of necessity evolve within the personal computer/Internet structure. Both parts of this environment—the personal computer software industry and the Internet—have a strong bias toward inexpensive, even free information. We doubt very much that there will be a continuing market for electronic information products priced higher than their paper counterparts.

Electronic products can add value to paper ones in at least three ways: They can be acquired immediately from the Internet, they can be searched effectively, and their content can be updated via the Internet. Other ways of adding value will no doubt be developed, but we believe that these three alone are sufficient to justify the existence of electronic information products. Accordingly, we believe that the future holds promise for publishers who can rapidly produce electronic information products derived from and marketed with established paper products. In this book, we will demonstrate how publishing with the PostScript-based Portable Document Format (PDF) is the best, and the only solution for rapid electronic document production. Publishers who delay their development of a PostScript-based electronic publishing system, or adopt an overly expensive approach to electronic publishing, do so at their peril.

Why Being on the Web Means Being a Publisher

The interesting part of this rush to get on the Web, from our perspective, is that so many people of different professions and pursuits are involved in what is probably their first publishing endeavor. No matter how simple the home page or document you put on the Web, you are effectively broadcasting it to millions of potential readers. And even if you don't have the budget of a traditional print publisher, your site has equal weight to theirs in cyberspace. There are no "superior" URL addresses for Fortune 500 companies. In the egalitarian, free space of the Web, you can publish quickly without having to answer to editors, advertisers, and other bureaucrats. Publicizing your site is also easy, by getting your URL listed in directories and putting links to your site on bigger sites related to yours. By using the right tools (hint: Acrobat is one of them), you can make your publication look as good as any printed publication out there. And your publications *should* look that good, because they will need to stand out among the volumes of mediocre-looking documents on the Web. Once you invest the effort in creating high-quality Web documents, you can create a publication that users can download, save, print, or store digitally, so you are making a lasting imprint both in cyberspace and in the real world.

Why Web Publishing Is Different

In the computer industry there's something called Moore's Law, which states that every eighteen months or so the computing power of a microprocessor doubles while its price falls by half. This claim might be slightly exaggerated, but it's a convenient way of showing how quickly our computer hardware is changing. The World Wide Web typifies a similar kind of sea-change in the realms of software development and information management. The Web breaks clear of the traditional mold for software development. Thanks to the URL, HTML, and the HTTP protocol, "application development" is simply the creation of new documents, with new URL links inside them. This is a huge contrast with traditional software development, which has been the realm of computer czars and software wizards. Today, the Web means that virtually anybody who can use a word processor can be, in effect, a developer of interactive electronic applications. In our humble opinion, the world will never go back to programming the same old way.

In fact, what the Web really represents is the emergence of something we call the "intelligent communicating document" as the fundamental unit of electronic information exchange and commerce. An intelligent communicating document is *intelligent* because it has been placed in a context by the editor, by virtue of the hypertext links that permit it to communicate with other related documents. Given these links and this context, an intelligent communicating document in fact comprises all the intelligence—via the links—of the documents it links to. In fact, by simply delivering a single one of these documents to a correspondent, you can effectively deliver the power of an entire Internet.

Acrobat PDF documents and the traditional HTML of the Web are both examples of intelligent communicating documents. For a host of reasons we'll explain in the course of this book, PDF is the superior format for publishing a wide variety—though not all—of electronic information products. Still, we believe that decades from now, when people look back at the mid-1990s and at the rise of the phenomenon of the Internet, what they'll remark on is not the famous "network of networks," but rather the emergence of a totally new form of computer application development based on linked sets of electronic documents.

Why PDF Will Become the Standard for Electronic Publishing

The overwhelming majority of information products in the market today are produced using desktop publishing tools based on Adobe's PostScript page description language (the basis for Acrobat PDF). The raw materials making up these documents may be stored in any number of forms and formats including HTML, but the finished product of the world's publishing companies is almost exclusively PostScript files. We believe that publishers will come to sell as a single package the electronic and paper versions of their products. In order for this to be done effectively, the two products must be produced simultaneously—the book and CD-ROM/WWW site must go on sale at the same time—and the former must, at a minimum, contain the same information as the latter.

At present, however, the tools for production of electronic information products are expensive, crude, and slow relative to those for print production. No available or announced non-PostScript tools—neither for the WWW nor for the multimedia CD-ROM market—can exactly represent a complex book, journal, or magazine. These tools rely on tagged text (e.g., HTML) and bitmap graphics to represent what PostScript represents as formatted text and vector graphics. In other words, non-PostScript tools create products that are simultaneously less effective at conveying information and more expensive to produce than the PostScript tools used in the print production process. In fact, PostScript was developed precisely to overcome the limitations of these tools.

It is true that electronic information products created specifically for the new medium, usually for CD-ROM, can be made to provide useful interactivity and exciting presentation. However, such products add their value to the print product by employing custom programming (in C++, Lingo, Java, etc.) that is much slower and much more expensive to produce than print. When a synchronized production of printed documents, Web sites, and CD-ROMs become the norm, publishers will not want to multiply their efforts in authoring for each medium. Instead of extending HTML authoring to print and CD-ROM media, which are capable of a much higher quality of document representation, publishers will opt to extend PostScript authoring for print to PDF authoring for the Web and CD-ROM. Put simply, we believe that publishers will choose PostScript authoring tools and PDF distribution over non-PostScript authoring tools and non-PostScript (e.g., HTML), distribution. Publishers will make this choice because PDF offers more functionality at less cost than any alternative system.

Why it Is Important to Invest in High-Quality Web Documents

What makes a high-quality document, and how much will it cost you? In our book, a quality online document is one that is well designed and well laid out, with the latest desktop publishing tools. It means full color combined with good compression techniques, with lots of links within the document as well as to other Web documents. And, if you are lucky enough to draw Web surfers into your document, be sure to reward them with good writing and interesting pictures. As the publisher, however, you need not consider yourself responsible for all of those elements. A good Web publication is always going to be the result of a productive cooperation of writers, designers, software experts, and Web experts. Even if all of those functions fall under your job description, make sure you consider them as separate tasks and bring each to its full potential. Why should you invest so much time and effort in your Web documents? Because on the Web, you never know who is coming to visit—they could be potential partners, customers, even investors in your organization. Impressing all of your visitors with high-quality documents will pay off, because praise spreads quickly on the Web (but not as fast as criticism). Particularly if you want people to pay for or subscribe to your publication, you should invest in good writing and design.

Fortunately, putting just a little extra effort into producing your Web documents, say as much as you would into a document that you would print out, will make your publication stand out on the Web. Most Web documents look pretty dull, because they are authored in the standard HTML (Hypertext Markup Language, which we'll discuss in more detail in Chapter 1). By authoring your Web documents in a format that can handle complex designs, as you can with Acrobat, you will give your site a very distinctive image. Many users recognize the PDF symbol as the mark of a visually rich document, so don't disappoint them. However much preparation you put into your documents, Acrobat will add to your cost only the price of the Acrobat software product you choose (ranging from about $200 to $600 for the authoring tools). Once you have Acrobat, you can make Web documents from the same document creation applications that you do now.

How Acrobat Will Help You Create High-Quality Web Documents Faster, More Easily, and Less Expensively

Acrobat is the only publishing software around that can take the documents you already have, in the applications you already use—word processing, spreadsheets, presentations, desktop publishing—and turn them into a format that is ready for the Web or for any digital medium. So unlike HTML, Acrobat allows you to reuse the documents you already have and get them up on your Web site quickly. There is no programming or encoding to learn, so you won't have to hire any new people or take any classes. Converting your documents to PDF is just like having a new printer for Web documents, except the output is a digital document that you can make interactive with a few clicks of the mouse. Once you buy the Acrobat authoring tool you need, you don't have to buy any extra software to get those PDFs up on your Web site; all you do is place them in your server's document directory right next to your HTML files. And there is no sacrifice at the user end for this ease of publishing; with Acrobat's new Amber enhancement, users can view PDF files one page at a time within the Netscape Navigator browser window. The end result is an inexpensive, speedy, and versatile Web publishing process that will please your colleagues and users alike.

How This Book Will Help You Start and Maintain a Cutting-Edge Web Publishing Venture Using Acrobat

This book will bring you up to speed with the Web and Acrobat, demonstrating how the two technologies can work together to make you a first-rate online publisher. We do not presume any foreknowledge either of Web technologies or of Acrobat, but we will tell you everything you need to know to go all the way with advanced production and Web server technologies. Working with Acrobat on the Web can be as simple or as complicated as you want to make it, because Acrobat is at once a user-friendly software tool and an intelligent, extensible platform for PostScript programming. We have tried to show all of the versatile ways in which you can incorporate Acrobat into your publishing process, according to your needs and ambitions.

Part One, Acrobat, PDF, and the Internet, explains in detail what the Web is and where it stands today, the significance of Acrobat in the space of the Web, and which Acrobat product is best for you. We also give you a look into the crystal ball, revealing some of Adobe's future plans for Acrobat, as well as how other exciting technologies are going to play into Acrobat publishing. Part One finishes off with a frank discussion of when to use PDF and when to use HTML on the Web, clarifying the advantages and limitations of both formats. Part Two, Creating and Designing PDF Documents, helps you gear up for and plan out your Web publishing project, tells you which kinds of documents you will need on your site, and then gets into the nitty-gritty of Acrobat production—using the PDF Writer, the Distiller, and Exchange, as well as third-party PDF enhancement tools. Part Three, Serving PDF from Your Web Server, brings you into the process of organizing your PDF documents on your Web server and integrating them with the other files on your site. We also introduce the various indexing and retrieval mechanisms for making the PDF documents on your site searchable for the user. Part Three ends with a discussion of Web server and PDF document security technologies, and describes a real-life implementation of one of the most advanced PDF encryption technologies. In Part Four, we move Beyond the Web to show you how you can also publish your PDF documents on CD-ROM, Lotus Notes, and other offline publishing media. Your same PDF documents can be republished over and over again on a wide variety of digital media, indefinitely extending the value of your work and broadening the audience for your information.

Without further ado, let's get started with your Acrobat initiation and PDF publishing project. We hope you enjoy the ride, and do some of your own Web surfing to check out all the interesting content out there in the Acrobat format. We will tell you where to go for fun and also to get help and more information on PDF publishing. Be sure to see the Appendices to learn how to configure your Web browser to view PDF files, how to navigate and search PDF documents, and how to install Acrobat Plug-ins, as well as for a list of the Web sites for the companies and products mentioned in this book.

Part One

Chapter 1

Web Publishing Standards

A vital part in your decision to use Acrobat for your Web publishing is to understand why the old ways are inadequate. As you will learn, Acrobat was not originally planned as a Web publishing application, but it became a compelling alternative to publishing with the standard World Wide Web (WWW) formats for representing text and images. This chapter will give a brief history of the Web and those standard formats, explaining when and why Acrobat moved onto the Web publishing scene. None of it is very old history; in fact every aspect of the Web is still in its early development. By getting a sense of the Web's relatively shallow roots and where Acrobat fits in, you can better plan your own Web publishing strategy.

For most of its young life, the World Wide Web has been synonymous with HTML, the HyperText Markup Language. HTML makes up the vast majority of the text you see on the Web—those long lines of text in a common font, often underlined to show that you can click on a word with your mouse to jump to another spot on the Web (Figure 1.1). That clickable attribute puts the "hyper" into hypertext, and "markup" just means the tagging system that is used to encode normal text as hyperlinks to specific locations. For those of us who are accustomed to using the Internet for email, or who browsed the Internet in the days before the Web, HTML is a dynamic enhancement to the "dead" ASCII text that had no formatting or linking capabilities. When the physicists at CERN (the European Laboratory for Particle Physics) in Switzerland invented the Web in 1989, it was intended to organize the

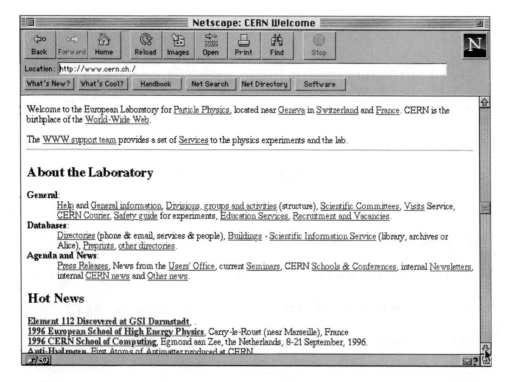

FIGURE 1.1 The common face of the Web, HTML text with underlined hyperlinks.

volumes of information on the Internet by creating simple hypertext links between those volumes[1] (Figure 1.2).

Why HTML Is the *Lingua Franca* of the Web

HTML is the standard method of encoding text for the dominant data transmission protocol of the Web, the HyperText Transfer Protocol, or HTTP (you'll recognize that term from the beginning of every Web address you enter). We call HTML a "standard" because it is a direct descendant of SGML (Standard Generalized Markup Language), an electronic system for representing documents online that was invented in the 1960s and adopted as an

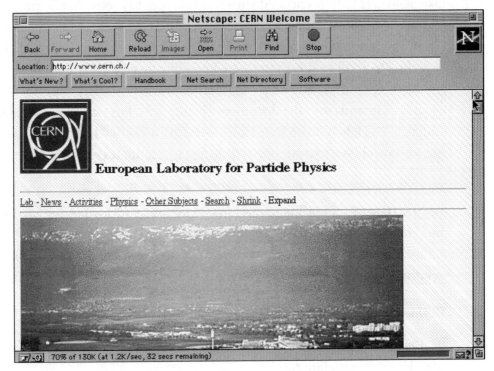

FIGURE 1.2 The CERN home page, where the Web began. An excellent resource for learning about the development of the Web and improvements to Web standards and protocols.

official standard by the ISO (International Standards Organization) in 1986 (Table 1.1). SGML is a cross-platform language that marks up regular ASCII text with "tags" that describe some structural and formatting attributes, such as headers or italics, to be represented in an SGML viewer displaying the document. For example, if we were to encode this book in SGML for a database, we would start with

```
<title>Web Publishing with Adobe Acrobat and PDF</title>
```

That way, the database would know that the above sentence is the title of the document. The government, libraries, and many publishing houses use SGML as an archival format for documents, since the structural information embedded in the text lends itself easily to indexing in document databases.

Like SGML, HTML is encoded with tags that identify some formatting information, but it adds a tagging system for embedding Web addresses, or URLs (Uniform Resource Locators) into the document so that it is a clickable hyperlink to another site on the Web. Encoding text for HTML is not a point-and-click operation, however—the author must physically type the rather arcane commands into the document (Figure 1.3). For example, to make the sentence "Click here to go to Adobe's Web site" an actual link to Adobe's Web site, you would have to add the following tags to the text:

```
<a href=http://www.adobe.com>Click here to go to Adobe's Web site</a>
```

Adding these essential links, marking structural and formatting attributes, and embedding image files amounts to a cumbersome job for the HTML author. Some software manufacturers, eyeing an opportunity here, have developed HTML "editors," such as Adobe's own PageMill, which provide a

TABLE 1.1 Evolution of Text Formats

Standard Internet Text Formats

ASCII	just plain text
SGML	ASCII + structural tags + limited formatting
HTML	ASCII + structural tags + limited formatting + hypertext

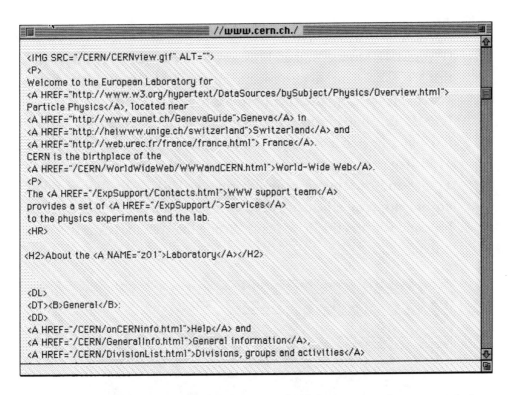

```
//www.cern.ch./

<IMG SRC="/CERN/CERNview.gif" ALT="">
<P>
Welcome to the European Laboratory for
<A HREF="http://www.w3.org/hypertext/DataSources/bySubject/Physics/Overview.html">
Particle Physics</A>, located near
<A HREF="http://www.eunet.ch/GenevaGuide">Geneva</A> in
<A HREF="http://heiwww.unige.ch/switzerland">Switzerland</A> and
<A HREF="http://web.urec.fr/france/france.html"> France</A>.
CERN is the birthplace of the
<A HREF="/CERN/WorldWideWeb/WWWandCERN.html">World-Wide Web</A>.
<P>
The <A HREF="/ExpSupport/Contacts.html">WWW support team</A>
provides a set of <A HREF="/ExpSupport/">Services</A>
to the physics experiments and the lab.
<HR>

<H2>About the <A NAME="z01">Laboratory</A></H2>



<DL>
<DT><B>General</B>:
<DD>
<A HREF="/CERN/onCERNinfo.html">Help</A> and
<A HREF="/CERN/GeneralInfo.html">General information</A>,
<A HREF="/CERN/DivisionList.html">Divisions, groups and activities</A>
```

FIGURE 1.3 HTML is derived from standard languages for transmitting text over the Internet.

point-and-click interface for the user to write in plain text, while the software converts it into HTML in the background. These editors have made it easier for beginners to author HTML, but still they have to learn to organize their documents to conform with official HTML document structure, in terms of headers, paragraphs, lists, and so on.

NCSA Mosaic and the Beginning of a Visual Web

Hypertext was an ingenious solution to the problem of navigating through the masses of text files on the Internet, but the nascent Web would remain the province of Internet geeks until NCSA (National Center for Supercomputing

Applications) invented the first graphics-capable Web "browser," Mosaic (Figure 1.4). Mosaic, and all browsers that followed it, is a type of software that acts as a "client" to retrieve information from a remote World Wide Web server (Figure 1.5). The client browser can download and display not only HTML files, but images in any of the standard image file formats—GIF (Graphics Interchange Format), JPEG (Joint Photographic Expert Group), TIFF (Tag Image File Format), and so on. At the user end, the browser acts as a point-and-click interface for entering the URL destination, scrolling down documents, saving them to a disk, saving locations as "bookmarks," and other bells and whistles that have made surfing the Web the easy experience that it is today.

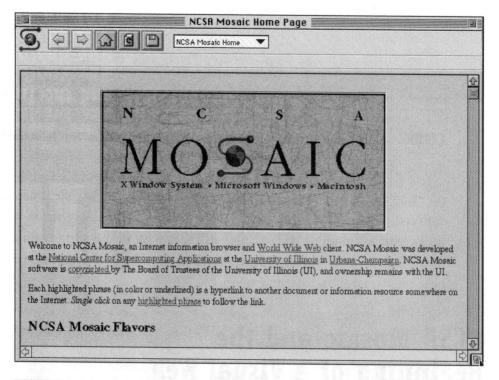

FIGURE 1.4 Look behind the curtain on HTML, and you'll see the labors of the HTML encoder. All formatting and links in HTML must be typed in special codes, unless you use a graphical HTML editor software.

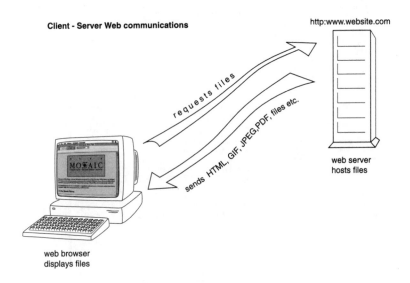

Client - Server Web communications

http:www.website.com

requests files

sends HTML, GIF, JPEG,PDF, files etc.

web server
hosts files

web browser
displays files

FIGURE 1.5 The NCSA Mosaic Web browser was the first software capable of displaying images along with hypertext on the Web.

The Web as we know it is a product of these two innovations, CERN's hypertext and NCSA's graphical browser software. Most Web pages feature a combination of hypertext and a few images that act as illustrations or as hyperlinked navigational buttons. Anyone browsing the Web today who knew what the Internet looked like just two years ago would say it has come a very long way. But the tide is changing nonetheless, as software makers, publishers, and users demand that the Web fulfill the promise of the information superhighway—interactivity, multimedia, animation, commerce—*now*. One modest step toward the fulfillment of that promise is simply to make Web documents convey information more effectively by adding more formatting, such as a greater variety of fonts, and the ability to combine text and graphics into columns, charts, and tables. Business users and traditional publishers in particular are pushing for Web documents to handle the same degree of formatting as the print documents they produce with desktop publishing software (Figure 1.6).

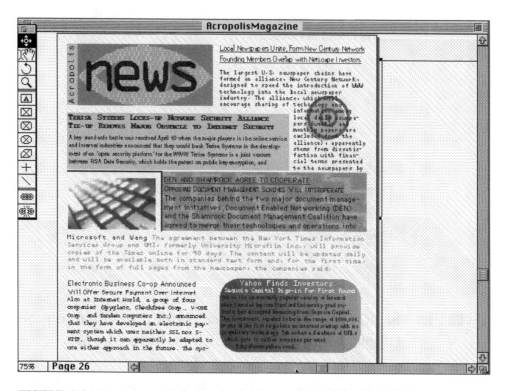

FIGURE 1.6 To view a page on the Web, your Web browser transmits the URL request to the remote Web server for the page you requested. The server receives the request and sends the data back to your browser, which displays the text and graphics. For each new URL you enter (or URL link you click on), your browser sends a new request to the remote Web server that hosts the page.

Official HTML versus Commercial "Dialects"

While the technology certainly exists to add more formatting capabilities to HTML, the process of changing an official standard is belabored and slow. Unlike software companies that frequently upgrade their products, HTML is governed by the Internet Engineering Task Force (IETF), a voluntary organization that is relatively immune to market pressures. Exasperated by the IETF's slowness to extend the HTML specification (it is currently in the 3.0 phase, allowing some forms and table capabilities), many browser vendors have taken it upon themselves to offer their own enhancements to the language (Netscape's NHTML, for example). This initiative has resulted in a splintering of the official HTML into proprietary "dialects" that only certain browser types can read. This means that a Web author may have to create several different versions of a page with varying degrees of formatting for each kind of browser the document may hit.

This is a doomed state of affairs, because while nobody wants to author a simplistic Web page, it just takes too long to author and reauthor for the different capabilities of all the browsers currently in the market. Some Web publishers, assuming that most visitors to their site will be using the very popular Netscape Navigator, may author their page just with Netscape's proprietary extensions, NHTML. But Netscape's domination of the browser market may not be permanent, especially considering Microsoft's entry into the Web with Windows 95. Furthermore, there is a limit to the amount HTML can be dressed up before the files become too large for current levels of bandwidth. As it is, the image files embedded in HTML documents make for lengthy download time.

Sidestepping HTML's Limitations with the Portable Document Format

HTML is the *lingua franca* of the Web because it conforms to the rules of HTTP, the HyperText Transfer Protocol. This means the text of an HTML file is guaranteed to reach any kind of Web browser, with only slight modifications to its appearance. In turn, you, the Web publisher, must conform to those rules when you think about what you want to present on your Web site. You sacrifice the quality of your presentation for the ubiquity of your information. Now for the good news: The Internet, the communications backbone of the Web, can transmit any kind of digital file, created with any kind of software program, to anyone who visits your Web site. The real issue is, how will they be able to see your file if they don't also have the software program with which you created it? It is precisely this dilemma that Adobe Systems solved with Acrobat's Portable Document Format (PDF), even before Acrobat was conceived of as a Web application. Acrobat's PDF is a platform-, operating system-, device-, and browser-independent solution to authoring visually rich Web pages. Publishing with PDF is fast becoming not just an alternative to HTML authoring, but a *de facto* standard on the Web.

Notes

1. Ben M. Segal, *A Short History of Internet Protocols at CERN*, 1995 (on CERN Web site at http://www.cern.ch/).

Chapter 2

Enter Acrobat: Raising the Standards of Online Publishing

In the first chapter, we discussed some Internet standards, such as HTTP, HTML, and the image formats. All of these standards have a common end—to transmit data from one point to another on the Web and display it with as much fidelity as possible to the content of that data. Conforming to the capabilities of the data communications infrastructure is the top priority of those formats and the reason why they are Internet standards. Adobe's Portable Document Format (PDF) is also a growing presence on the Web, but its background and raison d'être is completely different from HTML's. PDF has its roots not in the Internet, but in another technology that revolutionized the way we use computers about ten years ago—PostScript, and the ensuing desktop publishing industry.

The PostScript Revolution in Desktop Publishing

Most people don't know what PostScript is, but they use it every time they send a word-processed file to a desktop printer. Conceived by John Warnock, one of the founders of Adobe Systems, back in the early 1980s, PostScript is a device- and platform-independent programming language that graphically describes the text, shapes, and images that appear on a page. In its most common iteration, the PostScript technology is embedded as an interpreter inside a printer, allowing for WYSIWYG (What You See Is What You Get) printing of the document on the screen. When it was introduced in 1985, PostScript galvanized the desktop publishing revolution, making it possible for anyone with a PC and a printer to produce high-quality printed documents. Since then, PostScript has become a *de facto* standard in the printing and publishing industries, and has even spawned clones, such as Peter Deutsche's "Ghostscript." Adobe has remained largely in the background during the ascent of PostScript, but their experience with the language has fueled the development of their software applications products and firmly established them as the leader in desktop publishing tools.

Carousel and the Birth of Acrobat

For insiders of the publishing industry, the fact that Adobe invented the Portable Document Format and ushered in the age of electronic publishing comes as no surprise. Former Senior Art Director at the *New York Times*, Gary Cosimini, remembers his introduction to the Acrobat prototype:

> In my office at the New York Times, *I saw a demonstration of a software called "New Technology," the precursor to Carousel. I didn't know what it was, but I knew it would change my life. It was a very simple interface to an interactive document, that was fully zoomable and had interactive links. At the time, I had no idea what group it came from, but I knew what it was to be*

used for. That was apparent; I saw a million applications for it before I knew what it was. It was a cheap enlightenment, a moment of software nirvana.

Cosimini is now Adobe's Business Development Manager in New York City. He and other quick converts realized that the PDF language and *Carousel* (Adobe's code name for the Acrobat software prototype) signified an extension of the PostScript page description technology to the booming new media of CD-ROM and the Internet. This meant that just as PostScript let every PC become a virtual printing press for the desktop publishing era, PDF would let every PC become an electronic publishing house for the digital information age. Cosimini makes sense of the PostScript-PDF connection, this time from an Adobe insider's perspective (Figure 2.1):

Adobe creates baseline system tools for publishing. That starts with Post-Script, with hardware embodiments of the PostScript interpreters, then with applications that use PostScript technology. When you move beyond the world of printed information, into the world of information as a general class, the PostScript model has to be extended for general information, and that's what PDF is.

PDF the Language

PDF is quite unique among computer languages. Acrobat does not require you to know how to "write" PDF; it generates it automatically. Nevertheless, you may find it interesting to know how PDF is unique, particularly with regard to its parent PostScript.

Similarities to PostScript

The key characteristics that the PDF language takes from PostScript are its imaging model and its device independence. PDF's imaging model describes the text and graphics on a page by placing digital "paint" onto precise coordinates of a blank page. Like the pointillist painters of the late nineteenth

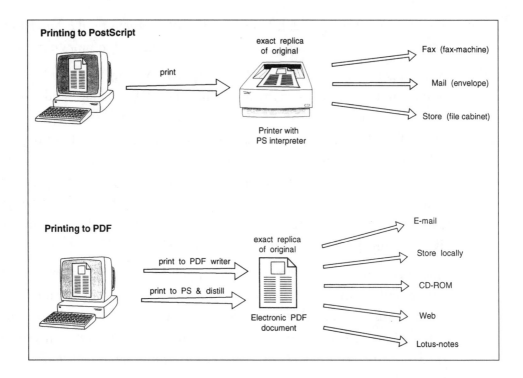

FIGURE 2.1 Both PostScript and PDF start out with a document authored on your computer. When you send that document to a PostScript printer, the PostScript interpreter inside the printer exactly reproduces the document on paper. But once on paper, your distribution options are limited to the traditional "snail mail," faxing, and inevitably, storage in the file cabinet. Printing the original document to PDF results in the same replica, but in a dynamic and portable electronic medium. Your distribution options expand to include the Web, email, the corporate network, Lotus Notes, and CD-ROM. (Of course, you can also print a PDF to paper.)

century, PDF paints a page one dot at a time, regardless of the different elements, text or graphics, the dots represent. Since PDF and PostScript share this imaging model, converting a document to PDF is much like printing a document to a PostScript printer. The resulting file is an exact WYSIWYG replica of the original. PDF also shares PostScript's device independence, which means that PDF files can be authored or viewed on any kind of computer platform, or even on a device that is not a computer, such as a projector. All the PDF file needs to operate is its Acrobat helper software. PDF's device independence is what puts the "portable" into the Portable Document Format, and what gives it the potential to become a standard as ubiquitous as its parent PostScript.

Differences from PostScript

PDF differs from PostScript in several ways that optimize PDF files for electronic exchange. Most importantly, PDF is not a programming language like PostScript. It has a unique, rigid file structure that limits user modification for enhanced portability and efficiency. As a result, PDF files are much more compact than PostScript files. Pam Deziel, Product Marketing Manager for Acrobat, points out, "PDF takes the benefits of PostScript and takes them further. A PostScript file in many cases is six or eight or ten times bigger than a PDF." Unlike PostScript, PDF files have features that are intended for digital display only, such as hyperlinks and article threads. PDF files are also designed for random access to allow for quick navigation of disparate parts of a document.[1] Table 2.1 lists the similarities and differences between PostScript and PDF.

Both PostScript and PDF are device-independent, portable languages, but the programmers at Adobe had a harder time keeping PDF portable because PDF documents must display on different computer platforms (Table 2.2). Although PostScript is a device-independent technology that can be embedded in any software or hardware, it is not crucial that everyone with whom you exchange information have the PostScript technology residing on their computers. The final output of PostScript is the very portable, but technologically challenged, printed page. With PDF, the goal is to exchange the digital file from your computer with a foreign computer over a network, and

TABLE 2.1 Similarities and Differences between PostScript and PDF

PostScript and PDF

Similarities:	Page description with digital "paint"
	Device independent; can be embedded technology
Differences:	PDF is not a programming language
	PDF has rigid file structure for random access
	PDF files are more compact, more easily compressed
	PDF files contain display information such as font metrics
	PDF files contain ASCII text for portability
	PDF files contain interactive elements such as hypertext

TABLE 2.2 The *Portable* Document Format

Media-Independent	Hard disk, CD-ROM, Internet & WWW, LAN, Lotus Notes
Platform-Independent	Windows, Macintosh OS, UNIX, DOS
Device-Independent	PC, projectors, navigation devices, portable reader devices

never have to go to print. This raised for Adobe the age-old problems of digital information exchange: "How will the computer at the other end understand and display the PDF document?" and "What if the computer doesn't have the right fonts to understand my text?" The first quandary Adobe has solved with a marketing tactic (giving the Acrobat Reader away for free), and the second one they solved with good old-fashioned engineering.

Solving the "Font Problem"

Before Adobe solved the font problem with PDF, any document that was not in ASCII could appear correctly only on a system that already had the fonts used in the document. If the receiving system did not have the fonts, the system would substitute a default font and the formatting of the document would be thrown off entirely. The sole alternatives were to send the fonts along with the document to the receiving computer (but that increased its file size tremendously), or to send a fixed-resolution facsimile (which also increased the file size). PDF resolves the problem with a new system that liberates a document from the fonts with which it was created. Every PDF file contains a "font descriptor" that describes to the host system the font name, character metrics, and style information for all the fonts used in the file. At just 1 to 2K per font, the font descriptor lets the host system simulate any missing fonts with a multiple master font, a technology that resides in the Acrobat Reader's ATM (Adobe Type Manager). With just the limited information proffered by the PDF file, multiple master fonts can mimic a wide variety of widths, sizes, weights, and type styles. The result is a compact PDF file that looks almost exactly the same as it did on its original system, yet retains its device and resolution independence. (In cases where "almost" is not good enough, Acrobat will allow you to embed exact fonts into the PDF files you create.) By providing display information separately from the actual PDF document, the document remains in a sort of flexible, metaformat for the resolution capabilities of the receiving hardware. As computer hardware improves its display resolutions, PDF files will look better and better. This flexibility contrasts with other file formats such as bitmaps, in which documents have a fixed resolution that will never improve.[2]

Making PDF a Standard

PDF is an extensible file format, meaning that it has an open structure for third parties to make improvements with software "Plug-ins." Adobe has published the PDF specification, in the *Portable Document Reference Manual* (Tim Bienz and Richard Cohn, Addison-Wesley, 1993), in order to hasten these developments. While such an open stance may invite competitors to Adobe's Acrobat product, it does increase the format's chances of becoming an industry standard. A file format that seems open instead of proprietary is also more likely to be embraced by consumers. However, Judy Kirkpatrick, Market Development Manager for Acrobat, remarks that the trade press has hindered this perception:

> *Almost every article I read, still always refers to PDF as being a proprietary standard. And yes, we have a group inside of Adobe called the PDF Language Committee, and they approve any changes or modifications to the spec. But the minute those changes are made, they're not kept at Adobe, they're published in the SDKs, on our Web site, anywhere we make the information available. So if Adobe were to go out of business, somebody could pick this stuff up and keep moving forward with it.*

The government has been more inclined to acknowledge PDF as a potential standard. The National Institute for Standards and Technology is considering making PDF a Federal Information Processing Standard (FIPS). The government has already embraced PDF as an electronic publishing tool, but if PDF were made a FIPS, government offices could exchange official documents in the format. Kirkpatrick says, "[The government] believes that PDF—not Acrobat, PDF—is a standard that they want to encourage for the exchange of information inside the government. And they say that because they fully understand that we've published the spec, and there's nothing in the spec that we have access to and somebody else doesn't."

Acrobat the Product

You may ask, *If Adobe is giving away the spec for PDF, how do they expect to make money on Acrobat?* Acrobat is the first, and presumably the best, software implementation of PDF and Adobe intends to keep it that way. Kevin Wandryk, Director of Business Development at Adobe's headquarters, says that the strategy for Acrobat will be similar to that of PostScript. "Not only did we build a business around development tools, we also built the best implementation of the technology. PostScript was a published standard that attracted clones, but we were the best implementor of the standard." So while other authoring programs may output directly to PDF, or plug-in developers add functionality to PDF documents, Adobe will make sure that the core product Acrobat is always a step ahead. Kirkpatrick explains, "I think it's important to make a distinction between Acrobat and PDF, because we want PDF to become the standard for the way digital information is shared and communicated. Acrobat is our answer; we believe that we have the best experience in how to author and publish PDF documents, and that's going to be what we focus on with Acrobat."

The Acrobat product line is diverse and ever growing, so it can be confusing to consumers who know they want to create PDF documents but are not sure how. It helps to think of it as a set of tools for manipulating PDF files in different ways—from very simple viewing with the Acrobat Reader, to conversion with the Distiller, to scanning paper documents into PDF with Capture. Together, the Acrobat products make it possible to create PDF files from virtually any kind of authoring tool and distribute them on all of the digital media—across corporate LANs and within databases, over the Internet as email attachments, on CD-ROM and other storage media, and of course on the World Wide Web. What follows is a breakdown of all the Acrobat products, so you can decide which ones you need in your Acrobat toolbox.

Acrobat Reader

The Reader lies at the bottom of the Acrobat totem pole, but it is all you need to view, navigate, and print a PDF file (but you cannot save it). Adobe made a marketing blunder in the beginning when they tried to sell the Reader, but since the 2.0 release they're distributing it by the millions for free. A good decision, especially now that most people download the Reader off of Adobe's Web site. And PDF publishers on other Web sites can point their visitors to download the Reader easily. You'll also find the Reader on floppies in all of the Acrobat off-the-shelf products, and on CD-ROMs that have PDFs, such as Adobe's Acrobat CD Sampler. Adobe is extending the functionality of the Reader especially for the CD-ROM market, integrating Acrobat Search and some selected third-party plug-ins. For the Web, they've made a special "Amber" Reader with Netscape, which improves PDF documents' performance by leaps and bounds. Read all about it in the next chapter. (Price: Free.)

Acrobat Exchange

Exchange is the Acrobat Reader with legs. In one box, it has everything the average business user needs to view, search, publish, and exchange PDF files across platforms and media. With Exchange, not only can you view somebody else's PDF file, but you can save it to your hard disk, add hyperlinks to it, annotate it with electronic "sticky notes," and add some security specifications to it. If the author of the PDF has indexed it using Acrobat Catalog (sold separately), with Exchange you use the Acrobat Search tool (featuring Verity Inc.'s search engine) to run a full-text search on the document. The Exchange box also includes the PDF Writer, a printer driver that can convert any word processed (i.e., MS Word or WordPerfect), spreadsheet (i.e., Excel or Lotus 1-2-3), and presentation (i.e., PowerPoint) documents into a PDF file. Writing one of these files to PDF is as easy as printing—you simply choose the PDF Writer as your printer instead. From there, the sky's the limit—you can publish the PDF on your corporate network, send it as an email attachment, burn it in on a CD, or put it up on your Web site. All the person at the other end needs to view it is the Acrobat Reader. (Price: $195 for Mac and Windows; $295 for UNIX.)[3]

Acrobat Pro

For the professional graphic designer or publisher, Acrobat Pro has everything Exchange has got, but it's packaged in a stylish Italian kidskin attaché case. Actually, the difference is in the Acrobat Distiller, the powerhouse Post-

Script-to-PDF conversion tool. For volume conversion jobs, or for documents created in any of the layout or image editing programs (i.e., Quark XPress, PhotoShop, Illustrator), Distiller can create a much smaller PDF file with total fidelity to the complex graphics and layout of the original. The Distiller shrinks these files using Joint Photographic Expert Group (JPEG) compression of color and greyscale images, and LZW (Lempel-Ziv-Welch) compression of text and graphics. There's just one catch—Distiller will only convert files that have already been written to PostScript files and that end with the suffix .PS, .EPS, or .EPSF. This is because the Distiller is a complete PostScript interpreter that can create a higher-quality PDF from files that have already been "printed" digitally to PostScript. No problem; all of the high-end graphic design and desktop publishing programs will output to .PS files. Then, you simply open them up in the Distiller program, and it goes to work, giving you a status report in progress and showing you thumbnail views of the PDF as it is created. You can give the Distiller as many .PS files as you like at one time, and it will churn them out in order, leaving you free to do something else. Since PDFs that come out of the Distiller are usually of superior quality and smaller in size, we recommend using it for any PDF document you want to publish on your Web site. (Price: $595 for Mac and Windows; $1,895 for UNIX.)

Acrobat for Workgroups

Acrobat for Workgroups is for a small company or office that wants to use Acrobat for internal document exchange and archiving. If you're serious about Acrobat publishing on the Web, this deluxe box has everything you'll need to run a start-to-finish PDF production operation. It comes with a ten-user license for Acrobat Exchange and the Acrobat Distiller, plus Acrobat Catalog, a tool that creates full-text indexes of PDFs so that users of the documents can perform full-text searches with the Acrobat Search tool in Exchange. The Catalog tool is ideal for Web publishers who want to keep track of the content of the PDF documents on their Web site. Your Web users, however, will not be able to access your Catalog indexes (see Chapter 11 for more on indexing PDFs). Catalog is also sold as a separate product, for $500. (Price: $1,595 for Mac and Windows; $3,295 for UNIX.)

Acrobat Capture

Introduced in spring 1995, Acrobat Capture is a revolutionary scanning software tool that creates smart PDF files from greyscale paper documents (not color, yet). Intended as an industrial-strength network tool, Capture works in batch-process mode only on 486 or better PCs with at least 16 MB of RAM and plenty of free disk space. Capture works with almost all of the scanners on the market to generate searchable PDF documents that retain the look and feel of the original, just like Acrobat does with digital files. Do you have file cabinets full of valuable "legacy" documents that have no digital counterparts? Do you want to bring them alive and publish them on your Web site, or just archive them on CD-ROM? Capture is the tool for you. Beware, however, that the current version 1.0 is reputed to be buggy, and you will probably need to muscle up your hardware to run Capture. Refer to Chapter 6 for tips on how to make Capture 1.0 work for you. (Price: $2,995—but you'll need only one copy for your whole organization.)

Which Acrobat Product You Need for Your Web Publishing Venture

When users download a PDF file off of a Web site, they may wait five, ten, even twenty minutes for it. And that's after they went to Adobe's site to download the Acrobat Reader for half an hour. They are willing to wait because they assume that they are going to be rewarded with a visually rich document that they'll want to save or print out. They are thinking, *This is going to be a document to which HTML could not have done justice.* Don't disappoint them! Invest in a good design for your Web publication, and pop for Acrobat Pro or Acrobat for Workgroups so you'll have the Distiller. You'll end up with a high-quality PDF that you'll be proud to launch on your Web site, and that you can repurpose again and again on other media such as CD-ROM. Even if you wouldn't call yourself a professional publisher at this point, how professional-looking your PDF document is may influence whether people return to your Web site. Anyone can throw a document up on a Web site, but not every Web site gets "bookmarked" by its visitors. So put your best foot forward and increase traffic on your Web site with a quality stock of PDFs. You and your organization's image will benefit. As Adobe's Pam Deziel says, "Compelling content is what pulls the people."

How Acrobat Interacts with Web Browsers

When Acrobat 1.0 was released in 1993, the Web was in its embryonic phase at CERN, and virtually no one except seasoned Internet surfers knew what the Web was. Kevin Wandryk, Director of Business Development at Adobe, remembers, "Back then, the Internet was primarily an academic tool for sending ASCII text email messages back and forth. Certainly the explosion of the Web over the last 18 months to some degree caught us by surprise, as it did a lot of other companies. And since then we've been pretty aggressive in trying to get Acrobat to play a role. But going back to day one, Acrobat was originally intended to be a corporate tool for delivering information across the corporate LAN." So when the Web did hit, and Mosaic and other browsers made it easy to access it, Acrobat became not just a local network and CD-ROM publishing tool, but a would-be Web publishing tool.

In the scurry to add Web features to the Acrobat 2.0 release, Adobe even considered making the Acrobat Reader behave like a fully functional Web browser, such as Netscape, but with the ability to download and view PDF files seamlessly. In the end, Adobe decided against it. Judy Kirkpatrick explains, "One of the things that Adobe does well, is it picks its market. We don't know browsers, we don't know that marketplace. So the decision was not to go forward in that, and that just shows that Adobe knows where its roots are, in publishing applications." Instead, they let the Acrobat Reader remain a separate viewer, and added only minimal communications abilities to it, in the Weblink plug-in. The Weblink plug-in, which didn't become a full-fledged part of Acrobat until the 2.1 release, lets the author of the PDF create hyperlinks that launch URLs in whichever browser users have on their system. The other side of Adobe's strategy has been to form alliances with browser makers such as Netscape, to embed the Acrobat Reader directly into their browser software. Netscape was the first to integrate Acrobat in this way, and most of the other browsers have plans to do the same. This way, Adobe does not have to compete in the unstable market of browser software; instead all of the browsers will offer support of Acrobat and help make PDF a standard format on the Web.

Acrobat as "Helper App"— Mosaic, Windows 95, MacWeb, and the Online Services

Currently, most of the Web browsers—Netscape 1.1, Enhanced Mosaic, Spry Mosaic, AIR Mosaic, Quarterdeck Mosaic, MacWeb, Cello, and the browsers used in Windows 95, CompuServe, and America Online—require that you configure the Acrobat Reader (or Exchange) as a "helper application" to view PDF files. (See Appendix A, "Configuring Your Web Browser to View PDF Files," for the specific steps to set up each of those browsers.) When you download a PDF file with one of those browsers, you will stay within the browser interface, watching the byte count, until the download is complete. At that point, your browser will automatically launch Acrobat Reader or Exchange, and display the downloaded PDF. Your browser is still running, and you are still online. To get back to the browser, alt-tab back to it in Windows, or choose it in the Finder menu on a Mac. The process of switching over to the Acrobat interface may be disorienting for users downloading PDFs from your Web site, so you may want to provide them with a little tutorial. The important thing is that no matter which browser the user has, the

PDF document will look exactly the same for all of them, because it is being displayed independently of the browser.

Acrobat as Inline Viewer—Netscape 2.0, the First PDF-Capable Web Browser

Adobe has worked closely with Netscape Communications Corporation since the two Silicon Valley companies announced an alliance to "bring commercial publishing to the Internet" in March 1995. They outlined a threefold plan for integration between Acrobat and the Netscape Navigator browser, which was realized over the years 1995 and 1996. The first step was for Netscape to support Acrobat's Weblink plug-in, so that PDF authors could include links to other Web sites in their documents. Second, Adobe worked with Netscape in their development of Netscape 2.0, to make the browser display PDF documents seamlessly, that is, as an "inline viewer" within the Netscape browser interface. Such seamless integration of PDFs, also under development with other browser types, solves the "disorientation problem" of leaving the browser interface altogether to view a PDF. The user retains the sense of still being online and browsing the Web. Finally, Adobe and Netscape worked together on the long-awaited "Johnny Cache" page-caching technology, the page-at-a-time downloading capability of Netscape 2.0 and the Acrobat Amber Reader. Page-at-a-time downloading means that you no longer have to download an entire PDF file in order to view it; instead the server that stores the PDF file sends down only one page at a time. This speeds up the PDF viewing process greatly, making PDFs as quick to navigate as HTML files. As a Web publisher, this technology makes it possible to store large PDF files on your server, of which users can access discrete parts. Of course, they will still have the option to save the file to disk, but this way they can preview the contents before making that time commitment. Also, Netscape will prompt any user lacking the Acrobat Reader to download it, eliminating the need for the user to navigate to Adobe's site. As the other browsers fall into line behind Netscape, there will be virtually no obstacles left to publishing and viewing PDF documents on the Web (Figure 2.2).

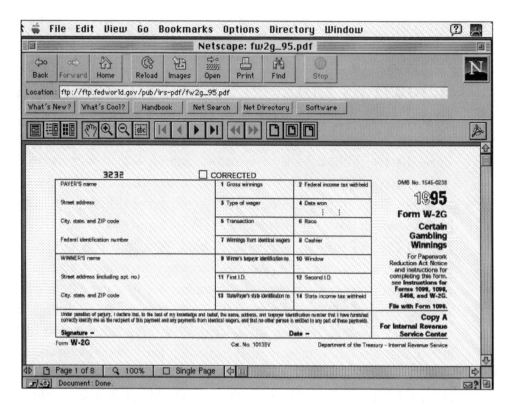

FIGURE 2.2 The amazing result of close cooperation between Adobe Systems and Netscape Communications Corporation: a PDF rendered inside the Netscape Navigator 2.0 window. Now, users with the Amber Reader and Netscape 2.0 can view PDF files automatically. If users do not have the Amber Reader, Netscape will prompt them to download it when they click on a link to a PDF.

A Quick Tour of Three Web Sites in and about PDF

The best way to learn about and experience PDF documents on the Web is to visit some sites that not only serve up PDF files, but are devoted to publishing information about Acrobat and PDF. Together, these sites make up a cyber-community of Acrobat publishers and developers that you will want to visit and interact with frequently. Each site offers a multitude of links to other PDF sites, brochures and journals devoted to Acrobat, and even downloadable Acrobat Plug-ins. Bookmark all three and no Acrobat news will escape you.

Adobe.com and the "Web Sites with Cool PDF" Page

URL: http://www.adobe.com

Naturally, the best resource for keeping abreast of Acrobat upgrades, new products, Plug-ins, and integration, is the Acrobat area on the Adobe Systems corporate Web site (Figure 2.3). It is the first place you and your Web site's

FIGURE 2.3 The Adobe Systems home page, at http://www.adobe.com, your primary resource for product information, help, free software, and the latest news on Adobe's activities in the software and publishing markets.

visitors can go to download the latest version of the Acrobat Reader, in a wide variety of flavors—for Windows, Macintosh, SunSPARC, HP, SGI, even for DOS (but not beyond release 1.0)—and in English, International English, French, Spanish, German, Dutch, Italian, and Swedish. Visitors to the Adobe site can also get all the information they need to purchase Acrobat products, including product features, pricing, system requirements, and distribution information. Adobe offers several free Acrobat Plug-ins for downloading, such as the AutoIndex Plug-in for automatically adding search index to PDF files, the Supercrop Plug-in for automatic cropping of PDF pages, and the OLE Server Plug-in that makes Acrobat Reader and Exchange act as an OLE server to display PDF documents embedded in other OLE-enabled container applications.

A great resource on Adobe's site, for browsers and publishers alike, is the "Web Sites with Cool PDF page" (Figure 2.4). Here, Adobe takes inventory of other sites on the Web that feature PDF files, giving a brief description of their content and linking each of them to their URLs. The chronology of the list, ordered from the first sites down to the most recent, bears testament to the brave souls who have been serving up PDF since the early days of the Web, such as the Wharton School of the University of Pennsylvania, whose Web site (http://www.upenn.wharton.edu) is loaded with magazines, reports, and useful guides in PDF. In fact, Kendall Whitehouse, Associate Director of Computing and Information Technology at Wharton, is willing to bet his site was the very first in the country to serve up PDF. Other early believers were Tandem Computers (http://www.tandem.com/), Dial-A-Book (http://dab.psi.net/Dial-ABook/index.html), and the Acropolis site. Now, PDF has won converts from such illustrious publishers as *Time* magazine (http://www.pathfinder. com/time), *PCWorld Online*, (http://www.pcworld.com/currentissue /toc.html), and *Fortune* magazine's Fortune 500 (http://www.pathfinder.com/). Very Impressive PDF sites get tagged with a red "VIP" tag, helping to guide you to the best sites. Since Adobe's Webmaster Andrew Shore began compiling this list, it has grown into several hundred sites, and it is "growing ever faster." Shore has said that he may adopt a more "Yahoo!-like" directory structure for the list in order to accommodate all the listings.

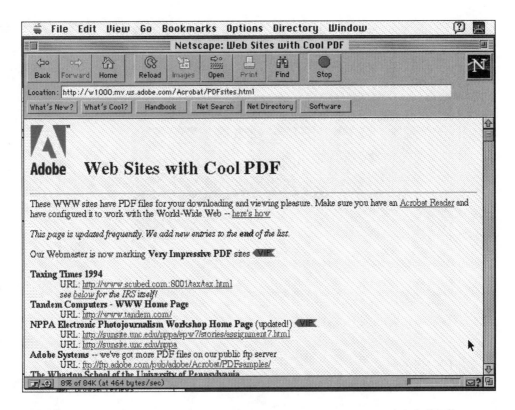

FIGURE 2.4 The "Web Sites with Cool PDF" page on Adobe's site, at
http://www.adobe.com/Acrobat/PDFsites.html. A history of
Acrobat Web publishing in linked URLs, this very long list is an
excellent resource of your fellow PDF publishers. Once you
launch your PDF documents on your site, get your site on this
list by sending email to webmaster@adobe.com.

Acropolis.com and *Acropolis* Magazine

    URL: http://www.acropolis.com/acropolis

Acropolis was launched in April 1995 as a site for the advancement of publishing with Acrobat and PDF, published by the New York-based electronic publishing and software developer Magnetic Press (Figure 2.5). The cornerstone of the Acropolis site is *Acropolis* magazine, a free, interactive journal

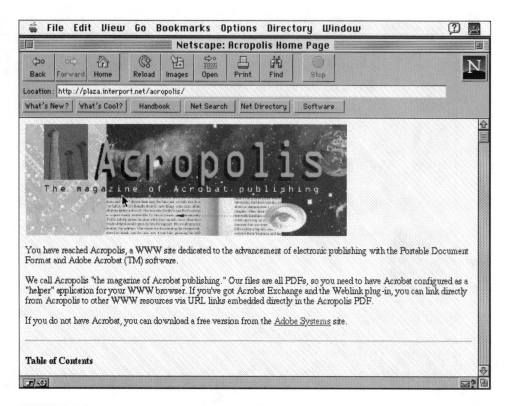

FIGURE 2.5 Our very own Acropolis home page, at http://www.acropolis. com/acropolis, the home of the first and only magazine for Acrobat publishing, *Acropolis.* We keep you abreast of the latest developments in the Acrobat world, and test out prerelease Acrobat technologies right on our site, like the Amber byte-server CGI script for page-at-a-time downloading of PDF files.

that covers the publishers, software makers, and technologies that are building the growing Acrobat industry (Figure 2.6). The magazine is presented in the PDF format, with high-quality editorial and graphic content. Each *Acropolis* issue features the latest news from Acrobat integrators and industry conferences, an in-depth feature article covering new Acrobat products and major industry developments, a case study focusing on a particular application of Acrobat, and a roundup of new Acrobat-related products. Since Acropolis operates independently of Adobe, our writers can give you candid,

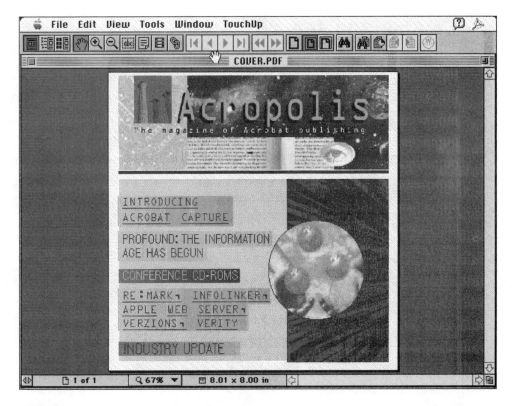

FIGURE 2.6 *Acropolis* magazine, in the PDF format. A full-color electronic magazine creatively designed by genuine New York City graphic designers. *Acropolis* can be viewed one page at a time using the Amber Reader within Netscape 2.0, or downloaded in its entirety and viewed offline. It contains Web links to lots of Acrobat-related sites.

objective coverage of Adobe's activities and products. The Acropolis site itself is a locus of new Acrobat activity, offering the magazine as an optimized Amber file for page-at-a-time downloading, and delivering new issues directly to subscribers via the Digital Delivery service. To keep abreast of everything that is happening in the Acrobat publishing industry, visit Acropolis and subscribe to *Acropolis* magazine.

Emerge and the PDF Zone

URL: http://www.emrg.com

Emerge is a Wisconsin-based Acrobat service bureau whose Web site mirrors much of Adobe.com's offerings, such as Acrobat Readers, and free Acrobat plug-ins for downloading. On the "PDF Zone" page, they provide links to other sources of Acrobat information on the Web, such as Adobe's own brochures and technical notes, third-party Acrobat journals such as *Acropolis* and the British quarterly *Acrobatics,* and other sources of tips and techniques for using Acrobat (Figure 2.7). The PDF Zone also links off to sources

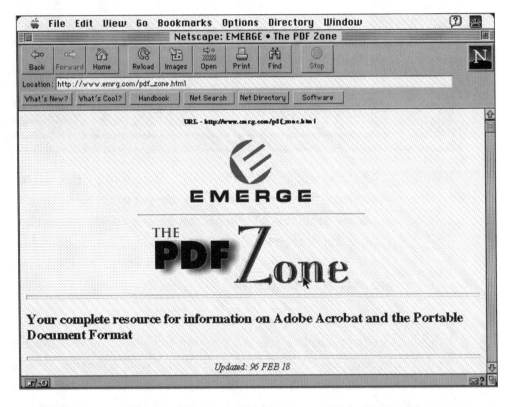

FIGURE 2.7 Emerge's PDF Zone, at http://www.emrg.com/pdf_zone.html, is a linked resource to documents and Web sites related to Acrobat. It includes links to Adobe's technical notes for common problems working with Acrobat products.

of demo PDF files, hosted by veteran PDF publishers like the Wharton School at the University of Pennsylvania and the Springer Press. For those of you who find Adobe's Web site overwhelming, Emerge's PDF Zone may be a good place to begin your exploration of PDF content on the Web.

Notes

1. Tim Bienz and Richard Cohn, *Portable Document Format Reference Manual* (Reading, MA: Addison-Wesley, 1993), 12.

2. Kenneth Grant and W. David Schwaderer, *Adobe Acrobat Handbook* (Sams Publishing, 1993), 7.

3. Prices as of January 1996 for Acrobat 2.1 product line.

Chapter 3

Acrobat: Present and Future

Acrobat 2.1 and the Weblink Plug-in: "The Universal Electronic Publishing Tool"

Released in September 1995 as an upgrade to the Acrobat 2.0 product line, Acrobat 2.1 incorporated several new features that made it a true Web publishing application. First, Adobe extended the range of platforms that Acrobat supports to Microsoft Windows NT, Windows 95, native Power Macintosh, SunOS, Sun Solaris, HP-UX, and Silicon Graphics IRIX systems. Now you can author and view PDF files on all of those platforms, and of course the originally supported Windows 3.1 and pre–Power Macintosh. Extending support for Acrobat across more platforms engendered a new slogan for Acrobat as the "universal electronic publishing tool." Judy Kirkpatrick, Market Development Manager for Acrobat, recalls, "We picked the word universal for three different reasons—you can universally create PDF files with your existing hardware and your existing software. You can universally use any tool you're already authoring in. And you can create it on whatever universe of computers you're in. So you could universally use an NT machine, or a DOS machine or a Macintosh, or a UNIX machine, to author PDF files in." Armed with a clear new message, Acrobat was ready to conquer the doubts of holdouts to the Acrobat 2.0 product.

Another major part of the strategy for 2.1 was to directly embed the Weblink Plug-in to the Windows, Macintosh, and UNIX versions of Acrobat Exchange, and support Weblinks in the free Acrobat Reader 2.1. The Weblink plug-in, which had been available as a separate free Plug-in since shortly after the release of Acrobat 2.0, gives the PDF author the option to embed URLs into the document's hyperlinks, so that when the user clicks on it he or she jump to another page or site on the Web. When the Weblink Plug-in was released, it resolved one of the primary gripes about Acrobat, that PDF documents could not interact with HTML documents. Making the Weblink technology an integral part of the Acrobat product would allow virtually every PDF file created to be a dynamic Web document, part of the navigable infrastructure of the Internet. The Weblink plug-in also gave PDF documents the unique capability to link off to the Web even when the user is browsing the PDF offline, by making the clicked Weblink launch the Internet connection software and Web browser resident on the user's desktop. The Weblink Plug-in was only the first in a series of improvements to Acrobat's performance as a Web publishing tool, however. As early as the launch of Acrobat 2.0, Adobe had laid out their direction for Acrobat on the Web. Pam Deziel, Product Marketing Manager for Acrobat, said, "First, you're going to have Weblink, then you're going to have PDF integrated into other browsers, and further on, you're going to have far better performance in terms of page-at-a-time downloading of PDF files."

By the end of 1995, the same year that Adobe released Acrobat 2.0, they were well on their way to accomplishing all three of those goals.

Adobe also added the Acrobat Movie Tool to the Macintosh and Windows versions of Exchange 2.1, letting PDF authors link off to QuickTime and AVI video and audio files from PDF documents. The Movie Tool lets the author determine the placement and appearance of a video file within the PDF document, allowing for more creative integration of multimedia elements than an HTML file offers. Both Macintosh and Windows versions of the Acrobat Reader 2.1 support Movie files, but beware of using too many in a PDF that's destined to be published on the Web. While Acrobat Movies may add a dynamic quality to your PDF, movie files can add greatly to the size of a PDF file and may take too long for the user to download. Acrobat movies do make a great addition to CD-ROMs in PDF, however, particularly in Adobe's own Acrobat CD Sampler.

Acrobat 3.0 and Amber—The Acrobat We've All Been Waiting For

If Acrobat 2.1 with the Weblink plug-in made Acrobat a real Web application, Acrobat 3.0, code-named *Amber,* makes Acrobat a "killer app" for the Web. Due in June 1996, Amber will change the face of the Web permanently, and for the better (Figure 3.1). Amber was developed closely with Netscape Communications for integration with the Netscape Navigator browser, primarily by Adobe Computer Scientist Amer Deeba (whose first name, misspelled "Amber" on his first set of business cards, became the software's code name). Amber is a series of extensions to the Acrobat API (Application Programming Interface) that make PDF files interact more closely with Web browsers and protocols, causing PDF files to perform much more elegantly online. Back when Amber was just a glimmer in the eyes of the Acrobat team, one of the primary features was nicknamed "Johnny Cache." Johnny Cache referred to a CGI script (now the Amber byteserver CGI script) that would allow Web servers to *cache,* or store without displaying, all of the pages of a PDF file, downloading only one page

FIGURE 3.1 The splash screen for the free Acrobat "Amber" Reader, with which you can view optimized PDF files one page at a time on the Web. The Amber Reader will also display PDF files within Netscape and render PDF pages progressively on the screen.

at a time to the online browser. Now called simply "page-at-a-time download-ing," this caching feature reverses the status of PDF files on the Web as big, bulky files that must first be downloaded in their entirety, and then browsed offline within the Acrobat interface. The Amber extensions, which now apply only to the Acrobat Reader and Acrobat Exchange 3.0, make PDF files dynamic online documents that can be navigated as quickly as HTML pages (without sacrificing their visual richness).

For page-at-a-time downloading to work, several Acrobat technologies must be working together (Figure 3.2). First, the PDF file must have been "opti-mized" by an Amber version of Acrobat Exchange (Acrobat 3.0 or above). Amber optimizes PDF files in a number of ways for viewing on the Web; for the purposes of page-at-a-time downloading, the PDF file must be able to be parsed by a server and compressed to the maximum extent. The PDF file should also contain Weblinks to other content on your Web site, whether in

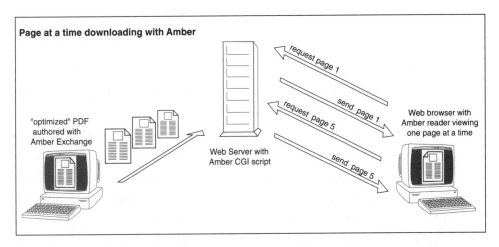

FIGURE 3.2 There are multiple components to the page-at-a-time download-ing process. First, the author of the PDF document must "opti-mize" the file using the Amber version of Exchange (3.0), which reorders the elements of the file for downloading over the Inter-net. Second, the WWW server on which the document is going to be published must have the Amber Byteserver CGI script running, to handle requests from users to serve only the number of bytes required to display one page of the document. Finally, the user at the other end must be equipped with the Amber Reader and an Amber-supporting browser such as Netscape Navigator 2.0.

PDF or HTML. Second, the Web server that is hosting the PDF file must have the Amber byteserver capability (the ability to parse out PDF files), which is native on those servers whose makers have licensed the Amber technology from Adobe—currently, the Netscape, Open Market, Quarterdeck, and Oracle Web server software. If you or your Internet service provider are using a different brand of server software for your Web site, you must employ the Amber Byteserver CGI script, which will be made available at no charge on Adobe's Web site. Third, the user on the other end must be equipped with the Amber Reader, as opposed to Acrobat Reader 2.1 or earlier, for page-at-a-time, online browsing of Amber PDF files. As with previous versions of the Acrobat Reader, Adobe will distribute the Amber Reader for free. Users of

Netscape 2.0 will be prompted to directly download the Amber Reader off of Netscape's server whenever they attempt to download a PDF file.

Not only does Amber parse PDF files by the page, it also reorders the data elements of the PDF file in a process called "linearization," or "progressive rendering." A linearized PDF file will cause the different elements to appear onscreen in order of complexity—first the text, then the images, and then the embedded fonts. For faster display of embedded fonts, Amber has a "font blitting" feature that displays embedded fonts first as substitution fonts while it looks for the embedded outline, then "blits" it onscreen. If the linearized PDF file has a series of pages with the same background elements, it will store that background as one object in the file, downloading text and images over it. Similar to the "forms" that can be created with Level II PostScript, this economical way of displaying backgrounds tremendously cuts down on the time it takes each page to render on the screen. Adobe has decided to reorder the elements of PDF files; Pam Deziel, Product Marketing Manager for Acrobat, explains, "The PDF file format is designed for random access. But if you're getting something over the wire, that's the opposite of the way you want to treat something that you're sending to the printer [when you want all the elements to appear at once]. So we're optimizing PDF files to put the objects in a more accessible order for downloading off the Internet." Using release 3.0 of Acrobat Exchange, publishers will be able to "Save As" PDF files as Amber PDFs, linearizing them for online use. The Acrobat Distiller 3.0 will initially mimic this "Save As" Amber function, but Adobe is planning to completely integrate the linearization process with a future version of the Distiller, and also with a batch linearization plug-in for Macintosh, Windows, and UNIX. Deziel also revealed that, in time, they expect to linearize all PDF files for all of the digital media. She says, "We haven't done any benchmarking, but linearization would likely give a small performance improvement with CD-ROM, and a little bit on local machines."

Not only will Amber let users browse PDF files more quickly, those PDF files will interact better within Web browser interfaces and even within HTML files. When integrated with a browser such as Netscape, Amber PDF files can be viewed seamlessly *within* the browser window, and navigated using the browser's toolbar. In Netscape 2.0, you can even "dock" the Acrobat toolbar on the bottom or sides of the screen to prevent confusion. This tight integration is a vast improvement on the old way of watching a PDF file download within the browser window, and then suddenly finding yourself inside the Acrobat window. With Netscape 2.0, you can even browse nonoptimized PDF files inside the Netscape window, as long as you are using the Amber Reader (but you must download the whole file first). Amber also offers "New Views" for optimized PDF files, such as continuous scrolling down PDF pages, and "two-up" viewing of two PDF pages at once. Another exciting aspect of the Netscape/Amber integration (also possible with other browsers) is that you can embed a visible PDF file within an HTML page. For example, you could have an HTML home page in which the pictures are actually PDF links to full-fledged PDF documents. This is a great alternative to the traditional way of indicating links to PDF files, with the "PDF" icons that are actually GIF images. Judy Kirkpatrick, Market Development Manager for Acrobat, charts the direction of all these changes. She explains, "Our real goal with Amber was to make the viewing of PDF files absolutely as seamless as viewing HTML documents. Amber achieves that with faster download times, and with the ability to use the Acrobat toolbar within the browser and zoom in on a document. That's something you can't do with HTML, in Netscape or with any browser."

With Amber, PDF files will interact so well with the standard language and protocol of the Web that the ratio of HTML to PDF files out there may lean less heavily on the HTML side. But will Amber ever completely eliminate the need for HTML files? Judy Kirkpatrick responds, "I don't think HTML will ever go away, because there's just too much content already in HTML. And with tools like PageMill, it's going to get easier and easier to create good-looking HTML documents. What I think we will see is people competing for other people's attention on the Web as more and more sites come up, and if they believe that they can design better with their existing tools than without, they're going to leverage those tools by publishing with PDF." And as more and more users become equipped with the Amber Reader, she continues, "I think you will start to see people building their whole Web site in PDF." John Monahan, Director of the Graphics Department of the Associated Press, echoes that prediction. He says, "This is why I believe PDF will win—it just enriches everyone's experience. The artist has a huge new opportunity to take content and start linking it, but it doesn't change the way the work is done—it just enhances it."

PDF Management with SiteMill

In September 1995, Adobe president John Warnock announced his company's acquisition of the six-person company Ceneca Communications and their HTML authoring tools, PageMill and SiteMill. Some were shocked at the price Adobe paid for the small outfit, and that they were purchasing tools for the previously reviled HTML format. But everyone came around when they saw these products demonstrated—here was a software program that brought the best of WYSIWYG technology to HTML authoring. In PageMill, you can design a Web page in minutes simply by typing in normal text, and dragging-and-dropping pictures into a template. All of the necessary conversions to HTML and the standard image formats are performed by the software in the background. Adding hyperlinks in PageMill is an easy copy-and-paste procedure that's impossible to screw up—the software won't let you create misplaced or dead links that go nowhere. The second product, SiteMill (Figure 3.3), is a program for keeping track of the names, locations, and links of all the files on your Web site. SiteMill performs a constant inventory, repairing all links so that they point to the right place and notifying you of the corrections. Capable of automatically solving all of the possible mishaps involved in maintaining a Web site, SiteMill is a real "why didn't I think of that?" software tool.

Ceneca did not originally design PageMill and SiteMill to handle PDF files, but you can be sure that's what Adobe had in mind when they scooped up those products. "We have some pretty big plans for what we want to accomplish with the Ceneca group," said Kevin Wandryk, Director of Business

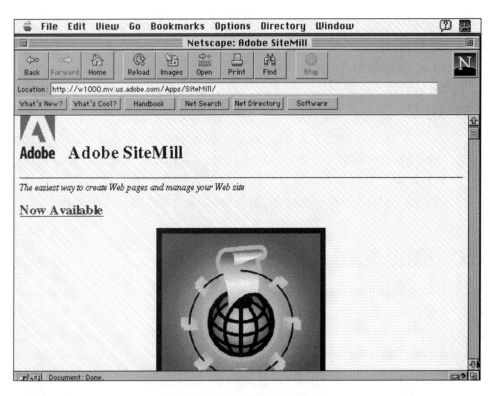

FIGURE 3.3 The SiteMill page on Adobe's Web site, at http://www.adobe.
com/Apps/SiteMill/. Check here for upgrades to the Web site
management software, which is destined to support PDF files
in a future release.

Development at Adobe. Adobe shipped off the first release of PageMill with
no PDF compatibility, since that integration may take a while to rationalize.
PDF documents are really intended to be created out of desktop publishing
applications, rendering a "PDFMill" sort of unnecessary. But once Amber is
released, we may see PageMill handling encapsulated PDF files as images
within HTML pages. The SiteMill product offers more potential for PDF, as
a management system for Web sites that combine HTML and PDF. The first
release of SiteMill offers minimal support for PDF files, but integration will
be tighter in subsequent releases. Presumably, SiteMill will eventually take

complete inventory not just of the names and locations of PDF files, but of all the links inside the PDFs, perhaps even keeping statistics on page-at-a-time downloading performance from the host Web server.

As for the heresy of Adobe's adopting HTML authoring tools, Product Marketing Manager Pam Deziel responds, "We don't really see PDF and HTML as competing. I look at PageMill and SiteMill and think, 'these are *great* products, they're terrific, and long overdue.' What we need to do now is make sure that PageMill and SiteMill handle PDF as well as they handle HTML in terms of managing links and the tasks of webmastering."

Acrobat and Java

If you are already a Web publisher, you've probably heard all about Java, Sun Microsystems' programming language that is able to create independent "applets" to perform operations on the Web. Java has sparked great interest among both the software and publishing industries, because it is a portable and dynamic language for creating interactive content on the Internet. Java can also be embedded into other software applications to extend their performance on the Web, on CD-ROM, and even in hardware appliances. Because Java applets can run independently of an operating system, the language has been seen as a potential threat to the monopoly of Microsoft Windows. Ideally, you could perform all the operations you need with Java applications, on a computer without Windows, DOS, or any of the operating systems. Whether or not Java contributes to the crumbling of the Microsoft empire, applications of the language are sure to crop up quickly and become a standard way of communicating on the Web.

In December 1995, Adobe announced an agreement with Sun Microsystems to license the Java programming language for integration with Acrobat and PageMill. The details of the integration have not yet been ironed out, but Adobe CEO John Warnock is aware of the implications of the agreement. He notes, "The huge installed base of Adobe customers will have the opportunity to merge their professional design and communication skills with the interactive capabilities of the Web in an unprecedented way. With technologies such as Java and Acrobat, Adobe and Sun can open Web publishing to a much wider range of content providers and end-users while significantly improving the Internet as a platform for business and consumer communications."

By integrating Java into Acrobat, Adobe is clarifying the distinction between Acrobat as a document format, and as a full-blown multimedia Web format. What Acrobat lacks in the way of interactivity, it can gain with Java applets embedded in PDF files. Pam Deziel comments on that distinction, "What Acrobat really is, is a product for composed electronic documents. What Java really is, is a programming language. For us, Java would be the little agent or program that gets embedded in a PDF document. Sun intends to create a set of authoring tools, and what Acrobat is all about is to work with authoring tools to be a delivery mechanism for content."

Cascade Systems is the first integrator of Java and Amber with their new MediaSphere W3, a search and retrieval system for all kinds of digital files. MediaSphere W3 can retrieve PDF files and byteserve them with Amber or display them as thumbnails in a "lightbox" viewer they created with Java. For more on MediaSphere W3, see the section on Cascade MediaSphere in Chapter 11, "Making Your Web Site Searchable."

Editable PDF Files?— Editability versus File Integrity

One of the guiding principles of Acrobat and the PDF format has been that, like paper, PDF documents are a final product, the content of which cannot be altered by the user. The PDF format is open to Plug-ins such as Re:Mark, which let an Acrobat Exchange user annotate a PDF with highlighted text, crossout lines, circles, and other marks. It is not possible to change the text or alter the images of a PDF without opening up the PDF in a design editing program such as Adobe Illustrator (but this is a shaky operation). For many publishers, the uneditability of PDF documents offers a welcome first layer of security to their content, especially when they are publishing on the Web. It has been a major distinction between PDF and HTML Web documents that the former cannot be altered and republished by readers of the document, while the latter's source file is visible and vulnerable to such republishing. Acrobat service bureaus and PDF publishers on corporate networks have, however, expressed the desire to integrate PDF into their production workflow by editing the contents of PDF files. John Monahan, Director of the Graphics Department at the Associated Press and leader of the crusade for editable PDFs, says, " I see PDF as being a core editing technology for Internet documents. PDF is not a final format. It has to be an intermediate format."

The architecture of the PDF format is not inherently read-only, but every PDF file has a level of encryption embedded in it that prohibits changes to the original content. The resistance to allowing editability, according to Monahan, lies with the Acrobat engineers at Adobe. He explains, "There's a lot of resistance in Engineering to this idea. They've got so much on their minds right now, editability was the thing they put out of their minds from the very beginning. I think they decided consciously not to make that a feature." Not only would including editability have threatened the hard-won features of cross-platform fidelity and device-independence, but it may have confused the direction of PDF as "digital paper," a final format for publishers and corporations to exchange. Monahan contends, however, that the market will continue to demand editable PDF files. He says, "There's going to be a hue and cry for support of groups, blocks of text, named colors, and styles in PDF files."

Now, two years after the release of Acrobat 1.0, Adobe has begun to develop a Plug-in called "Touch-Up," which offers limited editing of PDF files in Acrobat Exchange. Touch-Up is presently a very buggy Plug-in that has not yet been released by Adobe, but it will probably be included with Acrobat 3.0. It has four primary editing functions: to correct errors in PDF files generated from the Capture scanning software, to make limited changes to text, to "white out" a graphic, and to edit images using Adobe Photoshop. For a file format that was not designed to be editable, these functions can be considered major achievements, although they do not drill very deep into the contents of PDF files. Clearly, Touch-Up will not satisfy the needs of people like Monahan who want to integrate PDF into the newspaper production workflow, but it does make a great eleventh-hour tool for Web publishers and PDF production houses.

There is another editing feature under way for Acrobat 3.0 that *will* enable the level of editing required to make Acrobat a production workflow tool. Called *Layers* (a term that may be familiar to users of Adobe Photoshop), this feature allows the different elements of a document, such as a company letterhead and text of a letter, to be added or replaced independently. Each layer will be subject to encryption, so that the author of the PDF can determine which parts of the document can be altered by the user. This has intriguing implications for PDF files on the Web, as Web publishers will be able to fine-tune the level of interactivity of their PDF documents. Layers would also solve the problem of PDF forms, making it possible for a user to input information directly into a PDF document (the form would be one layer, and the filled-in portion a layer on top of the form). In the case of a production workflow process, changes could be made only to certain layers of a document, such as the images. At the end of the process, the entire PDF file could be encrypted to disallow any further changes.

Introducing editability to PDF files certainly broadens Acrobat's role in the software market, making it perform authoring tasks in addition to conversion and display tasks. Mohahan admits, "I have proposed a very complex PDF environment in which most of the heavy lifting would be managed by PDF, which really challenges the format." However, Monahan believes that editability is necessary to Acrobat's success in the publishing market. He maintains, "PDF is a natural display language for anyone in the publishing business today, because it is an extension, or subset, of PostScript. So it integrates with the existing infrastructure; the production of content is already happening.

The people who would do this are in place." HTML, by contrast, is an editable but nonPostScript language that is incapable of reproducing the efforts of an existing design staff (and which that staff is probably incapable of encoding).

Structured PDF?— Introducing Information about a Document's Content to PDF Files

In Chapter 1, we outlined the ways in which PDF is different from HTML and its forefather SGML. One of the primary differences listed was that an HTML file contains information about the structural contents of a document (e.g., title, Header 1, list 1, etc.), conveyed by the tags with which the author is required to encode the document. In HTML and SGML, including this information is necessary for the display of the document, whereas PDF's display information comes from PostScript. PostScript does not know and does not care about the actual content of a document; all it needs to know is where to place each dot that makes up the fonts and graphics on the page. There are, however, some instances in which it might be helpful for a PDF file to contain the kind of information contained in HTML tags. First, if a publisher is creating a PDF book and wants automatically to add Bookmarks for each chapter, it could be done in a flash if only Acrobat knew the titles of each chapter. Second, publishers may want to store all of their PDF publications in a database, with a simple index of the title and author of each one. With structured PDFs, you could perform a quick search on those elements without having to go through a full-text search engine. And last but not least (this was actually the impetus for structuring PDFs), people with vision disabilities are not able to read unstructured PDF files. Since special devices like Braille printers and screen readers cannot convey the formatting of a document that would give a seeing user a sense of its logical structure, information about titles, headers, and subsections would be of great help to visually challenged readers of a long document.

Adobe is well aware of these potential applications for structured PDFs. Rick Brown, Director of Public Relations for Acrobat, said "We solved a very hard problem at first—how do you come up with a way to display visually rich documents? Acrobat has achieved that. Now, we want to make PDF a more dynamic file format—outputting to different file formats, and including structure." Adobe has slated their project to introduce "logical structure" into the PDF language for completion in 1996. The technology to embed structural information in PDFs will be manifested as solutions-based extensions for regular and visually challenged Acrobat users. The first product will be an Accessibility Plug-in for the Windows version of Acrobat, which will enable people with limited vision to access PDF files with Windows screen-reading programs and print them to Braille printers. No further information about structure extensions has been released, but we can probably look for a basic structure plug-in, and eventually even an SGML-to-PDF conversion tool.

Acrobat Clones: Third-Party PDF Authoring Tools

One of the greatest indications of Acrobat's success will be the extent to which third parties imitate it with PDF viewers and manipulation tools. Although these companies essentially would be competing with Acrobat, they would expand the market for PDF documents. Pam Deziel, Product Marketing Manager for Acrobat, said, "There are actually half a dozen Acrobat clones out there, and we think that's a good thing because it's very difficult for us to get our coverage as broad as we'd like it to be to make PDF an international standard for electronic documents. And we like the competition. There are always one or two alternative products out there that push you to be innovative." From a publisher's perspective, these third-party PDF tools can be very helpful in solving a particular problem that Acrobat can't handle.

For example, the first commercial PDF clone, made by Zeon Corporation of Taiwan, handles the Double Byte Character Set for displaying the Chinese, Japanese, and Korean languages (Figure 3.4). Adobe Acrobat does not yet

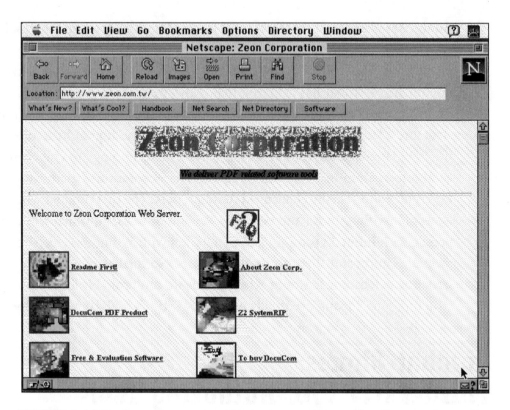

FIGURE 3.4 The home page for Zeon Corporation, the first makers of a commercial Acrobat clone. Their "DocuCom" suite of PDF publishing products supports direct editing of PDF files, and the Asian character sets.

support double byte characters, although it will in a future version of the Distiller (codenamed *Kirin*). Zeon also beat Adobe to the editing features that they are planning for the Touch-Up plug-in, with their DocuAuthor product. If you need those features *now,* you may want to contact Zeon on the Web at http://www.zeon.com.tw. The downside, however, is that Zeon's products are considerably more expensive than the Adobe originals. Their equivalent of Acrobat Exchange (without a Distiller), DocuPlus costs US$99.90. DocuAuthor, which adds editing features to DocuPlus, costs $799. And their high-end product DocuMaker, which adds a Distiller clone and a batch-server mode conversion tool to the DocuAuthor package, costs a hefty $1,799. But before long, Adobe or another third party will pick up on those now-costly features, and you may be able to get them for less.

Beyond 3.0

We asked a few of the Acrobat masterminds to look into the crystal ball and reveal some of the long-term goals for Acrobat. Kevin Wandryk, Director of Business Development, said, "In the future, the focus will be on creating building blocks for specific publishing solutions. Like the Reader with Search for CD-ROM publishers."

Pam Deziel, Product Marketing Manager, believes that "The direction from here will be more and more interactivity, higher quality of presentation on the screen. Probably the next order of business is forms. The Acrobat Pro product will be more of a composition-type product that would give the author of electronic documents everything he needs to create and publish documents. The Exchange product will evolve to become more of a business user's collaboration tool, so if I spend most of my day creating spreadsheets and word processing documents and using email, it gives me a set of tools to integrate them."

Judy Kirkpatrick, Market Development Manager, said, "One-button publishing is what we want to get to. You click a button, and you get a PDF file. And you'll find us continuing to push PDF authoring upstream. You'll see more and more support in Adobe applications, more organization for providing support to third-party applications." Simplification and streamlining of the Acrobat product line, and extending support for PDF beyond Acrobat, is Adobe's strategy for securing Acrobat's success and making PDF a standard. Publishers will benefit the most. "The future of Acrobat will have everything to do with authoring, and everything to do with removing barriers for a publisher to publish the PDF," according to Judy Kirkpatrick.

Future Developments in the Web Infrastructure

The Web is bound to grow and change at a rapid pace in the next few years. Here is a brief forecast of the developments that may affect Web publishing, borrowed from *The Internet Publishing Handbook* by Mike Franks.[1]

- *More people on the Net.* The most explosive growth on the Web is the number of users online, who are both launching sites and loading the popular servers. As hardware improves and communications bandwidth becomes greater, overpopulation on the Web won't be a problem. Increased bandwidth may come from any of these technologies—the integration of cable wires with the Internet, ATM (Asynchronous Transfer Mode), and ISDN (Integrated Services Digital Network). In the meantime, owners of very popular Web sites should consider setting up "mirror" sites to relieve the stress on their primary server.

- *Better search tools.* Automated indexing of Web content is leading to better Web directories. We may not continue to enjoy indexing and searching tools for free, however, as they are getting overloaded. Most likely, it will be more common for Web site owners to provide their own search engine, like the Verity Topic engine for PDF files.

- *Tighter security and full-fledged Web commerce.* Thanks to Terisa Systems' integration of the SSL and S-HTTP security mechanisms in 1995, the prospect of secure commercial transactions over the Internet is quickly becoming reality. Soon, corporations will be able to license the system, and Web browsers will support it. Better document-based encryption for PDF files is also under way, so that publishers can protect copyright as well as sell their content on the Web.

- *VRML and other multimedia data formats.* VRML (Virtual Reality Markup Language) is already being accepted as a new standard on the Web. Its applications for publishers and businesses are not readily evident, but virtual reality on the Web is sure to be popular with surfers.

- *Reverse Web document delivery.* With the development of Web "agent" software that can search and retrieve documents off of remote Web servers, Web publishing may become more of a two-way street (or superhighway, as it were). Netscape had developed the Server-Push and Client-Pull technologies, in which servers can be programmed to send documents at intervals to Web clients, and browsers can be programmed to continually check a server for updates. Another technology, the CCI (Common Client Interface), is under development. Not unlike Netscape's Client-Pull, the CCI is the reverse of the CGI (Common Gateway Interface), in that it lets the author script Web browsers to go out and grab documents at determined intervals.

- *More Web publications.* Not only is it the cool thing to do, publishing electronic periodicals on the Web is an attractive alternative to print publishing. With rising paper and postage costs, print is starting to look rather paltry by comparison to glowing Web journals, especially when they're in PDF. Besides, electronic journals are interactive, searchable, and don't take up storage space. Their distribution is also more easily tracked by publishers. One aspect of Web publishing yet to be ironed out is, should publishers charge for each download, or use advertising to cover all costs? The very concept of advertising is challenged by the Web, and few are sure on what basis to charge for them. The ability of publishers and advertisers to work out a new relationship will in part determine the success of e-journals.

It is hard not to be optimistic about the future of the Web, and PDF's role in it. The technology is already in place for first-class Web publishing, and with a faster, stronger infrastructure, it can only get better.

Notes

1. Mike Franks, *The Internet Publishing Handbook* (Reading, MA: Addison-Wesley, 1995), 329–340.

Chapter 4

When to Use HTML, and When to Use PDF: Determining the Optimal Mix for Your Site

In 1995, Adobe ran a print advertisement in several of the mainstream Internet magazines that showed two screenshots of a Web page, one in HTML and one in PDF. Above the HTML screenshot read the word "COMMONPLACE," in a rather aggressive boldface. Above the PDF screenshot, which looked much the same but had original fonts, read the word "COMPELLING." When we spoke to Judy Kirkpatrick, Market Development Manager for Acrobat, in September 1995, she said, "That's the last contentious ad I do against HTML." That advertisement provoked over 14,000 phone calls responding to its offer of a "free online publishing kit." September 1995 was the month that Adobe acquired Ceneca Communications and their HTML editing tools PageMill and SiteMill and announced HTML output options for several of their authoring software tools. Now that Adobe is the proud parent of Ceneca's popular HTML tools, its spokespeople have rescinded their attacks on HTML, instead advocating a peaceful coexistence between HTML and PDF on the Web. But what is that happy medium? The choice now comes down to you, the publisher, to combine the two formats successfully on your site. What follows are some tips to help you decide when to use PDF and when to use HTML.

When to Use PDF

When You Just Don't Want to Start from Scratch

Repurpose is a big word in electronic publishing these days. Gone is the stigma of your school days, when recycling term papers was tantamount to self-plagiarism. Repurposing your existing content for your Web site is an economical and speedy way to stake your claim in cyberspace. Acrobat is a shortcut to repurposing that content, since you can take the original files from your desktop publishing applications, zip them through the Distiller, and launch them on your Web site without writing so much as one HTML tag. The very same files you used to print out glossy-paper brochures become living digital documents on your Web site. With a few points, clicks, and drags, you can breathe new life into those documents by adding hyperlinks, Bookmarks, and article threads. And you're spending nothing over the cost of your Web site and the Acrobat box. (Or, you could hire a new designer and an HTML code writer, and buy whichever HTML software "helpers" that HTML encoder needs to keep his or her sanity.)

When the Design Matters

The practicality of the above argument notwithstanding, the guiding principle of Acrobat is to preserve the original "look and feel" of documents. Adobe prides itself on Acrobat's fidelity to those aspects of a document that are less tangible (formatting, fonts, etc.), but which communicate more about a document's content and its author than text alone. Even during Adobe's announcement of their acquisition of Ceneca's HTML tools, John Warnock put this principle above all else when he said, "It's going to be eons before you can express the content of today's authoring programs in HTML. If you want expressive control, you will go the PDF route." Acrobat's "expressive control" lets your Web document and your organization be more noticeable, more recognizable, more persuasive, and more memorable. We think the following types of Web documents must be rendered in well-designed PDF.

Official Corporate Documents

This would be anything where your corporate identity is at the forefront: fiscal reports, research reports, internal handbooks, promotional materials, catalogues. Design and production costs for these documents are probably already in the company budget. By publishing those same documents in PDF (Figure 4.1), you can leverage that investment to your Web site (and cut down on costly distribution of the print version).

Advertisements

Advertising is an essential application of Acrobat. It is particularly important that ads on the Web stand out from the crowd, since the medium is by nature less invasive than traditional advertising venues. GIF links to sponsors' sites are not enough—why would you want to lead your visitor astray from your site, anyway? Instead, you can include a visually striking PDF advertisement as a page within another PDF file, magazine-style. If you've already invested in

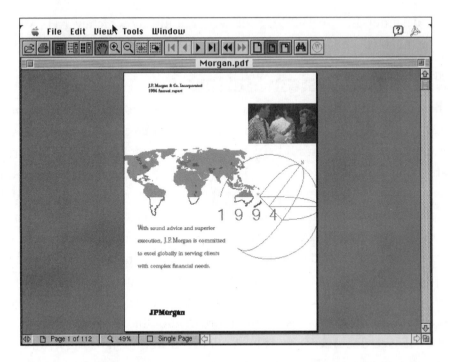

FIGURE 4.1   The *J.P. Morgan Annual Report* in PDF is a document in which they had already invested a design and published on paper. Distilling it into PDF and publishing it on their Web site preserves that original design at a negligible cost, and expands the potential audience for the document by the thousands.

print ads, you can just repurpose those ads in PDF on your own and others' Web sites (Figure 4.2).

Magazines and Journals

One of the great ironies of Web publishing is that *HotWired*, the Web version of the psychedelically designed print magazine *Wired*, is authored in HTML. These days, you have to shock your readers into attention with a striking design, especially when the content requires a longer-than-average attention span. Trying to achieve this in HTML is going to result in very large, image-heavy files. In PDF, your readers can preview the magazine in Amber, down-

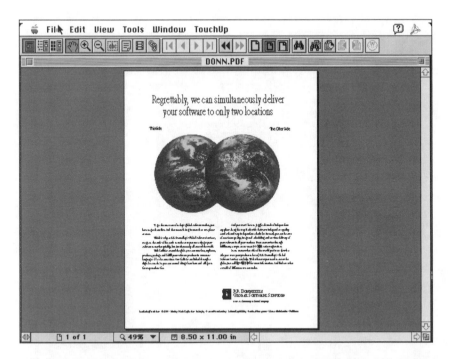

FIGURE 4.2 R&R Donnelley placed this advertisement as a PDF in *Acropolis* magazine, which is an exact copy of the print advertisement they have published in magazines like *Business Week.* Using the Web link tool in Acrobat, they added value to the ad by making their company logo, at the bottom of the page, a Web link to their own Web site.

load the whole file, and browse it offline at their leisure. Even if your magazine or journal does not aspire to the jolting appearance of *Wired*, you can easily publish an online version of your print publication with Acrobat (Figure 4.3).

And that's just the beginning. When you publish even the most modest PDF document you establish your Web site as a class act, as the British chef, Stephen Nigel Joshua Parkins, did when he published his curriculum vitae in PDF on his Web site (http://www.pow.com/culinarycreativity/face.html). We give him four stars.

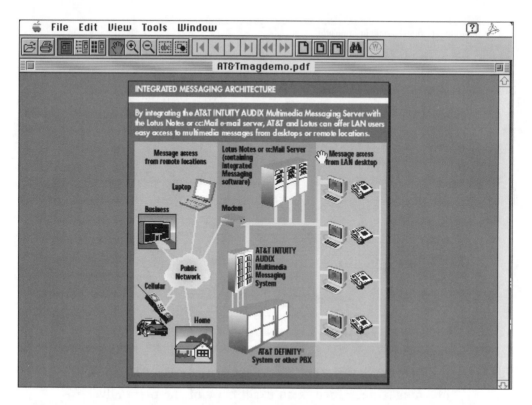

FIGURE 4.3 This is a sample page from the PDF version of *AT&T Technology* magazine. This same diagram in a Web image format like GIF would have a gigantic file size, while in PDF it is a well-compressed and beautifully rendered page. A page like this requires no more effort to distill into PDF than a simple text document.

When Your Document Is Long, and You Want a Compact File Size

Now that you're convinced that a richly designed PDF document is the way to go, you may start hearing that little voice in your head: *But the file size is going to go through the roof!* That little voice may be echoed by a lot of PDF naysayers, but the truth shall now set you free. Listen instead to Adobe's Pam Deziel:

There are a lot of myths about PDF on the Web. One is that PDF files are big. We know that a PDF file in most cases is significantly smaller than the original application file, but if you compare apples to apples in terms of content, PDF files in most cases are also smaller than a comparable HTML file with a couple of rich GIF images.

There are specific techniques you can employ to shrink down the file size of your PDF. One general guideline is, if you have the Acrobat Distiller, use it. The Distiller employs three different compression methods, each one maximized for specific types of information—text and graphics, color and greyscale images, and bilevel images (monochrome black and white). The Distiller also gives you the option to turn compression on and off, choose which kinds of compression you want and at which levels, and downsample files to a specific dpi. The PDF Writer, by contrast, uses one kind of compression for both color and greyscale images, and does not allow for user preferences. Becoming familiar with the various kinds and levels of compression offered by the Distiller will help you create very compact, efficient PDF files for Web transmission.

Another point that Judy Kirkpatrick makes is that even if an HTML version of a long document is a smaller file than the PDF version, people will be less inclined to read the long HTML document online:

If it's a short burst of information, like a page long of information, HTML is fine, because people will browse that online. But if you look at your magazine [Acropolis], or the TimesFax site, or reports that J. P. Morgan puts up, that stuff is 20, 30, 100 pages long, and people aren't going to browse that online. It's the kind of information that people want to take with them and stuff in their briefcase and read on the plane. In those circumstances, if you want to print it, if you want to deal with it offline, Acrobat is absolutely the way to go.

After all, your ultimate goal as a publisher is for people to read your content; the more options you give them for when, where, and how to read it, the better (Figure 4.4).

FIGURE 4.4 The *New York TimesFax,* a condensed eight-page version of the daily *Times,* was one of the first PDF experiments. Before Acrobat, the *TimesFax* was faxed to locations all over the globe, xeroxed, and then distributed. Now, remote readers like marines stationed on ships at sea can log in to the *TimesFax* site and get their daily news online. Here, the *TimesFax* is being rendered inside the Netscape 2.0 window.

When You Want an Independent, Secure Web Document

In the good old days of paper publishing, it was pretty difficult for content vandals to alter a book or pamphlet and redistribute it en masse. Instead, you would just round up as many copies as you could and hold a rousing book burning. On the Web, anyone with a mind to steal or ridicule your HTML content can view the source files right off of your server, edit them at will, and launch them on an "alternative" Web site. This practice has become almost obligatory for any Web site that goes up for a big Hollywood movie or political campaign. PDF imitates the security of paper because it is a static, final format that exists independently of the Web communications infrastructure. If somebody wanted to hack up your PDF document, they would have to start from scratch to redesign and regenerate it. Critics of PDF call this "inflexibility," but in the end a PDF file's static nature protects the information within it. Gary Cosimini, Adobe's New York business developer and Acrobat sage, puts it this way:

Information in a philosophical sense is something that has gone through a change of state, and with every transformation occurs a possibility for error. Computers, while they don't necessarily make errors, can transmit information in a way that loses information. HTML is information entropy; documents put into HTML lose or shed part of their structure. PDF is an attempt to create a stateless document that is designed for publication for printing.

The PDF format is also open to security restrictions that can be specified by the publisher. When you generate a PDF file in the Distiller, you have the option to require the end user to enter a password to open a file, to disable printing and editing, and disallow selecting text and graphics or adding or changing "sticky notes" within the document. When it's critical that users do not distribute a protected PDF document, as in a commercial Web publishing system, publishers can license a special copyright protection software called Keychain from Magnetic Press, an Acrobat software developer (visit http://www.acropolis.com/acropolis/mpihome.html). PDF, along with special security tools, can help to make the Web less of a jungle for publishers who want to sell content or simply protect their documents on the Web.

To Extend the Lifetime of Your Web Documents

Ever wonder how Acrobat got its name? From its ability to leap from one point and tumble onto just about anything, gracefully. When you publish a PDF document on your Web site, you are multiplying the usefulness and staying power of that document by as many different media as exist out there. If users have the Acrobat Reader, they can perform a full-text search on the document (if the publisher has indexed it with Catalog), and print it out after they browse it. If users have Acrobat Exchange, they can save the file to disk, CD-ROM, Syquest, DAT tape—whatever their digital storage medium. From there, they can distribute it via email or on their corporate LAN, and not have to worry about which platforms or software programs those people are running. If users are armed with Acrobat Catalog, they'll be able to create an actual archive of your Web publications and index them for searching by their colleagues. Judy Kirkpatrick thinks this archiving ability is a powerful reason in itself to publish with PDF:

> *Let's say you download every week's edition of the morbidity and mortality reports from the Center for Disease Control (Figure 4.5). That's 15 to 20 pages of charts and graphics which you could never retrieve in HTML. You'd have to do it as a GIF image. Somebody's not going to sit online and read 20 pages, they're just not going to do it. But, if I were a health care professional, if I knew I could download the reports every week, and I could index them using Catalog, I've got a resource at my desktop of all the latest public information I could ever want. You can't download HTML files and create indexes.*

As Judy demonstrates here, end users of your PDF document can actually add value to it and redistribute it if they have the right Acrobat tools. Not so with HTML documents, which have essentially no afterlife in the offline world. To extend the acrobat analogy, HTML documents fall flat on their face when they try to leap off of the Web. Users can save them only as ASCII text

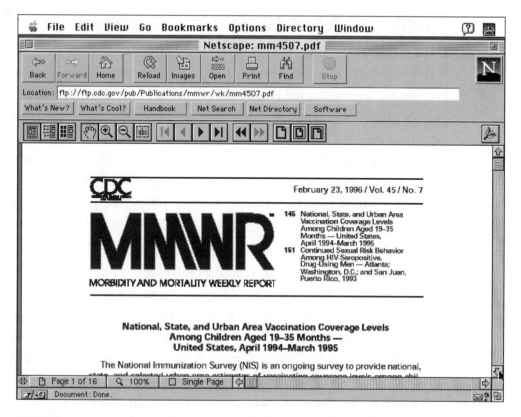

FIGURE 4.5 The *Morbidity and Mortality Weekly Report* is required reading for many health care professionals. The report has been published in PDF for over a year, making it possible for users to store an archive of the PDFs and even index them using Acrobat Catalog.

or as HTML source code, so if they print them out, all the formatting and images are gone. Printed ASCII is also hard to read—while Acrobat prints out quite nicely, having descended from PostScript, ASCII prints out at only 72 dpi. To truly experience the HTML document again, the user must log back online and navigate to your site. It's okay, even desirable, to get people back to your home page, but frustrating for a user who wants to reference one of your Web documents frequently.

When You Want to Publish Scanned Documents on Your Web Site

Let's say you are in charge of electronic publishing at a university and the English department wants to publish on the campus Web site the dissertations of all the famous writers who studied there. Naturally, you don't have digital sources for any of the papers; most of them have never seen a computer, having been typewritten. Many of them do exist on microfiche at the library, but microfiche doesn't jump onto the Web by itself either. Should you hire a bunch of undergrad minions to retype the papers and encode them in HTML? Think again.

Here's what you do have, being a university administrator: some very robust PCs on a local network, a scanner, and a budget at your disposal. From there, all you need is one box of Acrobat Capture, Adobe's paper-to-PDF scanning network software, which sells for $2,995. Capture will read those dissertations as they are scanned in, and generate fully searchable PDF files that reproduce the fonts and formatting of the originals. Itty-bitty footnotes are not a problem; users can magnify the text within the Acrobat Reader. As with all PDF files, the ones that come out of Capture are ready to be viewed on any medium you choose—from your hard disk to the Web and everything in between.

You can make your Web site a historical archive of important documents for which the source files are long gone or that never were digital files to begin with. On a corporate Web site, you could use Capture to publish your annual reports back to the beginning, all of the press items in which your company has been mentioned, even the company charter. Book and magazine publishers can republish out-of-print titles on their Web sites. Capture cannot handle color yet, but think of the possibilities for printed art images and photographs.

To get paper documents to appear magically on your Web site with minimal effort, there simply is no other way to do it than with Acrobat Capture.

When You Want to Deliver Your E-publication to Subscribers via the Web

Publishing with PDF goes part of the way to relieving users of having to navigate to your Web site every time they want to look at your documents. With Acrobat, the user can view your PDF file offline and store it on a different medium. But why should people have to keep visiting your Web site to find out if you've published something new? Remember, the wires that make up the Internet work both ways. With a new service called Digital Delivery, you can set up a subscription service on your Web site that will deliver your PDF publication to subscribers' desktops, alerting them when it has arrived.

As a complement to page-at-a-time viewing of PDF files with Amber, a service like Digital Delivery can eliminate the problem of waiting unnecessarily for a PDF file to download. Digital Delivery's delivery agent downloads the PDF in the background, leaving the user free to continue working. To see Digital Delivery in action, visit the Dial-A-Book Web site, at http://dab.psi.net/DialABook/index.html, and the CMP TechWeb site at http://techweb.cmp.com/techweb (Figure 4.6).

Delivering PDF publications over the Web extends the traditional print subscription model to the online world, letting you, the publisher, truly provide a service to your readers. A combination of a high-quality PDF and the means to deliver it directly to subscribers may be one of the few commodities that people are willing to pay money for on the Web. Instead of your Web site being an expense of dubious justifiability, you could be expanding the market for your publishing venture, even selling content online. (Isn't that what we've been promised, after all?)

When You Want to Establish High-Volume, High-Quality Production of PDF Documents

Digital Delivery is just one way that Acrobat publishing is going to ride the big Web wave to success. PDF is such an extensible format, and Adobe is so

FIGURE 4.6 CMP's TechWeb Direct was one of the first applications of the Digital Delivery agent technology. Users can download the agent for free, and then specify which CMP publications they would like to have automatically downloaded to their hard drive.

supportive of third-party development of the Acrobat software, that a number of software companies have quickly jumped on the bandwagon. A number of tools are on the way that are going to make PDF production happen at warp speed, with all of the features you could ask for, automatically generated. For example:

- Software Partners' Compose set of plug-ins automatically generates Acrobat Bookmarks simply by scanning the headers of the document. It also lets you copy hyperlinks to all the pages of the document. If you need to compile a number of PDF files into one large document, not only will Compose repaginate the composite file, but it will go in and white out the page number that appears within the page and replace it with the correct page number.

- Vertec Solutions' Verzions is a workflow tool that makes paper-to-PDF Capture production essentially a no-hands, batch process operation.

- Magnetic Press' Acrobot industrial-strength PDF generating tool will go right into your designed source files, or even your database, fiddle with them per your requests, and create huge batches of fully featured PDFs. Acrobot production is offered as a service to publishers by Magnetic Press, New York.

There are some HTML large-volume production tools, but the output applies only to mediocre Web publishing. By making the switch to PDF, you can lay the groundwork for large-scale production of high-quality documents that you can use not just on the Web, on CD-ROMs, or on your local network. Catch the wave—one high-speed, automated publishing process for all of the different media on which you want to publish.

When to Use HTML (and Some PDF Alternatives)

When It's Critical that the Information Reach All Visitors to Your Web Site

Despite the six million or so free Acrobat Readers that have been distributed, chances are most people visiting your Web site do not have the Reader. It's all well and good to point them to Adobe's site to download it, but that may take 15 minutes that potential investor does not have. So, if you can't afford to turn anybody away, put it in HTML, preferably on your home page.

PDF Alternative

Offer both HTML and PDF versions of important documents, so that Acrobat-equipped visitors can print out or save them. Or, email them as PDF attachments directly to people who have registered with your Web site.

When It's Your Home Page or Other Places Where Navigation Is Important

Your home page is the "lobby" of your Web site. It should be accessible by everyone and lead quickly and easily to the various departments. For the home page and the first few information-dense layers beneath it, HTML may be the way to go, so your visitors can navigate quickly to their point of interest. Once they've found it, then you can wow them with a rich PDF that they won't mind taking the time to download. Or, you can author the PDF to Amber so your visitors can browse it online a page at a time.

PDF Alternative

Create an "alternative" home page in PDF that links directly off of your HTML page. For Netscape 2.0 users, embed a PDF file into the HTML home page that they can click on to launch the PDF home page.

When Information Is Time-Sensitive and Frequently Updated

You don't want to be calling your Quark designer every time you want to edit your "What's New" page. It's quick enough to distill files into PDF, but all that preliminary design work can really slow up the process of getting a file up on your Web site. For pages that need to be updated daily or even weekly, and the appearance of the information is not critical, go with HTML. The designer's art cannot be rushed and, on the Web, "What's New" can very quickly become what's old.

When It's a Form or Other CGI Business

"Forms" on the Web are boxes into which the user can enter information and send it to the Web site's server, where a "gateway program" processes the information and generates a report that is returned to the user (Figure 4.7). Such transactions are governed by the Common Gateway Interface (CGI), the standard for communications between HTTP servers and server-side gateway programs. There is work under way to introduce forms

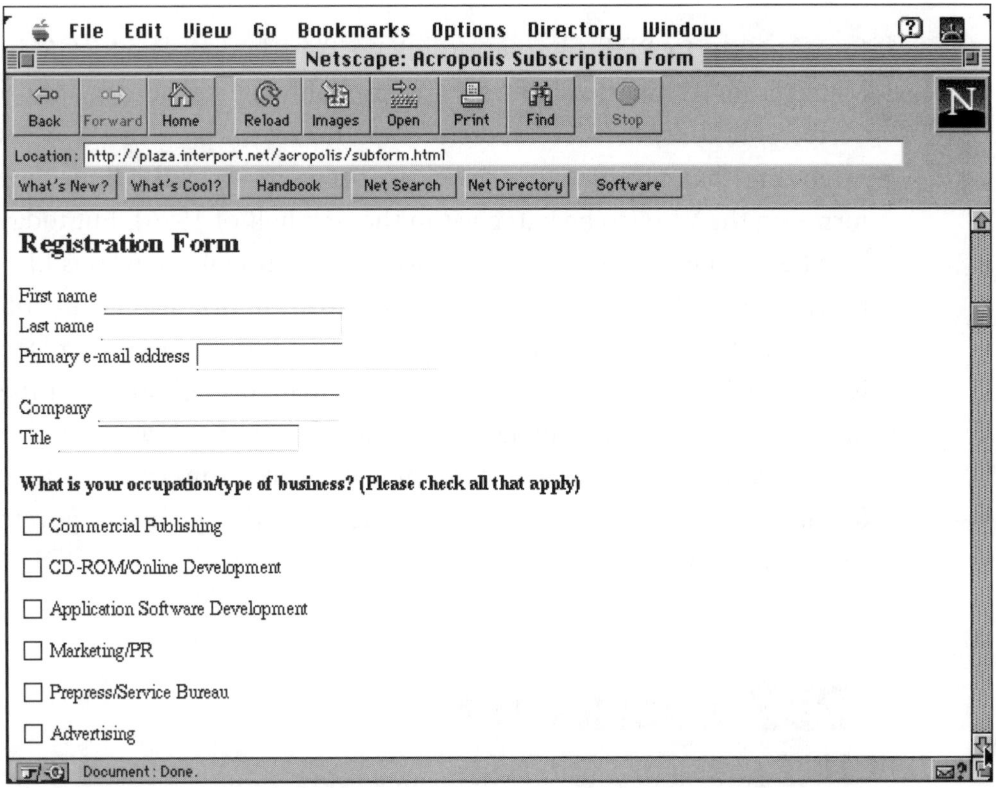

FIGURE 4.7 With an HTML form and a forms-capable Web server, you can have users fill in information in text fields, check boxes, and form menus. Unfortunately, most HTML forms look alike due to the language's formatting limitations.

PDF Alternative

If you are wedded to putting up PDF files frequently, one way to speed up the design process is to create a template in your favorite page layout program, so that all you have to do is add new text to the source file and distill it into PDF. Voila, you have up-to-date PDF files!

functionality to PDF files; according to Pam Deziel, Product Marketing Manager for Acrobat, PDF forms are "probably the next order of business." Vertec Solutions, the developers of the Tranzform plug-in for Acrobat, is extending that product to work with browsers to make bona fide PDF forms on the Web (to be launched in the first half of 1996). But today, your best bet is to generate forms in HTML, using special extensions like drop-down menus. After all, with forms it is most important that the information is understood by the gateway program, not that they look nice. There is a compelling case for designed, fully formatted PDF forms on the Web, however. For example, imagine actually doing the *New York TimesFax* crossword puzzle online, or filling in a PDF tax form, in the original IRS format, on the Web. See Figure 4.8. (Vertec is working with the government to develop a system called CyberTax for this purpose).

PDF Alternative

Have users fill in your HTML form, but program the Gateway Program to generate a PDF report with users' information, and send it back to them. You can see an operation like this demonstrated on the Dynamic PDF Web site, at http://www.best.com/~dglazer/adobe/.

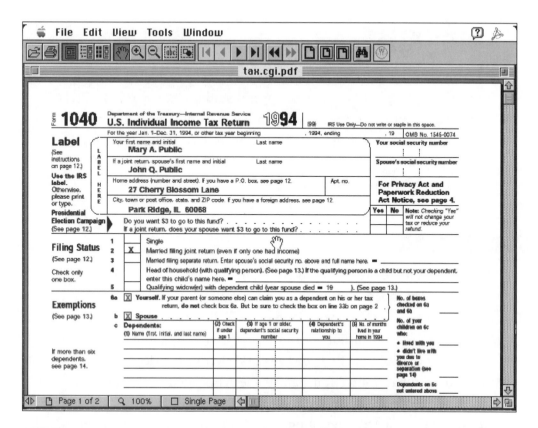

FIGURE 4.8 This PDF form is the result of HTML form input combined with a PDF template, generated on the fly with a custom CGI script. There is a tool being developed by Vertec Solutions, Inc. that would extend their user-friendly PDF forms tool Tranzform to a Web forms application. Ultimately, users will be able to fill in customized, visually rich PDF forms as they would HTML forms.

When It's a Lot of Information and the Presentation Doesn't Matter

If you need to publish a long list of raw data, and you don't care what it looks like, you may as well do it in HTML. The file size will probably end up being smaller, and the user will be able to quickly scroll down.

PDF Alternative

If you think users would rather browse and reference the list on paper, or store it on their hard drive, perhaps it would do better in PDF. PDF files print out at a higher resolution than text files, and are easier to read on-screen (the user can magnify the text). No elaborate design is necessary—just type it up in a word processing program, "print" it to the PDF Writer, and launch it on your site.

Conclusion

As more and more browsers provide seamless support for PDF, and as Adobe and other developers continue to improve PDF's performance on the Web, the need to use HTML on your Web site will diminish. In a year or two, it will be commonplace to author your home page in PDF, and have that page link off to other PDF files, so that your visitors never have to leave the visually rich world of Acrobat. John Monahan of the Associated Press envisions a PDF browsing experience devoid of toolbars and menus, "a wordless interface to an information space, navigating the Web as if it were a virtual mist." The visual quality of your content will matter much more in this "virtual mist," so you had better get started creating those artful documents! Part Two, Creating and Designing PDF Documents, will walk you through the process of turning those documents into Web-ready PDF files.

Part Two

Designing and Creating

PDF Documents

Chapter 5

Planning Your Web Publishing Project

Before You Begin— A Few Existential Inquiries

Now that you've read Part One, you've been instilled with the Acrobat gospel and can't wait to start your PDF publishing on the Web. Congratulations! You have taken the first step on your path to Web publishing success. But now is the time to step back and reflect on just what it is you would like to accomplish with your PDF Web publishing venture. While Acrobat is a great tool for creating interactive Web documents, it will not do the thinking and planning for you—only you can do the conceptual work that will give direction to your publishing project. Spending a few days or even weeks planning the goals, artistic and technological implementation, and long-term scope of your publishing project can save you money and anguish later on. Setting up PDF production and Web site maintenance processes can involve a great expenditure of time and human resources that cannot be replaced, so the mental legwork you do in the beginning will pay off. Also, it is important to realize that Acrobat is only one link in the Web publishing chain. You must also think about all of the skills and tools that go into creating a content package—writing, artwork, graphic design, even video and music, and the software and equipment to assemble them all in digital format—even before they are converted to the PDF format. Ready to throw in the towel? We wouldn't think of it. We will help you through every step of the planning stage, which, you will see, can be the most fun of the whole process. As the Adobe motto goes, "If you can *dream* it, you can *do* it." This is the time to let your imagination run free, and turn your ideas into (cyber)reality.

You are about to set foot in the still-uncharted territory of the Web. Sure, there are a lot of home pages out there, but it is still difficult to find a site that really stands out among the personal vanity pages, bland corporate sites, and gee-whiz jumbles of multimedia and virtual reality. The majority of these sites reveal remarkably little about their subject, in both senses of the word *(Who is speaking to me behind this veil of HTML? What is the point of this site?)*. As a result, these sites manage to speak to everybody and to nobody at the same time. They offer Web surfers no real incentive to penetrate the first layer, unless they are doggedly pursuing a specific piece of information (in which case their interest in you is probably a preexisting condition).

You can give your Web site a sense of identity, and reinforce your own, by asking yourself a few important questions:

Who Am I (Who Are We)?

For the purposes of this book, we're going to assume that you are not doing the entire Web publishing project by yourself. Let's say you are one in a group of people who have taken it upon themselves to publish documents on your organization's Web site. The direction of your Web publishing project must follow from the stated purpose of your organization. This purpose can be general. For example, you are a:

- *Publisher of books and magazines.* Purpose: to edit, print, publicize, and sell original written content (Figure 5.1).

- *College faculty.* Purpose: to teach, advise, assign papers to, test, and grade college students (Figure 5.2).

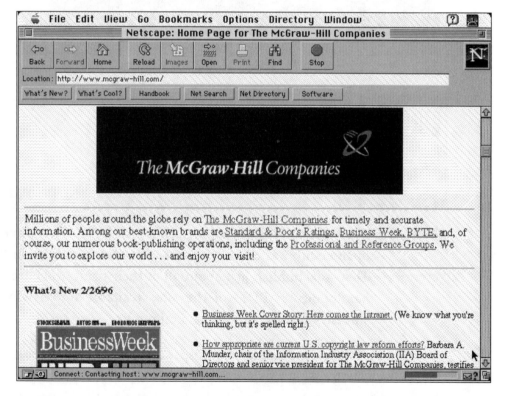

FIGURE 5.1 The McGraw-Hill home page, at http://www.mcgraw-hill.com. Established publishers such as this one are getting their feet wet in Web publishing, and Acrobat publishing in particular. But it may take a while for many of the large publishers to establish fully functional sites from which users can subscribe, download, and view PDF versions of their publications.

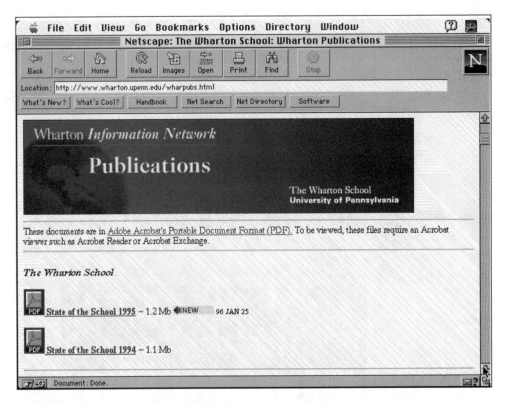

FIGURE 5.2 The Wharton Information Network, at http://www.wharton. upenn.edu/, was one of the first Web sites to publish in PDF. They now publish just about all of their print brochures and handbooks in PDF on the site, available for viewing by students, faculty, and the general public.

- *Church.* Purpose: to spread the Gospel (of God, not of Acrobat) and encourage people to join your flock (Figure 5.3).

- *WWW design house.* Purpose: to create cool Web sites (or the aforementioned "gee-whiz jumbles of multimedia and virtual reality"); (Figure 5.4).

All of these entities are very different, so their Web sites should ultimately be different, right? They will each be tailored to the driving purpose of their

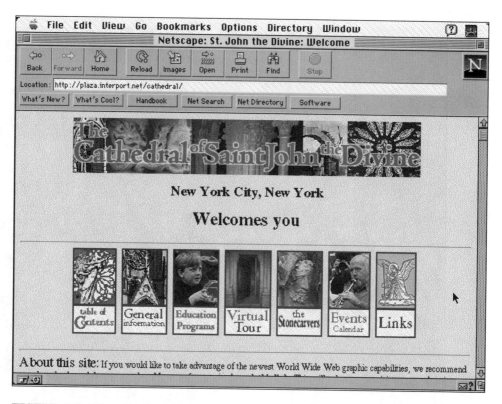

FIGURE 5.3 The site for the Cathedral of St. John the Divine in New York (http://plaza.interport.net/cathedral) does not have PDF documents, but it is a good example of a site that knows its audience. With an inviting welcome to visitors interested in the building, the stone masonry, the educational programs, the cultural events, and of course the church activities, this site will draw in just about anybody who crosses its path. And who knows, the Cathedral may decide that the photos of the Gothic structure might render much better in PDF.

parent organization. So if you were thinking that the purpose of your Web publishing project is to create a cool Web site, but you are not a WWW design house, think again.

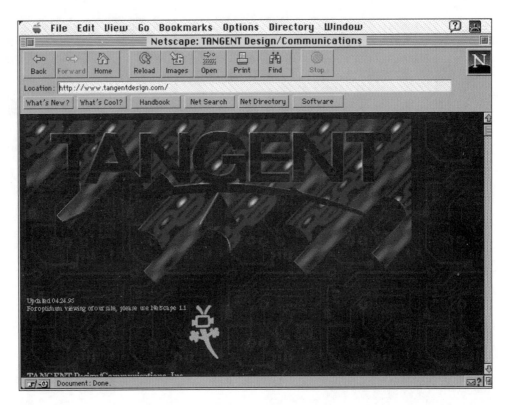

FIGURE 5.4 A home page for a Web design house. A groovy design, but for your page you would want to make the purpose of your organization clear at the outset.

What Is Our Product?

It also helps to think about what your commodity is. What do you have to offer that nobody else has? If you are the publisher, it may be a number of bestselling books. If you are the college faculty, it may be a set of dissertations and articles that embody original ideas on a range of subjects. If you are the church, you don't necessarily have a tangible product, but you may be the caretaker of a beautiful cathedral. All of these products should be leveraged and highlighted on your Web site.

Who Is Our Audience?

This is the single most important thing to consider before you begin your Web publishing project. Targeting your Web site to the right audience is the make-it-or-break-it factor in your survival in cyberspace. You may be setting up an internal Web site that is restricted to all but members of your organization. In that situation, determining their needs and interests will be easy (although you should poll your co-workers about what they would like to see on the site, and how to improve it once it is set up. If you are setting up a public Web site, the task of deciding who your audience is will be more of a challenge. You can be certain of a few demographic facts when you set up a public server. Most users of the WWW are more technologically savvy than the general population, so don't be afraid to use the correct Internet and computer terms on your site, and give them the opportunity to use forms and other interactive interfaces. Do *not*, however, make the mistake of assuming that your Web audience will be only young, white, male engineers. This may have been true in the early days of the Internet, but today Web users are men young and old, women both professional and at home, students of every possible race and persuasion, and of course kids, whose precocious surfing behavior often surpasses their parents' abilities. Finally, it is important not to forget the "World" in World Wide Web. Your public Web site will inevitably be accessed by users the world over, at every hour of the day and night. Once you set up your site for your North American audience, it may be a good idea to address your international audience, with multiple language offerings and links to other international sites (Figure 5.5).

Of course, not everybody is going to be interested in your site. Targeting your site to the people who already are interested in you or your products will help you achieve the results you want on the Web. If you are the book publisher, your audience is educated people who like to read and have money to buy books (this is a safe assumption, but of course formal market research would yield more sophisticated data). Your home page must zone in on their interests immediately. It should let them know that you know exactly who they are

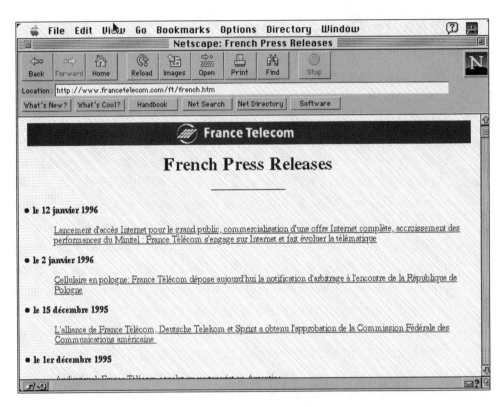

FIGURE 5.5 The France Telecom site (http://www.francetelecom.com) publishes French versions of their press releases. If you anticipate international visitors to your site (you will inevitably draw a few), or want to expand your market to other countries, offering multilingual documents is a great way to reach them.

and what they want. What do they want, anyway? They are looking to find information about your company and your products, yes, but on a more subconscious level to feel like an intelligent, Web-savvy, well-treated consumer. So you might draw them in with a trivia-question-of-the-day, or some sort of verbal puzzle that appeals to their natural inquisitiveness. Such tactics may sound silly, but remember that the purpose of the home page is not necessarily to give a table of contents of your site. It doesn't have to be "informative" at all; that is the role of the PDF documents that reside a few layers down in your site. The home page is like the entry way to a party—the user's first thought is not *who's inside?*, but *am I wanted here?* (Figure 5.6). Once visitors to your site feel welcome, they will explore your site for the golden nuggets, the richly informative documents in PDF.

The content of those documents, and the way they are designed should also depend 100 percent on their intended audience. First, let's deal with the content of the documents. What kind of information, and how much, is your audience looking for? If you are the college faculty, the students in your audience may just want to go in, get their grades, and get out. So the report cards should have only the information the audience is looking for: the grades. If you are the publisher, you'll want your documents to reflect the original

FIGURE 5.6 A bubbly welcome from the Moët site (http://www.moet.com). Home pages should be inviting so that visitors will want to burrow down to the valuable information in your documents.

content of your books and magazines, without necessarily duplicating them online. Whoever your audience is, try and get a feel for what they hope to find on your Web site, and how long their attention span is. (On the Web, attention spans are bound to be pretty short.) You'll want to provide enough information to give visitors a taste of what you have without overwhelming them with volumes of documents. You can always give visitors the option to download a long PDF file and browse it offline, after they've explored a few pages of it online with the Amber Reader. Don't forget to vary your content offerings frequently—you want to give your visitors the incentive to return again and again.

The design of your PDF documents should let your audience know what kind of a document it is, and speak to your audience's needs and tastes. For example, an annual report should have a crisp, simple design that projects an image of confidence and success, so that your audience will leave with that impression of your organization. You could take more creative liberties with a brochure or a magazine, where the persuasive nature of the document is determined in large part by the design. By contrast, some documents have such a strictly informational purpose that to design them would be a waste of your time. The report cards on a university site, for instance, do not require any design whatsover. The data within them is compelling enough to its audience. The level of design of a given document on your site should also depend on what your audience is going to want to do with the document once they see it. Will they want to print it? Are they likely to have a printer handy? Are they likely to have a *PostScript* printer handy? If yes, you'll want to design that document like you would a printed document, and make it a PDF. For documents that people are likely just to Save As text files, such as a long list of data, don't worry about the design.

One last thing to consider about your audience—it's going to take some extra work to find them in cyberspace and lead them to your site. The Web is one of the most *un*invasive communications mechanisms there is, so in order to get your message out you have to first decide for whom the message is intended, then go out and find them. The upshot of this uninvasiveness is

that once you do get your audience to come to you, there are all sorts of interactive techniques you can implement to keep them coming back. The first
step in getting them to find you is to post your site on one of the Web directories, like Yahoo! (Figure 5.7). You should also think about what paths your
audience is likely to take on the Web, and do a hyperlink exchange with the
sites that they may visit. For example, if you know your audience likes to read
about cultural events, post links on PBS Online (http://www.pbs.org), and on
the sites for your local museum and symphony orchestra. Most of the time,
other Web sites would be happy to post your link in exchange for a link to
them on your site. The more connected Web sites with similar audiences
become, the more traffic the sites get from just the people they want to reach.
Once you do start generating traffic from your targeted audience on your

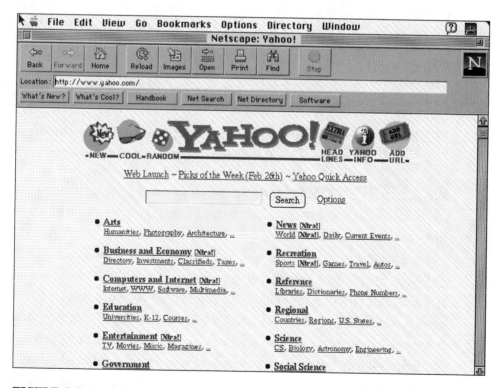

FIGURE 5.7 Posting your site in the Yahoo! directory is a great way to
generate traffic on your site.

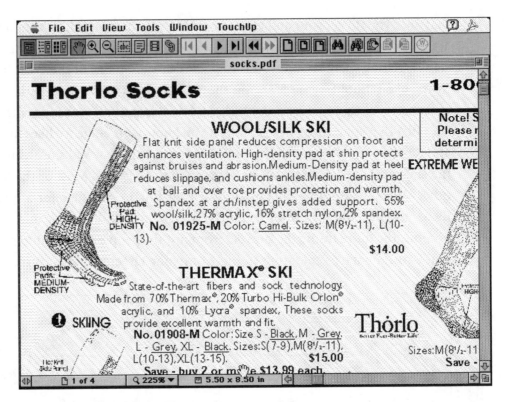

FIGURE 5.8 Catalogs are a perfect application of PDF on the Web, since their layout is often much too complex to render in HTML.

site, set up an FAQ (Frequently Asked Questions) page, so that first visitors to your site can learn from other users about the resources on your site. Post links to your email address all over your site, so that users can give you their input. Other ways to increase interaction with your audience are to provide online support for your products, to store a valuable database for users to reference, and to offer downloadable samples of your products. Make sure to serve up something that users will want to download to their local hard drive—that way they have a more permanent reminder of your product right on their desktop. Finally, don't swear off your traditional methods of advertisement in drawing visitors to your site—sending out a postcard with your URL may be the best way to get bookmarked in many people's Web browsers.

How Do We Communicate with Them Now?

Sum up all the ways in which you communicate with your audience now; by mail, over the phone, via email, in person? You probably use several methods, which upon scrutiny may prove to be redundant and expensive, or just plain retro. Examine what each of those methods does yield in terms of positive interaction with your audience: one-on-one interaction; getting their undivided attention; gaining valuable market information? You may be able to reproduce and consolidate these benefits on your Web site. For example, if you currently provide customer service for your book club over the phone, on the Web you could implement a system for starting and canceling subcriptions via forms, publishing interactive book catalogs in PDF in which they can order a book by clicking on a picture of its cover, and setting up a users' forum where customers can review and discuss the book of the month. However modest your first attempts to provide services on your Web site are, ultimately your Web site should relieve your organization of some of its more time-consuming and costly operations. You should start planning for it now, however, so that when you are ready to implement a new system, you have already laid the groundwork in your production process (Figure 5.8).

How Will We Improve Communication by Putting Documents on the Web?

Not only should you try to replace some of your old ways of doing things on your Web site, but you should think about new ways to communicate with your audience on the Web. Being a totally new kind of space, the opportunities to interact with your audience are limitless. Perhaps you've never really gotten to know your audience. On the Web, you have the technology to track their every step on your Web site, like observing lab rats in an experiment. Do they like to navigate the maze, or hang out in certain rooms of your Web site? Once you've discovered their patterns, you can tailor your content to better communicate with them.

What Are My Resources (People, Skills, Software, and Hardware)?

This could have been the rude awakening in your existential inquiry, but now that you've focused your goals for your Web site, it may not be. Evaluating your resources before you begin will help you focus your goals even more. First, make a list of all of the hardware you have available to put toward the project, including PCs, special data drives, extra hard drives for added memory, your Internet connection, and your Web server if you have one. (See the next section for a list of all the hardware you'll need.) Then, make a list of all the types of digital content you want on your site, such as HTML pages, GIF images, PDF documents, video and sound files, CGI scripts, and Java applets. From that list, determine how many of the appropriate software programs you have to create all of your content, and which people in your workgroup have the skills to work the software programs. Finally, decide how much time you are going to allot for the production process. If your time frame has been set for you, it is probably too short, so this is a good time to draw up a project plan as evidence that you will need more time. It is easy to underestimate the amount of time it takes to generate content and put it together on a Web site—at every step of the way, you will be faced with problems you've never encountered before. This is all the more reason to plan your project carefully.

For a more detailed discussion of what kinds of content you'll need for your Web site, see Chapter 6, "Getting Your Content Together."

Gearing Up for Acrobat Production: System and Software Requirements

Now that you have determined the goals for your Web site and assessed your resources, it's time to get down to the nitty-gritty of finding machines that can do the work for you. Chances are you already have the hardware in place, but we'll tell you how much system resources you'll need for the different kinds of PDF production, and at what point you might need to upgrade.

PDFWriter Production

If you need only create PDF documents through the PDFWriter in Acrobat Exchange, you will probably not have to gear up much. The following system requirements are based on Acrobat Exchange 2.1, but will probably remain the same for future versions. For Windows, you'll need a 386, 486, or Pentium-based PC, running Windows 3.1, Windows for Workgroups, Windows 95, Windows NT 3.5 or later, or OS/2 2.11 or Warp (running in Windows mode). Your PC must have at least 4 megabytes of RAM, and a 1.44-megabyte 3.5-inch floppy disk drive. For Macintosh, you will need a 68020 or later processor, running Apple System 7.0 or later. The Mac should have 2 megabytes of application RAM for pre-Power Mac computers, or 4MB of application RAM for Power Macs. If you plan to run the Distiller with Exchange, the system requirements will be somewhat greater. See the section on Distiller production below for Distiller system requirements. The following Exchange installation information is based on instructions in the *Getting Started* booklet that comes in the box with the Exchange software.[1]

To install Acrobat Exchange for Windows 3.1 and Workgroups:

1. Launch Windows, and make sure no other applications are running.

2. Insert Disk 1 into the floppy disk drive.

3. In the File Manager, select Run from the File menu.

4. Type "a:setup" ("b:setup" if you are using the B drive), and press Return. When the License Agreement appears, click Accept.

5. The Acrobat Exchange Installer dialog box appears. Choose whether you want to install ATM (Adobe Type Manager). ATM will give you better screen performance for Adobe Type 1 fonts, and better PCL (Printer Control Language) printing on HP Laser-Jet printers. Selecting ATM for Windows will install ATM 3.01 on

Note to Users of Windows 95 and UNIX

In the following chapters on production, we have separated our instructions, where necessary, into "Windows" and "Macintosh." Since the Acrobat program is highly independent of operating systems in its user interface, there are relatively few instances where Acrobat programs will behave differently on different operating systems. There is a divergence, however, in the terminology for accessing files and performing certain operations in Acrobat that are closely tied to the operating system, such as installation of programs. In our instructions, we have stuck to traditional Windows and Mac terminology, without giving specific instructions for users of Windows 95 and UNIX. In the case of Windows 95, Acrobat for Windows functions the same way; the program and its files are just accessed through the Windows 95 channels. For example, where we say "Program Manager," understand the Win 95 Start, Program menu, and where we say "File Manager," understand that to mean the "Explorer" program. If you are using Acrobat for UNIX, operations that interact

your system, but will not take effect until you reboot your system. When you are finished, click Install.

6. Select the target directory for Windows to install Exchange (should be C:\ACROEXCH).

7. Enter in your personal information and the serial number for your copy of Exchange (located on your registration card). Click OK.

8. Follow the Installer directions inserting Disks 2 through 4. When the Installation Complete box comes up, you have successfully installed the software. You do not need to reboot, unless you opted to install ATM.

9. You are now ready to produce PDF files through the PDFWriter, which has been installed as a printer driver in your system. To test closely with the operating system will happen differently from Windows and Macintosh versions. Please use the Windows instructions as general guidelines for using Acrobat for UNIX, and be sure to consult the online PDF guides supplied by Adobe with your Acrobat products for specific UNIX instructions.

If you are a UNIX user but have not yet purchased the Acrobat software, here are the system requirements for running Acrobat on UNIX systems. If you have a Sun SPARCstation workstation, it should be running Sun OS version 4.1.3 or later, Solaris 2.3 or 2.4, OpenWindows (3.0 or later) or the Motif window manager (version 1.2.3 or later) for Acrobat Reader or Acrobat Exchange. You will need 8 MB of free disk space for Acrobat Reader; 20 MB of free disk space for Acrobat Exchange; and 12 MB of disk space for Acrobat Distiller. If you have an HP Series 9000 workstation, it must be model 700 or higher, running HP-UX 9.0.3 or later in the HPVUE desktop environment. It must have 6 MB of free disk space for Acrobat Reader; and 14 MB of disk space for Acrobat Exchange. For detailed installation instructions for Acrobat for UNIX, refer to the *Getting Started* booklet accompanying your Acrobat product box.

out the PDFWriter, go to a simple word processed document and choose Print from the File menu. In the Print window, click on Printer and select Acrobat PDFWriter on DISK. Name the PDF file and Save it. In a matter of seconds, you will be able to view your new PDF in Exchange. For more on working with the PDFWriter, see Chapter 7, "Creating PDF Documents."

To install Acrobat Exchange for Macintosh:

1. Insert Disk 1 into the floppy disk drive and double-click on the Installer icon.

2. When the Installer splash screen appears, click Continue.

3. Click Continue in the License Agreement box.

Special Considerations for Windows

If your system has the minimum amount of RAM, 4 MB, you can set up a permanent swap file to give your system virtual memory and increase Exchange's performance. From the Control Panel, choose the 386 Enhanced icon. In the Enhanced window, click the Virtual Memory button. In the Virtual Memory box, click Change. In the New Swapfile Settings box, increase your virtual memory according to the Recommended Size. Click OK.

To install Exchange for Windows on a network using Acrobat for Workgroups, you will need to install the administrator's version of Exchange, and then install the standard version on users' machines. For further instructions, refer to your *Getting Started* guide.

To install Exchange for Windows 95, insert Disk 1 and click your Start button. Choose Run from the menu and type in "a:setup". Follow the installation instructions as described above.

4. In the Installation screen, choose Easy Install for automatic installation of Exchange into an Adobe Acrobat folder on your hard drive. Easy Install will not install QuickTime 2.0, the program required to run the Acrobat Movie Tool. Select Custom Install to pick and choose among Exchange files and the location of font software. Your choices for font locations are the System Folder or a Fonts folder within the Adobe Acrobat folder. If Quicktime is not installed on your system, select it and it will be installed to run Acrobat movies and other Quicktime movies. If you do not understand your options, you can click each one's information icon, located to its right. Or, you can click Help.

5. Choose the disk where you want the Exchange software to be installed, and click Install.

6. As the Installer asks you for Disks 2 through 4, insert them. An Installation Complete announcement will pop up when the software has been successfully installed.

7. Restart your Mac.

8. You are now ready to produce PDF files through the PDFWriter, which has been installed as an optional printer driver in your system. To test it out, go to the Chooser under the Apple menu and double-click on the Acrobat PDFWriter icon. Close out of the Chooser, and open up a simple word processed document. In the word processing program, select Print from the File menu and click OK in the PDFWriter dialog box. That's it—your new PDF will open up in Acrobat Exchange. For more on using the PDFWriter, see Chapter 7, "Creating PDF Documents."

Special Considerations for the Mac

If your Mac is on the low end of the 2 MB application RAM requirement (if pre–Power Mac) or 4 MB (Power Mac), you may not be able to open some PDF documents or use the Search tool. If you go into the Get Info dialog box (accessed through the File menu in the Finder), you will notice that the "preferred" amount of RAM is 3,200 K. There are two methods for improving Exchange performance in this situation. First, you can use the system version of ATM instead of the one installed by Exchange. The version of ATM that Exchange installs in the Adobe Acrobat Fonts folder works only with Exchange, and requires 1,000 K of system memory while Exchange is running. If you switch off the Exchange version of ATM and use a system version (which may have been bundled on your system), you can reduce the preferred memory size by 1,000 K. You must have one version of ATM running for Exchange to run. Second, you can disable the Acrobat Search Plug-in from loading every time, by placing it in the Optional Plug-Ins folder. This will let you reduce preferred memory by 510 K (360 K for the Search Plug-in and 150 K for three search indexes).

Distiller Production

Most probably you are going to be installing the Acrobat Distiller along with your copy of Exchange. For the PDFWriter alone does not a happening PDF Web publisher make! Here's what you are going to need in terms of hardware and software to run Distiller on Windows and Macintoshes. For Windows, you'll need a 386, 486, or Pentium-based PC running Windows 3.1, Windows 95, Windows NT 3.5, or OS2 2.2 or later running in Windows compatibility mode. The PC should have at least 8 MB of RAM, and a 1.44-MB, 3.5-inch floppy disk drive. For Mac, you'll need a 68020 or later processor (Power Mac is best), running Apple System 7 or later. The Mac should have at least 2 MB of application RAM for pre–Power Mac, or 4 MB of RAM for Power Macs.

To install Distiller for Windows 3.1 and Workgroups:

1. Quit all other applications in Windows.

2. Insert Disk 1 into the floppy drive.

3. In the File Manager, choose Run under the File menu. Type "a:setup" ("b:setup" if you are using the B drive) and press Return.

4. The license agreement appears. Click Accept.

5. The Distiller Installer screen appears. Enter the directory into which you want to install the Distiller, and click Install.

6. Enter your name, organization, and the serial number for your copy of Exchange, which you'll find on the registration card that came in your Acrobat box.

7. Insert the rest of the Distiller disks as you are prompted. A confirmation will appear when the Distiller has successfully installed.

8. You are now ready to produce PDF documents with the Distiller. We suggest, however, that you go straight to the Distiller online help guide, located under the Help menu in the Distiller program. You can also reach this document by selecting HELP_D.PDF in your File Manager, and viewing it in Acrobat Exchange. The Distiller guide is loaded with helpful instructions, many of which we will reproduce in Chapter 7, "Creating PDF Documents."

If memory is tight on your PC once Distiller has been loaded, try doing the file swap we described above, after the Exchange for Windows installation instructions.

To install the Distiller for Macintosh:

1. Insert Disk 1 into your floppy disk drive, and double-click on the Installer icon.

2. Click Continue in the Acrobat splash screen.

3. Click Accept in the License Agreement screen.

4. In the Install window, click Easy Install if you want automatically to install all Distiller files into a folder called Adobe Acrobat on your hard drive. Click Custom Install if you want to pick and choose among Distiller files (you can click the info icons next to each file to find out its purpose). You can install the right version of the Distiller (Power Mac or pre–Power Mac) by choosing the Adobe Distiller for Any Macintosh option. Select the destination disk for the Distiller software and click Install.

5. Enter your name, organization, and the serial number of your copy of Distiller, located on the registration card in your Acrobat box.

6. Insert additional Distiller disks as prompted. A confirmation will appear when the installation has successfully completed.

7. You are now ready to produce PDF files with the Distiller. First, however, you should browse through the online Help guide for the Distiller, accessible under the Help menu in the Distiller program. The Distiller online guide is an excellent resource for learning how to use the Distiller and understanding all your options when distilling files.

If your Mac is running low on application RAM after you load the Distiller, try the memory increasing techniques outlined above, after the installation instructions for Exchange for Macintosh.

Capture Production

If you have made the big leap and purchased Acrobat Capture 1.0, you know that the software runs only on Windows and requires quite a bit of free hard disk space. If you are just considering including Capture in your PDF production process, here are the specific system and software requirements. Capture can run on a 33 megahertz or faster 486 or Pentium-based PC (the faster the better), running on Windows 3.1 or later, or Windows for Workgroups 3.11 or later running in 386-enhanced mode. The system must have 16 MB of RAM, a hard disk with at least 15 MG of free space, 20 MB or more of permanent swap space, and an additional 2 MG for Win32 files. The PDF should have a 1.44-MG, 3.5-inch floppy disk drive and a VGA or better display adapter. Capture also installs Acrobat Exchange and ATM 3.1, so if you don't already have those programs running, you would need an additional 7.5 MG of free disk space. Obviously, you will also need a scanner and scanner software. Capture works with almost all brands of scanners, such as Canon, Epson, Fujitsu, HP, KOFAZ, Microtek, Ricoh, and UMAX.

The installation instructions for Capture are lengthy and are best referred to in the Capture *Getting Started* guide included with the software.[2] Once you've installed Capture successfully, check out the online guide for operating instructions. Also, Adobe's Web site has loads of technical notes for Capture users, located in the Support section of the site. In Chapter 7, "Creating PDF Documents," we provide a few tips for preparing Capture's ACD files to be compact PDFs for Web distribution.

Gearing Up for Web Site Production

This section will tell you how to integrate PDF publishing into your Web server if you already have a Web site. We also introduce the components of Web site hosting for those who have not yet established a presence on the Web.

For Existing Web Sites

If you already have a working Web site but have never served up PDF documents before, you will have to configure your Web server to host PDF documents. This is a fairly simple onetime procedure. The real challenge for owners of existing Web sites will be maintaining a constant flow of new PDF content on their site, which means coordinating writers, designers, PDF production people, and Webmasters to cooperate on an ongoing basis. Another challenge will be to stay on top of Adobe's developing Amber technology in its diverse forms—Amber Exchange, Amber Distiller, the Amber Reader, and the Amber byteserving technology. Adobe has moved very quickly with this technology and will continue to, so try to get involved in beta tests and upgrades. If your PDF content improves along with the Amber technology, your Web site will become more effective and draw more traffic.

Configuring Your Server to Serve PDF Files

Most Web servers are based on the NCSA or CERN HTTPD (HyperText Transfer Protocol Daemon) server software, which are the original UNIX-based Web servers. Some newer Web server software, such as MacHTTP and HTTPS for Windows NT, are not UNIX-based and are gaining popularity. To learn how to configure your server to publish PDFs on the Web, we have instructions for NCSA, CERN, and MacHTTP. If you are not using any of those servers but are using another UNIX-based server (i.e., Netscape, Open Market) or the NT server, follow the directions for the NCSA and CERN servers loosely. If you are using a server that is a few years old, you may want to consider upgrading. Some servers are automatically configured to serve PDFs, and there are many Amber-compatible servers on their way. Web server makers who have struck agreements with Adobe include Netscape, Apple, Open Market, Quarterdeck, and Oracle.

With the following commands for each of these server types, you are telling your server how to recognize the PDF file type, the .PDF file extension, and for the MacHTTP, how to handle PDF's binary data stream. You do this by adding PDF as a MIME (Multipurpose Internet Mail Extension) type to the server's list of application file extensions, so that the server can tell the browser on the receiving end what type of file is coming its way. In HTTPD servers, you can set the MIME type for PDF files in the configuration file in the Server Root. In a MacHTTP server, you tell the server how to handle the PDF binary stream in its configuration file.[3]

CONFIGURING THE NCSA HTTPD SERVER Look in the ServerRoot/conf/ mime.types file, and make sure that it contains the following line: application/pdf pdf.

CONFIGURING THE CERN HTTPD SERVER In the configuration file server_ root/config, add the line AddType .pdf application/pdf 8bit 1.0.

CONFIGURING THE MACHTTP SERVER In the MacHTTP.config file, add the line BINARY .PDF * CARO application/pdf.

Once you've configured your server along these lines, you are ready to serve up normal PDF files that users can download and view, using Acrobat as a helper application with their Web browser. To learn how to use the Amber byteserver CGI script in conjunction with Amber Exchange 3.0, so that users can view your PDFs one page at a time online, see Chapter 10, "Launching PDF Files on Your Web Site."

For New Web Sites

If you do not yet have a Web site, your first decision should be whether to host the site yourself or to engage an Internet Service Provider (ISP) to host your site on their server. ISPs will lease you space on their server to host your Web site, at a fee of about $100 per month (not including setup). Using an ISP is a good way to relieve yourself of the duties of maintaining the server, but in return you are at the mercy of their server. If your ISP is hosting many sites, users of your site may get slow service as a result. It will also be more of a hassle to get into the files on your site on a daily basis and tweak with CGI and other scripted activity. The following section will explain what is involved with hosting your Web site yourself, so you can make the right decision for your organization.

Hosting a Web site yourself involves three elements:

1. *A direct TCP/IP connection to the Internet, with a minimum bandwidth of 64 KB per second.* Your Internet connection can be established by a growing number of eager ISPs, particularly in urban areas. How much bandwidth you need is a function of the number of user requests for documents and the size of those documents. The higher both of these factors are, the more bandwidth you will need, culminating in a dedicated T1 line for heavily trafficked sites. If you are serving up a number of large PDF files for downloading, that will extend the duration of each file transfer and slow down performance on your site. For example, with a bandwidth of 64 KB per second, and one user connection per minute, your average file size could be 64 KB. But with 60 connections per minute at the same bandwidth, your average file size could be only 1.1 KB. When you upgrade to a bandwidth of 1.5 MB per second, at one connection per minute, your average file size shoots up to 1,500 K. But with 1,200 connections per minute at that bandwidth, the average manageable file size degrades to 1.25 KB, at which point you would want to increase your bandwidth even further.[4]

2. *A host computer.* When most people think of a Web server, they envision a large computer whose sole purpose is to run a Web site. In a sense, that's true, but the hardware component of a Web server is simply a powerful computer that runs Web server software. So your Web server could be a machine that you happen to have around, which you simply need to connect to the Internet and load with Web HTTP server software (the different kinds of server software are discussed next). Which computer you choose to host your Web site depends on the complexity of actions you want your Web site to perform, the anticipated number of connections per

minute, your budget, and which operating system you (or your Webmaster) feels comfortable with. Regardless of the platform, the host computer should be dedicated to its Web-serverhood, with lots of disk space and room to grow. UNIX machines are the most widely used and highly recommended server hosts, because the CERN and NCSA HTTPD server software were written for UNIX, and many other servers are based on UNIX. UNIX machines make it easy to run executable scripts, and are best at multitasking. If your budget does not permit a UNIX machine, the Linux system is a cheaper UNIX clone that runs on Intel-based machines, and does very well as a server host. A second-best option for hosting your server would be a PC running Windows NT, especially because it is much easier to install and maintain than a UNIX server. Finally, a Power Macintosh running MacHTTP (commercially known as WebSTAR) is a very easy way to establish a simple Web site for small groups and individuals. Power Macs do not offer the stability of UNIX and Windows NT systems, however.

3. *Web server software.* This is where the real action begins. Server software tells the operating system of your host computer everything it must do to receive connections and process file requests and transfers, and create documents on the fly with CGI scripts. Servers also communicate with the Web browser at the other end of the connection, telling them the rate of download, sending error messages, and so on. Many types of server software are available at no cost over the Web, and those that cost have added value such as HTML authoring software and CGI scripts for common transactions.

Following is a short list of publicly available, widely supported Web servers.

Web Servers for UNIX

The first web servers were UNIX-based, and most web servers today continue to run on UNIX. There are several versions of the orginal CERN and NCSA servers available, many of them for free. But UNIX servers are generally quite difficult to set up and require an experienced systems administrator to maintain.

CERN HTTPD

This is the true-blue original from the folks who invented the Web, and free to boot! Because it is the original, it has had the most features added to it, and may be complicated to install and configure. Its unique features include the ability to act as a proxy through a firewall, to locally cache remote documents, and to choose among multiple versions of a document according to the browser that is requesting it.[5] You can download the CERN server at http://www.w3.org/hypertext/WWW/Daemon/Status.html.

NCSA HTTPD

This one is the most popular in the United States, from the most accomplished Web developers in the United States. Also available for free, the NCSA HTTPD offers all the features you could ask for in a server, such as security based on IP addresses or passwords and the ability to execute CGI scripts. It is easier to install than the CERN server, so it is a good one to start out with. You can download the NCSA server from http://hoohoo.ncsa.uiuc.edu/docs/.

Netscape

Netscape offers two UNIX-based servers, the Netsite Communications, which sells for $1,500 (free to nonprofit educational and charitable groups), and the Netsite Commerce Server for $5,000. Why the high prices? While they are based on the NCSA and CERN servers, these ones are faster and perform better under a heavy load. They are easier to configure as well, because they have a user-friendly graphic interface for configuring the server. The Commerce Server lets your Web site perform secure financial transactions with credit card numbers (although the customer must be using the Netscape Navigator browser). Netscape servers are also preconfigured to handle Acrobat PDF files. To find out more about Netscape servers, and to test drive one for a limited period, go to http://www.netscape.com.

Open Market

Open Market sells two UNIX servers, the WebServer for information services ($1,495) and the Secure WebServer for online commerce ($4,995). The Secure WebServer supports Netscape's Secure Socket Layer (SSL) as well as S-HTTP (Secure Hypertext Transfer Protocol).[6] Both of Open Market's servers offer direct support for Acrobat PDF files.

Web Servers for Windows NT

Netscape

Netscape sells a Windows NT version of the Netsite Communications Server for the same price, $1,500 for commercial users, and free to educational and charitable nonprofits. The NT version has the same set of features as the UNIX version. For more information, go to http://www.netscape.com.

Web site

Created by Robert Denny, who wrote Windows HTTPD, Web site is a 32-bit server for Windows NT 3.5. It sells for $499, and is also compatible with Windows 95. Web site provides a graphical interface for configuring the server, creating HTML documents, and CGI scripts. It can also run Microsoft Excel, relational databases, and OLE applications right in the server. To find out more, go to http://www.ora.com/gnn/bus/ora/news/c.Web site.html/.[7]

InterNotes Web Publisher

Lotus Development Corporation (now a subsidiary of IBM) is selling a Web server for $7,500 that acts as a gateway between Lotus Notes and the Web. We address InterNotes in detail in Chapter 14, "PDF and Lotus Notes." You can also visit Lotus at http://www.lotus.com/inotes/.

Web Servers for Macintosh

MacHTTP/WebSTAR

MacHTTP, the first Web server protocol for the Mac, started out as shareware but has now adopted the name WebSTAR under the ownership of StarNine

Corporation. WebSTAR runs on Apple System 7 or higher, and supports both 68000 and Power Macs. It allows for easy graphical installation and configuration and creation of forms and image maps on HTML pages. For more on WebSTAR, visit http://www.biap.com.[8]

Apple Internet Server Solution

In 1995, Apple unveiled its version of the MacHTTP server, bundled in a PowerPC with Netscape Navigator, AppleSearch, CGI scripts, and Acrobat Pro. The Internet Server Solution ranges in price from $2,909 to $8,209. For more information, visit Apple at http://www.apple.com.

Once you decide on a Web server, you will want to register a main URL for your Web site with the main Web directories, managed by the Web Consortium (http://www.w3.org), NCSA (http://www.ncsa.uiuc.edu), and Yahoo! (http://www.yahoo!.com), among others. Your main URL should be simple and easily guessed by users looking for your site: http://www.yourfirm.com is the model to follow. Your main URL signifies three things to the Web browser and user—"http," that your server speaks the HTTP Web protocol; "www.yourname," the name of your host machine; and ".com," that you are a commercial organization. If you are an educational organization, use the .edu extension; if you are a government organization, use the .gov extension; if you are a military organization, use .mil; and if you don't fit into any of those categories, assign the .org extension to your host name. If your host server name does not have the official name "www.yourfirm," that's okay; most URLs are aliases of the actual host names. Creating a general alias makes it easier for people to find you on the Web, and it also makes it easier for you to switch your Web server to a different host machine if you need to, since the alias can remain the same. Your server software should allow you to make URL and file name aliases.

You may need to configure your new server to recognize the PDF file type and PDF's binary data stream. For instructions on how to configure HTTPD-based and MacHTTP servers to serve PDFs, see the above section on existing Web sites.

Conclusion

You should now have a good idea of what you want to accomplish with your Web site and how you can tool up to make it all possible. In Chapter 6, "Getting Your Content Together," we will tell you what kinds of documents make up a Web site and give you tips on preparing PDF content and authoring HTML pages. In Chapter 7, "Creating PDF Documents," we will get down to business and tell you how to produce PDF from your applications using the PDFWriter and the Distiller. Chapter 8, "Enhancing your PDF in Acrobat Exchange," will cover how to turn your PDFs into interactive Web documents. To learn more about serving PDF on your server, and the Amber Byteserver CGI script, refer to Chapter 10, "Launching PDF Files on Your Web Site."

Notes

1. *Adobe Acrobat Exchange 2.1/Distiller 2.1 Getting Started Guide* (Adobe Systems Incorporated, 1995).

2. *Adobe Acrobat Capture 1.0 Getting Started Guide* (Adobe Systems Incorporated, 1995).

3. *Adobe Acrobat Publishing on the World Wide Web* (Adobe Systems Incorporated, 1995) 14.

4. Lincoln D. Stein, *How to Set Up and Maintain a World Wide Web Site* (Reading, MA: Addison-Wesley, 1995), 55–56.

5. Stein, 59.

6. Franks, 138.

7. Stein, 64–65.

8. Stein, 63.

Chapter 6

Getting Your Content Together

"Content" is an unfortunately geeky word that came into its current usage around the birth of the Web, presumably to differentiate the connectivity and protocols and HTML encoding and browser software from the words and pictures that finally appear on your screen. Listening to a few HTML encoders, Internet service providers, and Netscape programmers talk shop, you'd think that content was the least essential part of the Web, an incidental. But without content, there would be nothing for the HTML encoders to encode, nothing for ISPs to serve up, and nothing for Netscape to display. And now, especially with the help of Acrobat, content is coming into its own. With the technology to publish lengthy, well-designed multimedia documents in PDF, there has been a sudden clamor for the English majors and artists of the world to come out of hiding. There *is* a place for you creative types in cyberspace, after all!

This chapter will help you decide what kinds of content you want to bring together to make your dream Web site. This is the stage that should take the most time, because once you begin the conversion and Web-launching process it is very difficult to go back and change the content you started out with. Fortunately, this is also the stage that requires the least technical skills and lets your creativity reign. So start gathering all the drawings, photographs, logos, and other visual material you think you may use. And get ready to do some writing, as well. If writing is not your forte, find somebody who knows your organization and can write clearly and concisely for the Web (in English, not HTML). You'll be glad you invested in creative images and good writing when it comes time to unveil your site to the world. Even if you are planning to put up a no-frills Web site with content that you already have available, this chapter will tell you how to assemble the elements you need to make a home page, navigational pages, and PDF documents created from digital files, as well as from paper with Acrobat Capture.

What Kinds of Documents You Will Need

It will help to understand all the different types of documents that make up even the most bare-bones Web site (Figure 6.1). Together, they should establish a navigational path that leads from content-chunk to content-chunk in a logical manner. Their interaction will create the environment for your whole Web site, so that no matter which path your visitor decides to take, it will feel like an exploration through a coherent space. To achieve this natural flow will take a different kind of thinking on your part. It must be different, because a Web site is unlike a linear document, or a billboard, or a television ad, or any kind of traditional communications you are used to. The model that has emerged in the three-year-old life of the Web is an HTML home page, linked to several other HTML pages. With Acrobat and Amber, you have the opportunity to break out of that mold with visually dynamic PDF pages that down-

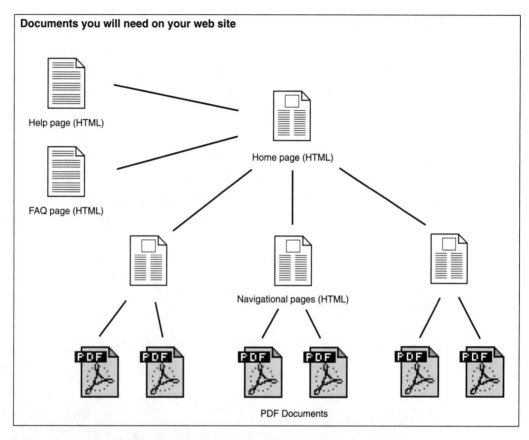

Documents you will need on your web site

Help page (HTML)

FAQ page (HTML)

Home page (HTML)

Navigational pages (HTML)

PDF Documents

FIGURE 6.1 The kinds of documents that make up a basic Web site, organized in terms of their "levels" on your site. The home page, help, and FAQ files are close to the top for easy access to the user, navigational pages are one level deep, and documents are at the bottom in special folders.

load one page at a time, and link off to other PDF pages. Your options for linking them together are much less constricted, with Weblinks and links to other views and files. Keep these expanded options in mind when you begin your content gathering.

Here are descriptions is a list of the kinds of documents you will definitely need for your Web site. Once you've established the basic structure for your site that these documents provide, the sky's the limit!

Home Page

The "home page" is a relatively new concept that evolved from the "main menu" of the old DOS days. More than a table of contents to a document, a home page is a carefully designed orientation to an interactive document (Figure 6.2). The home page is a vital element of any interactive product; while no one stays there very long, it is the most simple point of reference to a document. The home page, in general, should be informative about the contents of a document without giving too much away. It should have an inviting, colorful, simple interface. It should have a compact file size so that it does not take a long time to load. Normally, your Web home page will have

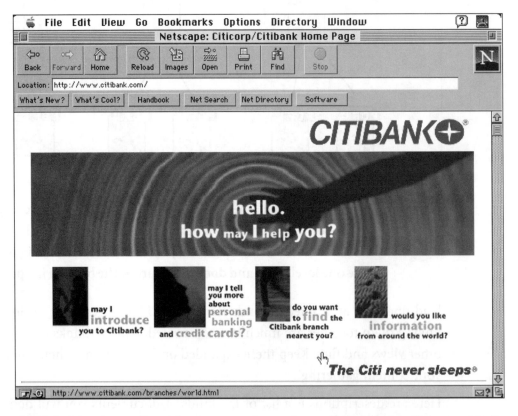

FIGURE 6.2 The Citibank home page draws users right in with the same kinds of questions that greet users of their ATM machines. (Unfortunately, "Get Cash" is not one of them.)

to be authored in HTML, so that everybody who visits your site can at least get in the front door without needing the Acrobat Reader. (You can provide a link to Adobe's web site here for people to download the Reader.) Since your home page will have references to the navigational pages and documents on your site, it should be the last thing you do. Some tips on HTML authoring are provided later in this chapter.

Navigational Pages

These pages form the second layer of content beneath the home page, serving to narrow visitors' paths along their line of interest (Figure 6.3). For example, on your home page you could list out the four main subsections of content on your

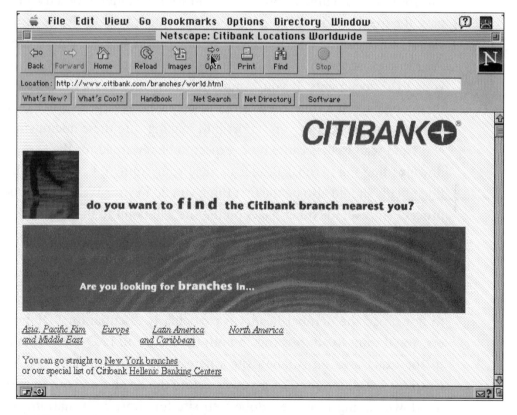

FIGURE 6.3 A Navigational page can be nothing more than a more specific set of links to a region of your site.

site—Our company, our products, our customers, our publications—and link off to four mini-home pages for each of those subsections. From there, you could link to the related documents. If your volume of content is so great that your navigational pages are too long, just add another layer of pages to further narrow your visitors' paths. Navigational pages should be simple and compact, without a busy design. They are usually done in HTML because navigation is their only function (that's what HTML does best). But that's not to say you couldn't make your navigational pages the first pages of a longer Acrobat Amber document that downloads to the user one page at a time.

Documents

The meat of your content should reside in your documents, because here you have the freedom to publish great-looking content in PDF. By the time your visitors navigate the first few layers of navigational pages, you've captured their interest sufficiently and have the opportunity to really wow them with your PDF documents. If you "Amberize" these files so that users can view them one page at a time, they can in principle be as large as you like. You'll want to put the bulk of your effort into making sure these documents look good and read well, because users expect to be rewarded for their trouble in downloading the Acrobat Reader to view your content. Creating your PDF documents should also be the first thing you do in your Web site production process, since all the other pages on the site will point to them.

Help and FAQ Files

You can avoid frustrated users by providing Help and FAQ (Frequently Asked Questions) files on your site (Figure 6.4). Explaining where and how to download the Acrobat Reader is particularly essential for PDF publishers. You'll want to address this in both the Help and FAQ files. Offer a link to the exact area on Adobe's site where users can download the Reader (http://www.adobe.com/). Or you can store the Reader on your own server for downloading (see the Adobe web site for more information). If you

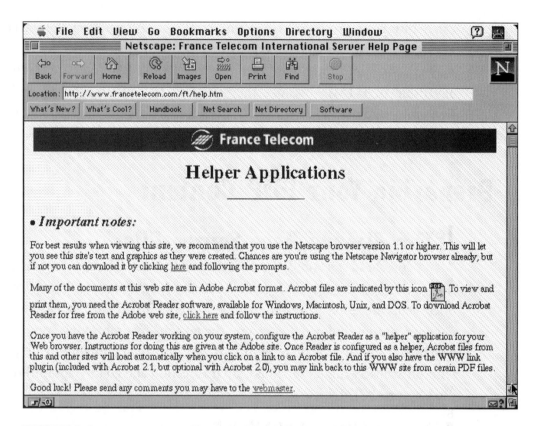

FIGURE 6.4 France Telecom's Help file explains which browsers work best with their site, how to view PDF files, and whom to contact with further questions.

have optimized your PDFs for Amber, tell visitors to make sure they have the Amber Reader. If not, explain the downloading process, and how users can configure the Acrobat Reader as a helper application for their Web browser (see Appendix A, "Configuring Your Web Browser to View PDF Files," for a sample explanation). Also in the Help file, you'll want to explain the navigational structure of your site in case the user gets lost. In the FAQ file, post email inquiries from users that may be informative for all visitors to your site. In the beginning, you may want to anticipate these inquiries with questions and answers of your own making. Typical questions will be "How do I view the PDF files?" or "How often is your site updated" or "How can I buy your product?" Giving users all the information they need to navigate your site and download your PDFs will ensure their return, and may get you some good word of mouth. Help and FAQ files are traditionally done in HTML, because they need to be viewable by all and are frequently updated. They should be authored before the navigational pages and the home page.

Preparing Your PDF Content

If You Already Have Source Files

You've got a head start on PDF production. But you still have to "tweak" these files to get them ready to be interactive electronic documents. If your source documents are word processed files, desktop published files, spreadsheets, or database output, following are some suggestions for improving your source files before you convert them to PDF. If your source documents are on paper without available digital versions, skip this section and go to "Tips for Preparing Capture ACD Files."

Add Cross-File and Weblink Text

If you are planning on having this document link to other documents on your site and to other locations on the Web, be sure to add the text for those links before you begin PDF production. For example, your PDFs should always have a link back to your Home Page, so where you want the link you should write in "Back to Home Page" or a little house icon. For remote Weblinks, write in the names and URLs of the sites. Later, in Acrobat Exchange, you can make these live links. It is a good idea to give all of your hyperlinks a consistent appearance, so that their function is obvious to the user each time. Your options for distinguishing links in Acrobat Exchange are pretty limited (a box or dotted line around the word or picture), so you should let your word processing or desktop publishing program do the link emphasis. This is also a good time to plan out the official names of all the files on your Web site so that your links will be accurate. To learn how to set base URLs for your files, see the section on setting document info in Chapter 8, "Enhancing Your PDF in Acrobat Exchange."

Add Navigational Notations

People reading your PDF files may not understand how to use the Acrobat toolbar to navigate the document. So you should be prepared to include some links of your own, right on the pages of your document (Figure 6.5). You can add the links later in Acrobat Exchange, but you should put in the necessary arrows or pointers like "Next Page," "Help," and "Home Page," at this stage of the game. The more button-like you can make them, the better, so that they stand out as functional tools. That means drawing boxes around them, making them shadowed, and so on.

Add an Introduction to the Electronic Version

If your document had previously been published on paper, you may want to write an introduction to the PDF version and stick it in at the beginning of the document. There you can highlight the improvements to the document and note its interactive features.

Change the Page Size to Fit the Screen

You'll have to experiment with custom page sizes in the Page Setup box in your application, but see if you can change the page size to something that will fit in the average-size computer screen (something like 8.5 × 6 inches is close). The resulting PDF will look much more like it was intended as an electronic document, and it will save the user from having to scroll down your pages (Figure 6.6). Of course, if you think the user is going to want to print out the PDF to paper, keep it letter-size. And remember, the page sizes in a PDF document do not all have to be the same—each one can be a different size. In Acrobat, users will have so many different ways to view the pages that you can afford to be original.

FIGURE 6.5 Buttons do not have to look like icons, as long as their function is clear. Adobe's Amber advertisement uses a creative design for navigational buttons—arrows that look like paper airplanes.

Jazz It Up!

Especially if you are working from a word processed file or a spreadsheet file, liven up the document for your online readers. The information in these documents needs to pop out, so pump up the font size and bold the most important words. And add some color—having Acrobat is like having a high-end, fullcolor laser printer at your fingertips. On the Web, your document will be competing with some pretty vibrant colors, so it is well worth it to put some bright, saturated colors into your PDFs.

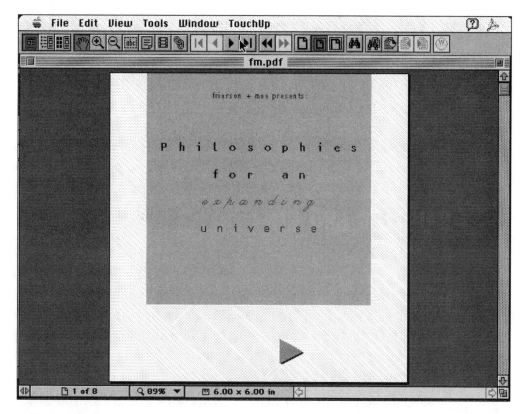

FIGURE 6.6 Documents that have a screen-size, horizontal orientation are better suited to interactive Web documents. The less scrolling users must do, the better.

Make Any and All Final Changes

You want the PDF file that ends up on your Web site to be perfect, so make sure that your content is perfect at this stage. There's quite a bit that can go wrong during the later stages of production; this is one aspect you can absolutely pretty much control. So proofread and spell check the document until you are comfortable with publishing it for, potentially, millions of readers.

Now your source files are ready to go into PDF production. If you also have files you've scanned in with Acrobat Capture (ACD files), read on. If not, skip ahead to "Creating Your HTML Documents."

Tips for Preparing Capture ACD Files

Once you have installed Capture and done a few scans, follow these tips for maximizing the quality and compactness of your intermediate ACD files.

1. In Reviewer's Setup Suspect-Word Options box, keep the default 95% word confidence setting. Assuming that you used a high-resolution scanner setting, Capture's level of word confidence should be appropriate. Click all four boxes of conditions for suspect words to be highlighted by Capture, and then click OK.

2. As you tab through the highlighted selections, keep an eye out for nonhighlighted errors. Sometimes, Capture will misread a word as another word, but not make it a suspect because it is in its dictionary. Capture is only somewhat artificially intelligent, so we recommend zooming in on each page and reading through it carefully. (A Capture plug-in called Reviewz, by Vertec Solutions, will extract all the highlighted errors and display them in a two-column window with the original. For more information on Reviewz, call (910) 855-1766).

3. Once you've finished making corrections to the text, you can fix any errors Capture made in page layout. Capture sees pages as combinations of two kinds of regions, text and graphics. Sometimes, it will confuse one for the other in the scanning process. So in the Reviewer you can select a region that was mistaken for a graphics region and make it a text region. You can also add and delete text and graphics regions or resize them. But you must delete a region before you add a new one in its place. It is possible to overlay graphics regions with text regions with the Move to Back command (available in the right mouse button menu). Experimenting with the page layout will eventually give you a document that is good enough for publishing on the Web.

4. In the Reviewer Preferences box, select "Use PDF Writer Settings" so you can set specific compression levels and font-embedding options

for the final PDF document. Capture Defaults automatically selects compression, which may not be appropriate for Web documents. In Chapter 7, go to the section "Using the PDFWriter" for advice on setting options in the PDFWriter. The same rules of compression and font embedding apply to ACD files and normal source documents.

5. Go to File, Save As for a list of possible output formats. You will see that you have a number of options, including three different kinds of PDF—Normal, Image Only, and Image+Text. We strongly recommend that for Web documents you choose PDF Normal, because it has the smallest file size of all the options. If your files are image-only, you may want to choose Image Only. Never choose Image+Text for your Web documents, because that option creates one big nonscalable bitmap, that you cannot clean up in the Reviewer.

6. Once you have your PDF, add Acrobat features as outlined in Chapter 8, "Enhancing Your PDF in Acrobat Exchange."

Alternatives to Using Capture

There are some instances in which you may not want to use Capture. If you simply want to scan images on paper for use within a desktop published document, you can scan in the images as TIFF or GIF. Then you can insert the pictures into your document and distill the whole file into PDF. This way, you can preserve color in your scanned images. Another instance is black-and-white line drawings—these you can scan in as greyscale images at a relatively low resolution, and they will look fine when you insert them into documents.[1]

If You Are Going to Make New Documents

Chances are you'll need to create some PDF documents fresh for your Web site, especially if you are publishing a periodical. In this section, we'll give you some tips on choosing the best authoring tool for each kind of document. We will also give you some general design guidelines for creating documents that will perform well on the Web. For more detailed coverage on design programs and creating interactive documents, we recommend these titles, which have been extremely helpful to us: *Production Essentials* (Mountain View: Adobe Press, 1994), and *Interactivity by Design* (Mountain View: Adobe Press, 1995).

Tips for Choosing the Right Authoring Tool

Acrobat will create PDF files from any application, but some applications are better for certain kinds of documents.

When to use a word processor

A word processing application with some graphics capabilities, such as Microsoft Word, should be used for documents where the content of the text is the most important element, and all the illustrations needed are simple tables and bitmapped pictures. A technical "white paper" or a press release are two examples,. Since word processing applications are easy to use, they are ideal for authoring information that needs to be published quickly, or which are part of your internal document exchange. Also, most word processed files will output directly to PDF through the PDFWriter.

When to Use a Desktop Publisher

Desktop publishing applications are programs that handle professional page layout and a wide range of image formats and control slight variations in color and resolution of documents. Most of them were intended to output to high-quality printers, but they all work well with the Acrobat Distiller to create visually rich PDFs. Some desktop publishing programs, such as Adobe PageMaker 6 and FrameMaker 5, and Corel Ventura 5 provide integration with Acrobat conversion and interactive features. There are also plug-ins for extending the PDF compatability of some programs, such as Cascade's QuarkXtensions for QuarkXPress. (For more on these programs, see Chapter 9, "Special-Purpose PDF Production Tools.")

Although these programs often require professional design skills, you should use a desktop publishing application to create a document that needs to be publication-quality, such as a product brochure or a magazine. Any document that you would like to have several colors, lots of images and interactive interface controls, such as buttons, must be created in a desktop publishing program. These programs are able to handle text and images from multiple sources, and lend themselves easily to the integration of multimedia effects once they become PDFs. To preserve the quality of files created with your desktop publishing application, you must first print them to PostScript (all of them have this feature in their print driver), and convert them in the Distiller. See Chapter 7, "Creating PDF Documents," for more on using the Distiller.

When to Use a Presentation Program

If you simply want to get a few key points across to your audience, without a lot of bells and whistles, you may want to use a presentation program such as Microsoft PowerPoint or Adobe Persuasion. These programs generate slide-show style documents that contain short chunks of text in a large point size and relatively sophisticated charts and graphs. Once converted to PDF, presentation documents lend themselves easily to navigation with Acrobat's hyperlinks. Possible examples of such documents would be a company profile, a training guide, or a new product announcement. Since presentation files involve colors and graphics, you should use the Distiller to convert them to PDF.

When to Use a Spreadsheet Program

Organizations that already use spreadsheets to circulate numeric information may want to repurpose them on their Web site. Spreadsheet applications like Microsoft Excel and Lotus 1-2-3 output nicely to PDF through the PDFWriter. Once in PDF, users can zoom in on the spreadsheet to examine specific numbers. They can be inserted as pages into a larger PDF document that was created in another program.

When to Use a Database Report

If you have a database that you use internally, and you would like to make some of it available on your Web server, you can save a lot of hassle by generating a report from your database program. Most database applications offer this feature, allowing you to choose certain categories and display the information in lists or charts. Rather than give users crippled access to your actual database, simply decide which categories are not for public access and exclude them from the report. Then you can take those report pages and print them to the PDFWriter. As PDFs, your reports will provide valuable information to users and they can be updated easily.

Tips for Layout and Design

When we asked the Acrobat people at Adobe what they thought we should write about in this book, they all brought up the issue of design. While design is not exactly the turf of the Acrobat software or of this book, it is an integral part of the electronic publishing process that culminates in conversion to PDF and distribution via the Web. For Adobe's customer base, primarily graphic designers and print publishers, designing for the screen has posed a challenge. Acrobat Product Marketing Manager Pam Deziel says, "Designers look at Acrobat and say, 'This is really neat, I can make an electronic document that's exactly the same thing I would do in print.' That's absolutely true, but what people are learning is that we don't necessarily want to." Judy Kirkpatrick, Market Development Manager for Acrobat, has seen the same learning curve among Adobe customers. She says, "Designers everywhere are going to have to make that leap from designing for print, and designing for online. People are going to struggle with it for a while, until they get really good at what makes a page easy to read and deal with online." We can offer some guidelines to help you with that learning curve, but your own experience with interactive documents, and experimentation with your own, will yield the best results. After all, it is a new medium with no set rules.

Just as you did with the design of your whole Web site, planning out the design of your document before you begin will truly pay off. Follow these few steps, and you will be able to begin quickly with a clear design roadmap[2] (Figure 6.7).

1. Determine the Overall Visual Theme of the Document

The visual theme of your document should be a cohesive set of design elements—colors, shapes, lines—that unify the pages and help convey the message of your content. This thought process harks back to Chapter 5, where we discuss the goals of your Web site. Here again you should consider how you can leverage your product and communicate most effectively with your audience.

2. Plan the Interface Design

The elements that make up the interface of the document, from the background to the controls to the text, should look relatively consistant. These elements don't have to look the same on every screen of the document, but they should look like logical offspring of the home page design. They should also interact together well, both visually and functionally, to achieve the overall theme of your document. Following are descriptions of the items that make up an interface, in the order in which they should be designed.

BACKGROUND The background of the interface will be the setting for everything that comes after it, so it is an important factor in the environment of your document. The background can be a solid color, blocks of color, or a pattern. In most cases, the brightness and sharp edges in the background will need to be toned down and blurred so they don't overwhelm the elements that go over it. One benefit to making your background the same for all pages of the document is that if you optimize that file to Amber, it will store the background as just one object in the file. When users download the file with the Amber Reader, the text and images will download much more quickly while the background remains the same on their screen.

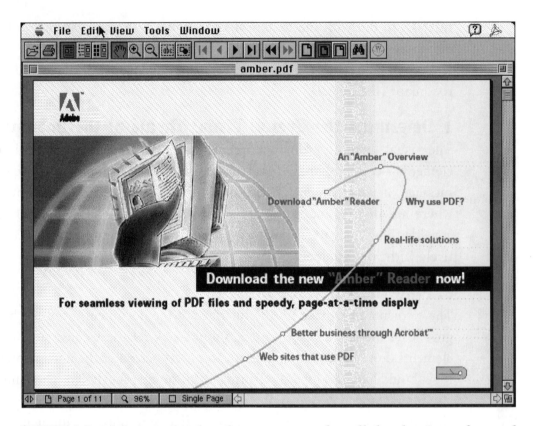

FIGURE 6.7 Adobe's Amber brochure puts together all the elements of a good interactive design—a screen-sized page, a consistent template of colors and panels, innovative use of buttons and links, and well-positioned images and text.

WINDOWS AND PANELS Windows and panels are regions of the interface that help to demarcate content matter, or simply to break up a monotonous background with overlaid shapes. Most desktop publishing programs have sophisticated mechanisms for creating transparent and translucent areas that are ideal for windows and panels. Using them in your interface design will help you set off specific areas for the frontal elements of the design.

BUTTONS AND CONTROLS These are the interface elements that are going to make your document interactive once it is a PDF. But what's going to make them *seem* interactive is the way they are designed, even before they do anything. It's important that your buttons (little rectangles or circles that express a navigational function) and controls (any kind of symbol that lets the user change part of the interface), express their function clearly. This means that not only must they have a clear symbol on them or say outright what they do, but each recurring button or control should look and act the same way on every screen. For example, a control that starts an Acrobat Movie should bear some relationship to a film device, and look the same for every Movie link. Be sure not to overcrowd your interface with buttons and controls—they will end up distracting the user and diminish the quality of your design. That aside, don't be afraid to be creative with their appearance. As long as their function is clear and they are inviting to users, buttons and controls can be as original as you can make them.

IMAGES Your photographs, line art, and graphical flourishes should overlay the windows and panels, and cohabitate the space with your buttons and controls. Since your images will be different on each page, you should take care to ensure that they all work well with the other interface elements. You can integrate images creatively with the background by varying their placement on the page, giving them a unique window, or making them interact with the text. Of course, images can be links in themselves to other parts of the document. If so, the content of the image should be an obvious metaphor for the linked destination and perhaps have some link-like attributes, such as a border (this can be added in Acrobat Exchange).

Your images will give your document the visual richness and variety it needs to retain the user's interest. Unfortunately, images also bring on problems of resolution, color fidelity, and large file sizes. When you are integrating images into your document, keep in mind that most users' computers are capable of displaying only 256 colors, at 72 dpi. By reducing the color depth (number of colors) and the resolution (dpi) of your images within your authoring program, you will end up with a document that will display better and have a smaller file size once you convert it to PDF. Using the Distiller, your file size will be further compressed to the maximum extent, without sacrificing the quality of the display.

TEXT How you display the text of your document could be the make-it-or-break-it factor in its success. First and foremost, the text must be large enough so that it is legible onscreen. As a general rule, do not go below 12 points. Second, the text should be a color that contrasts strongly with the background color—dark blue on yellow, or white on dark green. If your background has a variety of light colors, black text is usually the best way to go. Text that will be made into hyperlinks in Acrobat should be made bold or a different color, consistently for all link text. Third, you should limit the number of fonts you use to two or three, and reserve each one for the different structural parts of your content—titles, headers, body, and so on. Use fonts that are relatively common, such as those that reside in Adobe Type Manager, or else you will have to embed the entire fonts in the PDF document. If you must use a custom font, you should embed those words in the file. Embedded fonts will increase your file size, but at least you can be sure that the Acrobat Reader will not try to substitute them at the user end. Finally, don't crowd too much text on one page. Text should be displayed in bite-size amounts, with links to more information if the user is interested. Most users are not accustomed to reading as much onscreen as they would on a printed page, so go easy on them.

Once you put the finishing touches on your design, you are ready to make a PDF prototype of the document. It will be a prototype, because inevitably you will find that you have to go back and make some changes. But it's easy to distill documents in PDF, and give them the interactive features they need for your vision to really come alive. So even if you have to go through the process a few times, you won't lose a lot of time and you'll learn some important things about PDF production. See Chapter 7, "Creating PDF Documents," to get started.

The remainder of this chapter presents tips on creating HTML documents for your Web home page and the first few layers of pages on your Web site.

Creating Your HTML Documents

Recall from Chapter 4 that you might want to use HTML for your Web documents under these circumstances:

- When it's critical that the information reach all visitors to your Web site

- When it's your home page or other places where navigation is important

- When information is time-sensitive and frequently updated

- When it's a form or other CGI business

- When it's a lot of information and the presentation doesn't matter

It is hard to avoid doing some HTML authoring for at least one of those circumstances, especially for your home page. While it is not within the parameters of this book to explain how to encode text with HTML, we can give you some starting tips and point you in the right direction to get more specific information. The following tips are geared toward home page authoring, but also apply to other kinds of HTML pages as described above.

Look Behind the Curtain on Some Cool Web Pages

A good way to begin is to browse the Web in search of a home page that approximates how you want yours to look. Then, in your browser program, choose View Source to see the HTML encoding behind the page (Netscape and most other browsers will let you do this). Seeing the complexity of the underlying code will help you understand what you're getting yourself into before you start trying to replicate it. HTML pages that include image maps (linked images arrayed on the page), fancy backgrounds and fonts from HTML 3.0 or NHTML (Netscape's version), and many URL links are going to have very intimidating source files. Do not despair, however; if you want a sophisticated home page, there are many HTML editors that can make your authoring tasks easier.

Keep It Simple

When you are planning your home page design, remember that while your home page should be impressive and inviting, it need not be complicated or even informative. Images, well-compressed and shallow in color depth for faster downloading, should dominate the page, with links to other documents either embedded in an image map or written out in HTML. You'll want to keep your HTML text brief on your home page—just enough to describe succinctly who you are and what your Web site is about. All tolled, your home page should not require more than one scroll down the screen. You can use your home page as the primary navigational page, listing links to all the documents on the server, but we recommend spreading out your user's navigation. To keep your home page brief, just include links to a few pages that are devoted to linking off to other documents. When you write out the content of these links, be sure to make them informative about their destination. For example, instead of writing "To read our 1996 Annual Report, Click here," write simply "Read our 1996 Annual Report." Users will know that the underlined HTML text is a link to the annual report, and Web search engines will be able to index the content of your site more easily. (In the first example, a search on "annual reports" would have missed the "click here" link.) Finally, if you want your home page to link directly to a PDF document, be sure to include the official PDF GIF icon to mark the link. The icon, available in three different sizes, is available off of Adobe's Web site (http://www.adobe.com). To learn how to insert the icon into your HTML page, see Chapter 10, "Launching PDF Files on Your Web Site."

Does Your Authoring Program Output to HTML?

Before you start learning all those HTML tags, find out which of your authoring programs offers automatic HTML conversion. Currently, Microsoft Word, WordPerfect, FrameMaker, QuarkXPress, and PageMaker have Plug-ins which will convert documents to HTML. This is a great way to author HTML automatically, but beware of the limitations on converting complex desktop published documents into HTML. You will probably need to simplify them a great deal, separating text from graphics clearly, before running the conversion.

For HTML Do-it-Yourselfers

Once you have a good idea of how you want your home page to look and read, you should determine whether you can do the HTML encoding manually, or need the help of an HTML program. If you want to brave it manually, you should first visit a few HTML-related Web sites for their tutorials, such as the WWW Organization Committee (http://www.w3.org), or CERN (http://www.cern.ch). There is no dearth of books on the subject, either—try the *HTML Sourcebook* by Ian S. Graham (John Wiley & Sons), or the *HTML Manual of Style* by Larry Aronson. You should also make sure you understand the various standard image formats and how to insert them into your HTML pages. The three standard inline image formats (meaning that they can be viewed within a Web browser) are GIF (CompuServe's Graphics Interchange Format), JPEG (Joint Photographic Experts Group), and black-and-white bitmaps (.XBM).

Use HTML Editing Software

Doing HTML encoding manually may allow you to fine tune your pages, using specific tags for HTML 3.0 and other new extensions. But for most publishers' needs, an HTML software editor can do good work in a fraction of the time in a user-friendly environment. The most impressive HTML editor we've seen thus far is Adobe's PageMill, the WYSIWYG drag-and-drop software developed by Ceneca Communications. Aimed at publishers and designers who are accustomed to a visual editing interface, PageMill lets you drag images and text from other applications into an HTML page, performing all the necessary data conversions in the background. It retails for $99, but alas, is available only for Macintosh. A Windows version is under way, however. Other HTML editors include HoTMetaL from SoftQuad (http://www.sq.com), WebAuthor from Quarterdeck (Word for Windows only, at http://www.qdeck.com), and InContext's Spider (Windows only, http://www.incontext.com).

Get Your HTML Checked Out

It is easy to author "illegal" HTML, which doesn't conform to the HTML standard and won't display properly on all browsers. Even if your HTML displays fine in your browser, it is worthwhile to have your syntax checked by an authority. There are a few Web sites that will perform this service for free: Htmlchek (http://uts.cc.utexas.edu/churchh/htmlchek.html), Weblint (http://www.khoros.umn.edu/staff/ncilb/weblint.html), and the Online HTML Validation Service (http://www.halsoft.com/html-val-svc/).[3] You can rest easy if you authored your HTML with PageMill, or HoTMetaL—these programs won't let you author illegal HTML.

Save Your Multimedia for PDFs and Other Downloadables

It is possible to link off to sound and video files from HTML pages, but it takes a long time to download them and they are often disappointing. Instead, save your sound and movies for PDF files, so they can be downloaded with the PDF file and locally accessed. If you want to include a file with greater animation than Acrobat allows, such as one created with Macromedia Director, you can offer that for downloading as well (Netscape offers a Macromedia viewer as a helper application for Director files).

We revisit the world of HTML in Chapter 10, "Launching PDF Files on Your Web Site." Now, back to the fun stuff—the next chapter will tell you how to create interactive PDF files from your document source files.

Notes

1. Chris Converse, *Designing for Acrobat*, 1994 (a PDF-only guide on the Web).

2. The following tips were borrowed by the excellent design handbook by Ray Kristof and Amy Satran, *Interactivity by Design* (Mountain View: Adobe Press, 1995, distributed by Hayden Books).

3. Lincoln D. Stein, *How to Set Up and Maintain a World Wide Web Site* (Reading, MA: Addison-Wesley, 1995), 216.

Chapter 7

Creating PDF Documents

Now that your beautifully designed source document is ready to be "PDF'd," it's time to consider the different ways you can create PDF files and enhance your PDFs with Acrobat Exchange. In this chapter, you'll learn how to make PDF files from a simple one-page document with the PDF Writer to bulk document conversion with the Distiller. We'll give you special tips on how to use both of the PDF creation tools to their best potential so you can cut down your production time. Once you master setting the right job options in the PDF Writer and Distiller, and learn our shortcuts for volume conversion, the conversion part of PDF production will be a speedy process with few headaches. Then, you can proceed to the fun stuff—adding interactive features to your PDFs and launching them on your Web site.

Using the PDF Writer

The Acrobat PDF Writer, which comes with every copy of Acrobat Exchange, is the ideal PDF creation tool for the business user or publishers of simple, text-heavy documents. It can generate PDF files directly from word processing, spreadsheet, or presentation documents that do not contain complex graphics and colors. The PDF Writer is actually a printer driver that becomes an optional output format for all of your documents. Creating a PDF this way is as simple as configuring the PDF Writer as your printer of choice, and going through the normal print process. As quickly as you could print a document to paper, you can get a PDF that's ready to put on your Web site.

The PDF Writer is also embedded in Acrobat Capture for output of scanned documents into PDF. If you have purchased Capture, you need not purchase the PDF Writer separately; you can simply "Save As PDF" in Capture. You do not need to use the Distiller for Capture ACD files, because those documents are all black and white with simple bitmapped or greyscale images. Once Capture supports color documents, we may see Adobe embedding the Distiller inside the scanning software, to handle more complex graphics.

When Not to Use the PDF Writer

The PDF Writer is an easy-to-use tool for creating PDFs, but it does have its limitations. That's why Adobe made the Acrobat Distiller—an industrial-strength PostScript-to-PDF conversion tool that comes with the Acrobat Pro and Acrobat for Workgroups products. If your document fits any of the following descriptions, skip the PDF Writer section and head right for our discussion of the Acrobat Distiller.

- *If the document was authored in a desktop publishing program, such as QuarkXPress, PageMaker, FrameMaker, Illustrator, PhotoShop, Corel*

Ventura, Harvard Draw or Harvard Graphics, Micrografx Designer, or QuickDraw GX. These documents are likely to have complicated layouts and images that only the Acrobat Distiller would be able to handle.

- *If your document contains EPS files.* Do not use the PDF Writer in this case, because it does not support EPS files. If you have the Distiller, use that to convert the document. Otherwise, save your EPS files as TIFF files if they are images, and as PICT or BMP if they are text and graphics.

- *If you're working on the UNIX or DOS platforms.* The PDF Writer is available only for the Windows and Macintosh platforms. To convert simple and complex documents on the UNIX and DOS platforms, use the Distiller (in DOS, you'll have to use the Distiller 1.0, the first and last release for DOS).

- *If you already have PostScript files for your documents.* These can be dropped onto the Distiller easily, and would not be handled well by the PDF Writer.

The following list of steps is deceptively long—printing to PDF with the PDF Writer can take only seconds. But assuming that this is your first time, we've outlined all of the "printer" options the PDF Writer provides so that you can fine-tune the results of your digital print job.

To print to PDF from a Windows Application:

1. *Put the finishing touches on your document.* In the authoring application (e.g., Microsoft Word), make all final changes to the document and Save it.

2. *Print.* Select the Print command from the File Menu.

3. *Choose the PDF Writer.* (See Figure 7.1.) In the Print dialog box, click the Printer button. When the Print Setup dialog box appears, select Acrobat PDF Writer on DISK from the Specific Printer list. Click the Set as Default Printer button.

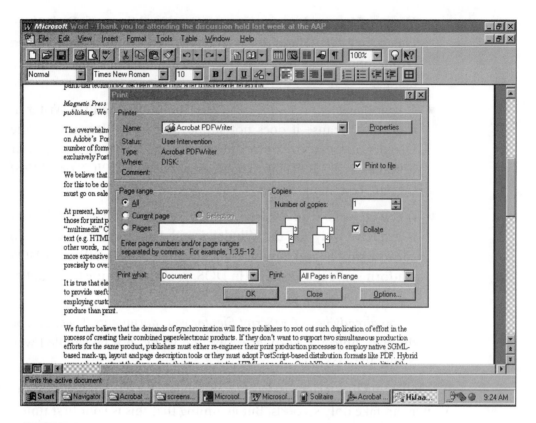

FIGURE 7.1 Selecting the PDF Writer in the Windows Print Setup window.

4. *Set Page Display Options.* (See Figure 7.2.) From the Print Setup box, click the Options button. From there, you can adjust the page size, orientation, scaling, and resolution of the PDF file printed by the PDF Writer. If the pages of your document have a unique page size, enter the dimensions in the Page Size menu. If you want to set the resolution of the PDF file other than the default dpi (equal to the dpi of your screen), choose an alternative from the menu— 150, 300, or 600 dpi. (Choose 600 dpi only if you're planning to print the PDF out on a high-resolution printer; normal screens and printers cannot display 600 dpi.) The default orientation is vertical, or "Portrait," but you can change it to horizontal by selecting the "Landscape" option. The default scale is 100 percent, but you can enter a different percentage if you want to shrink or enlarge the pages of your document during the printing process.

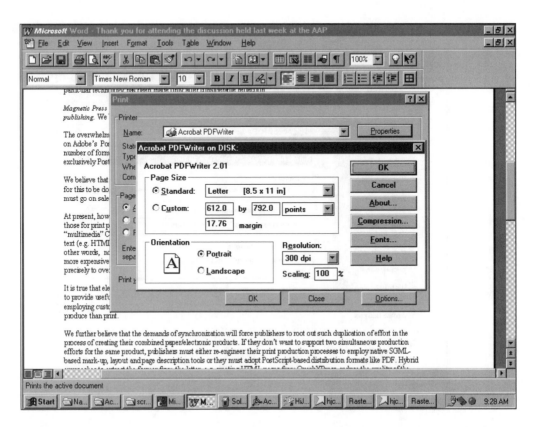

FIGURE 7.2 Setting Page Display options in Windows (using Microsoft Word).

5. *Set Compression.* (See Figure 7.3.) To change the compression settings, click the Compression box in the Print Options window. You may want to choose a particular type of compression to reduce the size of the resulting PDF, which may be large if the document contains color or greyscale images. Text, graphics, and monochrome images can also benefit from compression. Under "General" in the Compressions box, the PDF Writer is set to compress the file to the binary format. The other option is ASCII, but Adobe recommends the equally portable binary format because it makes for a smaller file size and better transmission through email gateways. Compression of color and greyscale

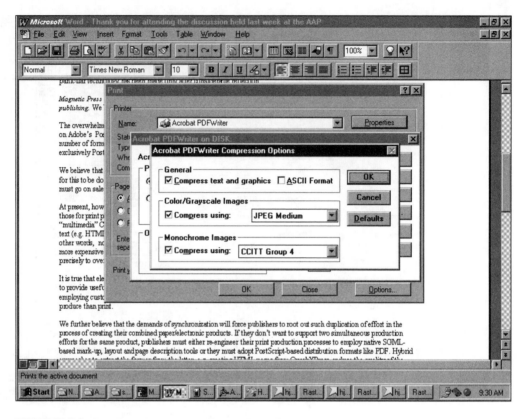

FIGURE 7.3 Setting Compression in Windows.

images is set to Compress using JPEG Medium, which offers extensive compression with moderate loss of data. You can change this option to low or high JPEG, with high giving you the most compression and data loss and low giving you the least. Or, you can set color and greyscale image compression to LZW, which is better for large color blocks and simple images. LZW compression does not lose any image data. But it is not recommended for complex images such as photographs, and 24-bit continuous-tone images, in which cases the compression will not result in a smaller file size. For complex images, JPEG is the way to go, especially if the images contain detail that would never be visible at most screen and printer resolutions.

The final compression category, Monochrome Images, is set to CCITT Group 4, a general method that compresses without losing any data. Other options are CCITT Group 3, which compresses monochrome bitmaps one column at a time, LZW, which is best for images with repeating patterns, and Run Length, which is best for images with large blocks of white or black. All of these options compress monochrome images without data loss.

We recommend practicing with the various compression options before you work on the final PDF, to get a feel for the results. If, in the end, you think that the Default settings are the best, you can automatically revert to them by clicking on the Defaults button in the Compressions Options box.

6. *Embed Fonts.* (See Figure 7.4.) If the computer on the receiving end of your PDF document does not have the fonts you used in the original, Acrobat's ATM font substitution system will kick in. It will substitute multiple master fonts for the missing ones, mimicking as well as possible their size and style. Acrobat's font substitution is very impressive, but if your document requires *exact* fidelity to fonts you may want to embed your fonts into the PDF file itself. Be warned, however, that embedding fonts will dramatically increase the PDF file's size. Using font embedding with compression methods may help you achieve a good balance.

In the Printer Options box (window title reads "Acrobat PDFWriter on DISK"), click on Fonts. You will be shown a list of available fonts, and given a set of three embedding options. First, you can choose to Embed All Fonts that are in the document. This is a safe choice if the document does not contain too many fonts. The second option is the customized Always Embed List. In this box, you can drag and drop specific fonts that you always use from the Available Fonts list into the Always Embed box. That way you can be sure that people viewing your document will always see those fonts. Finally, there is a Never Embed List, so that if you click on Embed

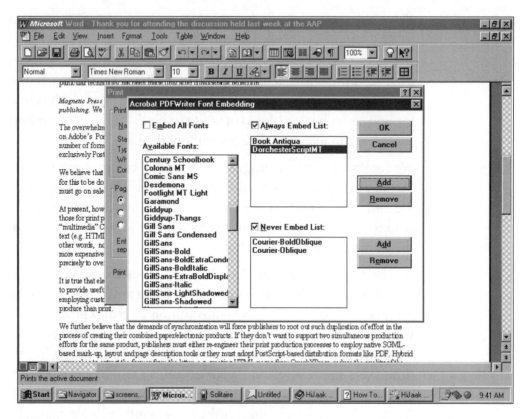

FIGURE 7.4 Embedding fonts in Windows.

All Fonts up top, you can specify items from the Available Fonts list that you do not want embedded.

7. *Select number of copies and page range.* Back in the Print window, select the number of copies and page range you want, and then click OK.

8. *Save the PDF File As....* (See Figure 7.5.) The Save As PDF window appears. It will suggest a name for the file that is the name of the source file with the .PDF extension. You can change the name of the file, but it must be under eight letters and have the .PDF suffix. Choose the right directory for the PDF document. At the bottom of the Save As window, you are given the options to Prompt for Document Info, and View PDF File. Check the Prompt for Document

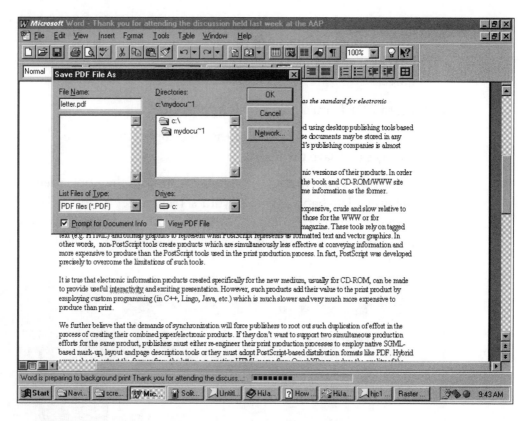

FIGURE 7.5 Saving the document as PDF in Windows.

Info box if you want to enter the title, author, and other information about the document (this information will be available to users of the document). Check the View PDF File box if you want to see the resulting PDF in the Acrobat Reader. When you're done, click OK.

9. *Wait while the PDF Writer does its thing.* Watch the little Acrobat "A" spin around as your PDF file is created. When it's finished, Acrobat will automatically open up the PDF, or you can open it up yourself with the Reader or in Exchange.

10. *Look at your shiny new PDF.* Check the PDF file for fidelity to the original. If the PDF Writer had a problem reproducing the fonts, formatting, or images of the source file, it may have been too

complex a document. You may want to experiment with the compression options until you get a good result. Or, use the Acrobat Distiller to convert it. It usually succeeds where the PDF Writer fails.

To print to PDF from a Macintosh Application:

1. *Save the original.* In your authoring application, make all final changes and save the file.

2. *Choose the PDF Writer.* (See Figure 7.6.) Under the Apple menu on the upper left-hand corner of your screen, select "Chooser." In the Chooser window, double click on the PDF Writer icon, identified by a little printer icon with the red "A" peeking out. A PDF Writer

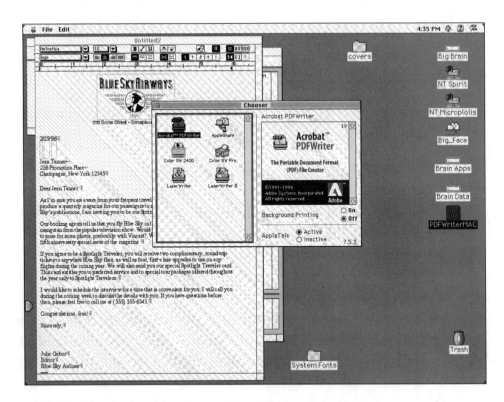

FIGURE 7.6 The Macintosh Chooser for the PDF Writer.

graphic will appear on the right side of the window. You have the option to turn "background printing" on or off. Turn it on if you want to work in another application while the PDF Writer is printing. Close out of the Chooser window.

3. *Go to Page Setup.* (See Figure 7.7.) Back in your authoring application, go to Page Setup under the File menu. In the Page Setup dialog box, you can set the page size, orientation, scale, and options for document margins, compression, and fonts.

4. *Select page size.* You have a number of Standard options. The default is Letter size (8.5 × 11 inches), but you can also choose from Legal, Tabloid, basic Screen size, and four international page size standards (A4, A3, B5, and B4). If your document fits none of

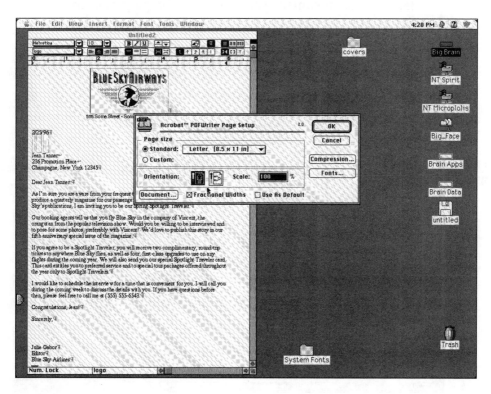

FIGURE 7.7 The Mac Page Setup box.

those standards, you can select a Custom size. When you click Custom, boxes will appear in which you can enter numbers for the size and margins. You can also select the measurement—in inches, millimeters, or points.

5. *Select orientation and scale.* The default orientation is vertical, but you can switch it to horizontal by clicking on the icon with the figure on its side. If you want to shrink or enlarge the size of your document (its actual size—not the magnification), enter a percentage number next to "Scale."

6. *Select compression.* (See Figure 7.8.) In the Page Setup box, click the Compression button. You may want to choose a particular type of compression to reduce the size of the resulting PDF, which may be large if the document contains color or greyscale images. Text,

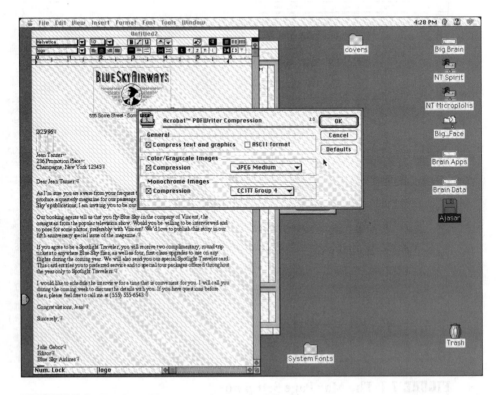

FIGURE 7.8 Setting Compression on a Mac.

graphics, and monochrome images can also benefit from compression. Under "General" in the Compressions box, the PDF Writer is set to compress the file to the binary format. The other option is ASCII, but Adobe recommends the equally portable binary format because it makes for a smaller file size and better transmission through email gateways. Compression of color and greyscale images is set to Compress using JPEG Medium, which offers extensive compression with moderate loss of data. You can change this option to low or high JPEG, with high giving you the most compression and data loss and low giving you the least. Or you can set color and greyscale image compression to LZW, which is better for large color blocks and simple images. LZW compression does not lose any image data. But it is not recommended for complex images such as photographs, and 24-bit continuous-tone images, in which cases the compression will not result in a smaller file size. For complex images, JPEG is the way to go, especially if the images contain detail that would never be visible at most screen and printer resolutions.

The final compression category, Monochrome Images, is set to CCITT Group 4, a general method that compresses without losing any data. Other options are CCITT Group 3, which compresses monochrome bitmaps one column at a time, LZW, which is best for images with repeating patterns, and Run Length, which is best for images with large blocks of white or black. All of these options compress monochrome images without data loss.

We recommend practicing with the various compression options before you work on the final PDF, to get a feel for the results. If, in the end, you think that the Default settings are the best, you can automatically revert to them by clicking on the Defaults button in the Compressions options box.

7. *Embed Fonts.* (See Figure 7.9.) If the computer on the receiving end of your PDF document does not have the fonts you used in the original, Acrobat's ATM font substitution system will kick in.

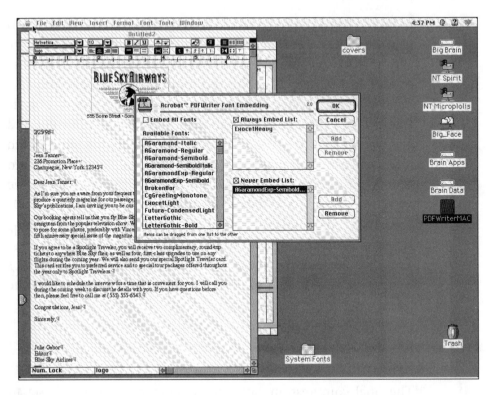

FIGURE 7.9 Embedding fonts on a Mac.

It will substitute multiple master fonts for the missing ones, mimicking as well as possible their size and style. Acrobat's font substitution is very impressive, but if your document requires *exact* fidelity to fonts you may want to embed your fonts into the PDF file itself. Be warned, however, that embedding fonts will dramatically increase the PDF file's size. Using font embedding with compression methods may help you achieve a good balance.

In the Page Setup box, click on Fonts. In the PDF Writer Font Embedding box, you will be shown a list of available fonts, and given a set of three embedding options. First, you can choose to Embed All Fonts that are in the document. This is a safe choice if the document does not contain too many fonts. The second option is the customized Always Embed List. In this box, you can drag and drop specific fonts that you always use from the Available Fonts list into the Always Embed box. That way you can be sure that people viewing your document will always see those fonts. Finally, there is a Never Embed List, so that if you click on Embed All Fonts up top, you can specify items from the Available Fonts list that you do not want embedded. Click OK, and click OK in the Page Setup box. (Ignore the Document button and Fractional Widths checkbox at the bottom of the Page Setup box. These functions apply only to paper printing and are not part of the Acrobat software.)

8. *Print.* (See Figure 7.10.) Select the Print command from the File menu. Choose the page range of the document you want to print to PDF. Check the View PDF File box if you want Acrobat to

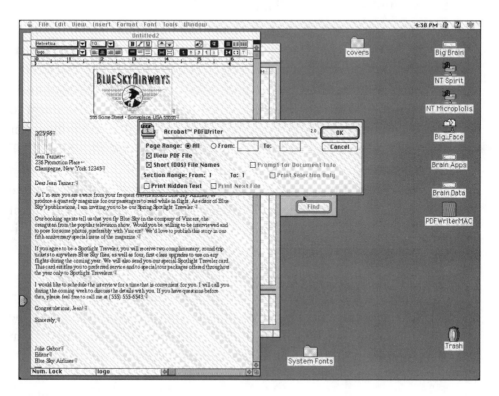

FIGURE 7.10 The Mac Print Dialog box.

launch and display the "printed" PDF when it's completed. Otherwise, you will have to start up Acrobat and open the new file yourself. Below, you have the option to require Short (DOS) File Names for the PDF files you create. Although the Macintosh does not care if your PDF file names are long, on the Web your PDF files will be accessed by people with DOS-based systems, like Windows. So if your Mac-generated file is called "Spring Catalog 1996.pdf," that long name is going to be truncated and unrecognizable when the user's system tries to make an eight-letter DOS name out of it. We recommend checking that box, so that if you try to enter a long name, the PDF Writer will not accept it. Instead you will have to name the file, for example, "Spring96.pdf." Finally, you can choose to Print Hidden Text in the PDF document any text that you may have marked "Hidden" in your word processing program. Click OK.

Mac users have the option to use the PDFWriter shortcut key to print to PDF, once you've set all your compression and font embedding options the first time. Using this shortcut, you'll be able to side-step going to the Chooser and switching to the PDFWriter every time you want to print a document to PDF. With the document to be printed open, hold down the Control key and choose Print under the File menu. Select Print options, Save As the document as a .PDF file, select a destination folder, and click Save. To change the settings for the PDFWriter shortcut key, go to Control Panels under the Apple menu, and select PDFWriter Shortcut. In this box, you can Enable or Disable the shortcut and change the keystroke that activates the shortcut from Control to Option, or Shift.

9. *Save PDF File As....* (See Figure 7.11.) The Save As dialog box appears. The PDFWriter will suggest a name that is a combination of the original file's name and the .pdf extension. You can alter the file name, but be sure to include the .pdf extension, as it is an important indicator of the file format. Click on Save.

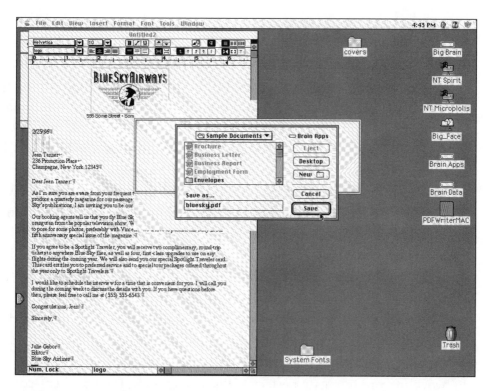

FIGURE 7.11 Saving As PDF on a Mac.

10. *Wait while the PDF Writer does its thing.* Watch the little Acrobat "A" spin around as your PDF file is created. When it's finished, Acrobat will automatically open up the PDF, or you can open it up yourself with the Reader or in Exchange.

11. *Look at your shiny new PDF.* Check the PDF file for fidelity to the original. If the PDF Writer had a problem reproducing the fonts, formatting, or images of the source file, it may have been too complex a document. You may want to experiment with the compression options until you get a good result. Or use the Acrobat Distiller to convert it. It usually succeeds where the PDF Writer fails.

Using the Distiller

The Acrobat Distiller is a powerful publishing tool, unlike any software you may have seen. Not a printer driver like the PDFWriter, nor an application conversion filter, the Acrobat Distiller is a complete PostScript processing engine. It gets its name from the verb "to distill," which comes from the Latin *distillare,* or "to alter." In modern scientific terms, to distill means to extract the essence of a substance, to purify it, or to create a new substance from it. The Acrobat Distiller takes files that have been saved as PostScript files in authoring applications, and extracts from them the information Acrobat needs to display them as PDF files. The Distiller weeds out unnecessary file data and compresses files a great deal. The Distiller can also handle PostScript run files—special scripts that automatically add interactive features to the resulting PDF files. How the Distiller does all this remains a mystery to most, and you certainly do not need to be intimately familiar with its inner workings to operate it. But the more you get to know the Distiller's capabilities, the more you can make it work for you to create perfect PDFs. Fortunately, the Distiller's complexity is hidden by an easy-to-use interface.

Recall from the discussion of when not to use the PDFWriter that you should always use the Distiller to convert files to PDF (1) if they were authored in a graphic design program, (2) if the documents contain EPS (Encapsulated PostScript Files), and (3) if you need a compact file size for a complex document (this will almost always be true for Web-based PDF documents). Because the Distiller generates PDF from PostScript, its output is very high-quality, high-fidelity reproduction of the original. As such, you should use the Distiller for any document that you will be distributing to a mass audience.

This section will show you how to generate clean PostScript files from your authoring application, how to set Distiller Job Options, how to Distill multiple PostScript files at a time, how to monitor the Distiller's progress, and how to troubleshoot "crashed" Distiller jobs. You also have Adobe's jam-packed Distiller online help guide at your fingertips, accessible under the Help menu within the Distiller program[1] (Figure 7.12).

Generating PostScript Files from Your Application

Before you can convert your application files to PDF through the Distiller, first you must print the files to PostScript (.PS) files within your authoring application. To do this, you must select a PostScript printer driver on your

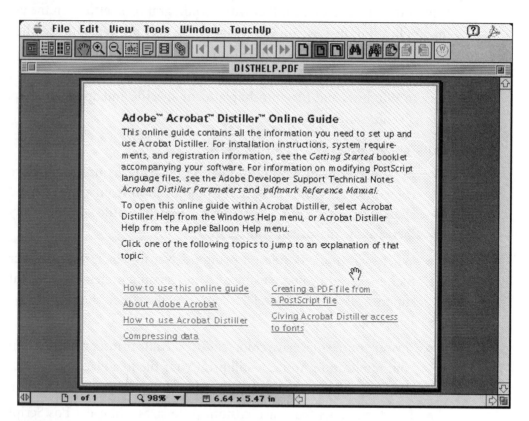

FIGURE 7.12 The Distiller Help online guide, called "HELP_D.PDF" in your Distiller Help folder or directory.

system (both Mac and Windows systems come with at least one). Once you choose a printer driver, you will see that you have the option to Print to File in the Print dialog box of your authoring application. For each file that you want to run through the Distiller, "print" each one to PostScript by selecting the Print to File option and saving the file with the .PS extension. This will not overwrite the original file; it will just create a PostScript version.

You can avoid Distiller problems, and faulty PDF files, by starting out on the right track with clean PostScript files. "Bad" PostScript files are those that have a larger-than-necessary file size, that come out of outdated PostScript printer drivers, and that conflict with certain graphics settings in the authoring application. Just as you have page setup and printer options when you print your files to paper, you have options when you print to PostScript that can change the Distiller's PDF output significantly. The following tips apply both to Windows and Macintosh; platform-specific and application-specific tips will come after.

General PostScript File Printing Tips:

- In your design program, do not use fill patterns unless they are color fills. This will prevent your application from using Type 3 characters to create fill patterns, which would dramatically increase the file size of your PDF.

- When selecting a PostScript printer driver to which to print your files, make sure you are using a recent version, preferably one that supports PostScript Level 2. Your actual printer should also be PostScript Level 2.

- If your source files have color, choose a color printer driver within your application. You can still print your file to a black-and-white PostScript printer, but the printer driver must support color.

- For documents that have custom page sizes, choose a PostScript printer that supports custom page sizes. The maximum page size for which the Distiller can create a PDF is 45 inches by 45 inches.

Printing to PostScript on a Macintosh

Before you begin printing your files to PostScript on the Mac, you should be aware of a potential problem that Adobe stresses in their literature. If your document was authored in a graphics program, do not choose the Smooth Graphics option in the Page Setup box, and uncheck it if it has been selected by default. Smooth Graphics would add much more image data to your file than is necessary for screen display, and would result in a very large PDF file.

This process will slightly vary depending on the authoring application and the printer drivers you have available, so use these instructions as general guidelines.

1. Go to the Chooser under the Apple menu, and click on the Laser-Writer icon, or any other PostScript printer you have available. Close the Chooser.

2. In your authoring application, open the document you wish to convert to PDF.

3. Select the Print command under the File menu. In the Print dialog box, select the Print to File option.

4. If your document contains color or greyscale images, select the Color/Greyscale option (you may have to click Options to find this option). Click OK.

5. The Save As dialog box appears. (See Figure 7.13.) Choose a destination file for the PostScript file (you should create a folder/directory for all the .PS files you want to Distill and name it accordingly). Name the PostScript file with a descriptive (eight-letter) name, and the extension .PS. It is extremely important to include the .PS extension to help you keep track of the various file types in your production process—original, .PS, and .PDF.

6. If there is a Font Inclusion menu in your Print Dialog box, select it and choose the All But Standard 13 option, so that all of the fonts on your system will be available for embedding in the Post-Script file.

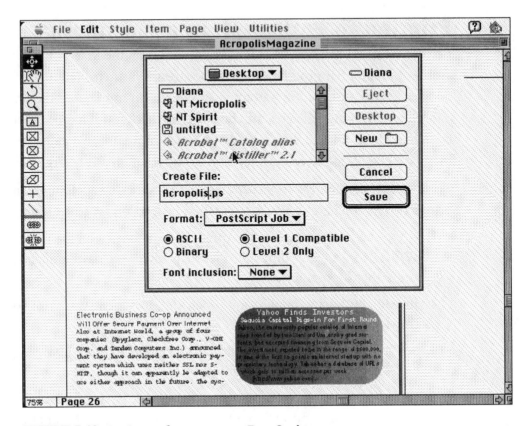

FIGURE 7.13 Saving a document as PostScript.

7. Click Save. When the print is complete, you should be able to locate the .PS file in the folder you chose. Do not try and open the .PS file—you will not be able to see the results of your print until you Distill to PDF.

Printing to PostScript from a Windows Application

There are two ways to create PostScript files in Windows: by printing to file in your authoring application, and by using the Distiller Assistant. Printing to PostScript in Windows requires that you have a PostScript printer driver loaded, but it is not necessary that you actually have a PostScript printer connected to your PC. You must install a PostScript printer driver in the Control Panel for it to be active, however. Once you have loaded and selected a PostScript printer driver, you can print directly to PostScript within your application. The other method, using the Distiller Assistant, is a shortcut for Windows that automates the production of a PostScript file and converts it to PDF. It mimics the PDFWriter by acting as an optional printer driver. The downside is that you always have to be running the Assistant in your StartUp file, and you cannot program the Distiller with special PostScript commands.

Special Considerations for Windows PostScript Files

Before you begin printing to PostScript with your Windows applications, you should be aware of some potential juggernauts. First, you may not have the option to print to file in your application. If not, you must add a new printer entry in the Windows Control Panel. Open the Printers icon, and click Add in the Printers dialog box. A list of possible printers appears. Select "PostScript Printer" from the list, and click Install. You will be returned to the Printers dialog box, where PostScript Printer has been added to the list of installed printers. Select the PostScript printer listing, and click Connect. In the Connect dialog box, select File from the Ports list, and click OK. You will be returned to the Printers dialog box, where you will notice that the PostScript printer is now connected to File. Click Close, and then Exit the Control Panel. Now you are ready to Print to File from any of your Windows authoring applications.

Second, if your source document uses TrueType fonts, you will need to convert those fonts to Adobe Type 1 fonts in the PostScript file you send to the Distiller. (You can tell by going to the Fonts information box for your document and checking if there is a "TT" icon next to the font you are using.) To program your PostScript printer driver to perform these conversions, go to the Windows Control Panel and select Printers. Select the PostScript printer you have installed, and click Options. In the Options box, click Advanced. In the Advanced Options dialog box, select Adobe Type 1 in the pull-down menu next to the words True Type Fonts: Send to Printer As. Click OK.

Printing to File from a Windows Application:

1. In your authoring application, select the Print command from the File menu. In the Print dialog box, select Print to File.

2. In the Print dialog box, click Setup. From the list of printers, choose the PostScript printer that is connected to File. Click OK.

3. In the Print to File dialog box, choose a directory and file name for the PostScript file. Make sure that you include the .PS extension so that you can distinguish it from the original file and the resulting PDF file.

4. The PostScript file will be printed and placed in the directory you chose. Do not attempt to open the PostScript file; you will be able to view it only once it has been Distilled into PDF.

Using the Distiller Assistant

The Distiller Assistant is a Windows-only tool that operates as an icon that you put in your Windows StartUp group in the Program Manager. When you load the Distiller for Windows, the Distiller Assistant is placed in the Adobe Acrobat program group. To activate it, copy it into the StartUp group so that it initializes every time you start your PC. When it is running, you can print files to PostScript and to PDF by choosing the printer \DISTASST.PS in the Print Setup dialog box. The process is similar to printing to the PDF Writer, but in the background the Assistant is actually writing a PostScript file and feeding it to the Distiller.

Before you try out the Distiller Assistant you should set Distiller Assistant options by clicking once on its icon in the Program Manager. The options appear as menu items, which show a check mark when you activate them. View PDF file will automatically launch Acrobat Exchange to display the PDF file resulting from its print to PostScript and Distill job. Exit Distiller when Idle will quit out of the Distiller program when the distill is complete. Ask for PDF File Destination prompts you to name and save the files that you are printing to PostScript and Distilling. If you do not select this, the files will go into the Distiller directory.

Not only can you "print" to the Distiller Assistant, but you can also drop a file that has already been printed to PostScript and drop it onto the Assistant icon. It will Distill the .PS file and launch Acrobat Exchange to display it. If you are running the Distiller on a network (we'll tell you how to do that later in the chapter), the Assistant will monitor the Distiller's "watched" folders and distill any files that appear.

A few words of warning about using the Distiller Assistant. First, the Assistant will infer a .PDF file name from the .PS file you print to, so make sure that your naming scheme is consistent for each step. Second, the Distiller automatically deletes the .PS file once it has distilled it to PDF. If you want to keep a record of the source .PS files, it is best to use the drag and drop Distilling method, which we will explain later in this chapter. Third, the Distiller Assistant cannot handle PDFmark runfiles, which the more advanced PDF publishers among you may want to use to automate the production of certain Acrobat features. For more on PDFmark, see Chapter 9, "Special-Purpose PDF Production Tools."

The next three sections provide some tips for producing PostScript from three common design applications for which Adobe has provided special information. If you are using another design application, follow the Printing to PostScript instructions above as rough guidelines, and refer to that application's manual for specific steps.

Generating PostScript from Adobe PageMaker

When you go to Print, select "Acrobat Distiller" as the Type, or PPD (PostScript Printer Description) in the Print Document box. The PPD file tells PageMaker what the Acrobat Distiller needs to generate PDF from the PostScript file, such as built-in fonts, paper sizes, and resolution capabilities.

If your PageMaker document has a custom page size, note the dimensions that you entered in the Page Setup box, and go back to the Print Document box. If you are in Macintosh, click the Paper button; in Windows, click Setup. Select Custom as the size. In the Custom Paper Size dialog box, type in the dimensions that you noted from the Page Setup box. Set the Paper margin and Paper feed values at 0, and the Page orientation at Normal. Click OK.

After you set the page size, click Options in the Print Document box. Select Write PostScript to File in the PostScript section of the Options box. Page-Maker will suggest a name and location for the file. You can change the name and location by clicking Save As on the Mac, or Browse in Windows. If you are on a Mac and it has suggested a file name longer than eight letters, abbreviate the name to eight letters and make sure it has the .PS extension. Select Normal. Select Include Downloadable Fonts to include fonts with the Post-Script file if you will be Distilling the files on a different system that may not have the fonts. When you are finished setting options, click Save and the .PS file will be written. After you write the first PostScript file from PageMaker, you do not need to reset Options to print other PageMaker files to PostScript. Just go to Print, click Options, and Save the file as .PS.

PageMaker 6.0 offers a Create Adobe PDF option that walks you through the process of generating PostScript for the Distiller. For more information on PageMaker 6's integration with Acrobat, see Chapter 9, "Special-Purpose PDF Production Tools."

Generating PostScript from QuarkXPress

If you are going to generate .PS files from QuarkXPress 3.3, but Distill the .PS files on another machine, you will need to install the Acrobat Distiller PPD on the system that is running Quark. First, find the file called Acrobat Distiller PPD in the Acrobat Distiller Xtras folder on the machine that has the Distiller. On a Mac, move the PPD to the Printer Descriptions folder, in the Extensions folder of the System Folder. In Windows, move the file ACRODIST.PPD to the Windows System folder. If you are running an earlier version of QuarkXPress for Mac, copy the XPress PDF from the Acrobat Distiller file in the Xtras folder into the QuarkXPress application folder.

To print a Quark file to PostScript on a Mac, go to the Chooser under the Apple menu and select a LaserWriter or another PS printer. In Windows, you will have to configure your printer to print to a PostScript printer on FILE, as was discussed earlier in the section on printing to PostScript from a Windows application.

Inside the Quark document, select Page Setup if you are on a Mac. Select the Acrobat Distiller from the Printer Type menu. In Windows, choose Printer Setup within the document, and select the Acrobat Distiller where it says Use PDF For. On both platforms, enter the width of the document. Set the Page Offset and Page Gap amounts at 0. Select Portrait as the orientation, even if some or all of the document is in Landscape orientation. The resulting PDF will carry the original orientation.

- On a Mac, click Options, and disable Smooth Graphics. Click OK.

- In Windows, click Options, Advanced and deselect Compress Bitmaps. Click OK.

- You are now ready to print to PostScript from your Quark document. Select the Print command, choose File as the destination, and click Save. In the Save As box, enter the file name and correct folder for your file, using an eight-letter file name and the .PS extension. If you will be Distilling the Quark files on a different machine, you should include the fonts with the PostScript files. On a Mac, select All or All but Standard 13 to embed the fonts in the document. In Windows, choose Options, Advanced in the Printer Setup box, and select the fonts used by the document. Click Save and the .PS file will be written.

Generating PostScript from Adobe Illustrator EPS Files

Although the Acrobat Distiller can handle EPS (Encapsulated PostScript Files), it will always create a PDF document from them which has an 8-1/2-

by-11-inch page size, regardless of the original size of the Illustrator document. Insert the EPS file into a page design application such as PageMaker or QuarkXPress, and then print it to PostScript using a PS Printer driver; the resulting PDF file will maintain the original size of the artwork.

Inserting EPS files into PostScript-capable applications will also give the Distiller access to the fonts used in the EPS file. When printing to the PostScript driver from the application, choose All But Standard 13 from the Font Inclusion menu to send the fonts to the PostScript file.

If you want to directly distill an EPS file, there is another option for dealing with page size problems for those familiar with the PostScript language. After you've created the .PS file from the EPS, open it up in a word processing or text program. Add the following PostScript Level 2 command to the header of the file: <</PageSize [*width height*]>> setpagedevice. Do not write out "width height" in the brackets; there you should enter the dimensions of the page in terms of PostScript "units." (In PostScript, there are 72 units per inch.) Enter the width unit numbers first, and then the height unit numbers, separated by a space, like this: [792 1008] (this would create an 11-by-14-inch page size). To set a default page size for all Distiller jobs, you can add this command to the Distiller's Startup folder.

We've covered many bases toward producing clean PostScript files from Macintosh, Windows, and some common desktop publishing applications. One final measure to ensure that your .PS files are clean is to print them on paper to the PostScript printer to which your system is connected. If printing to paper works well, printing to PDF through the Distiller is likely to work well. If not, you may want to go back and recreate the .PS files from your applications, making sure you are connected to the right printer driver and printer and tinkering with printing options a little more.

Setting Distiller Job Options

Now that you have prepared your PostScript files and placed them in a special folder for the Distiller (this can be a folder of your making or the Distiller In

Folder), you are ready to set Job Options within the Distiller program (Figure 7.14). The Job Options box sets compression types and levels, downsampling of images, and a few other features. Start the Distiller program by double-clicking on its icon in the Adobe Acrobat program group. You will see the Distiller program window, which does not take up the whole screen. From the menu items at the top of the screen, select Job Options. In the Job Options box, you can set the following Distiller commands:

COMPRESS (LZW) TEXT AND GRAPHICS Definitely take advantage of this powerful file compression method. LZW compresses everything in a document except bitmaps, and loses no data. This compression method will be

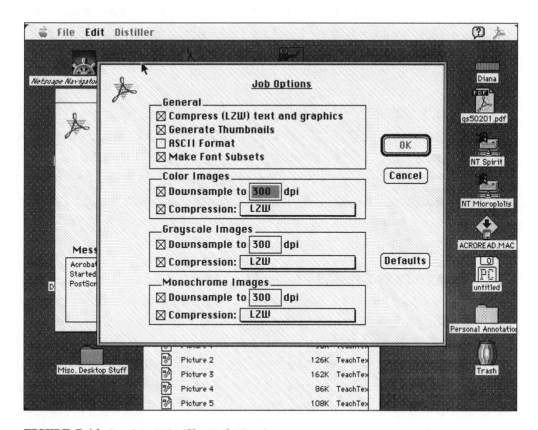

FIGURE 7.14 Setting Distiller Job Options.

responsible for the marked decrease in file size from the PS source file, because it compresses all of the display information contained in the .PS file. You can also use LZW compression to further compress color, greyscale, and monochrome images, but they are dealt with separately in the Job Options box.

GENERATE THUMBNAILS Thumbnail views are a great way for your user to navigate your document, and also handy for shuffling pages around in Exchange. Checking this box will automatically generate Thumbnails for the document, so you don't have to do it in Exchange. Thumbnails will add from 1 to 3 KB per page of your document, however. You may not want to generate Thumbnails if your document does not have many images or tables, because at such a reduced size all the pages will look the same as Thumbnails. Remember, you can always Create All and Delete All Thumbnails in Exchange.

ASCII FORMAT We recommend that you do not select the ASCII Format option, because PDF's 8-bit binary format results in a file size that is 20 percent smaller, and ASCII-formatted PDF files may be corrupted by file transfer programs. Eight-bit binary files are the best for electronic transmission over email, networks, and the Web. Adobe provides the option only because some older versions of file-transfer programs do not support 8-bit binary files, but you would be hard-pressed to find one that does not support them today.

MAKE FONT SUBSETS This option will select only those characters of an embedded font that are used in the document, to reduce file size dramatically (30 to 40 K per Type 1 font). This option should always be turned on, or else the Distiller will embed entire fonts into your document. The only instance in which you should not make font subsets is if your document contains fonts that do not use the Roman character set, such as symbolic fonts. If you do not embed those entire fonts into the PDF, the Acrobat

Reader on the user end will try to substitute them with Roman-character-based multiple-master fonts, resulting in an incomprehensible jumble of characters. Also, be aware that once you make a font subset, you will not be able to edit the text of the PDF or add text that uses characters that are not in the font subset. You would run into this problem only if you tried to alter the text of the PDF with the Touch Up plug-in, or open up the PDF in Adobe Illustrator and edit the text. One final consideration for font subsets: If you combine multiple PDF files into one after you have distilled them, font subsets will not be combined. Even if they are the same font subsets, both will reside in the file and add to the file's size. In this situation, you should embed the entire font at the outset when you distill the files.

DOWNSAMPLING COLOR AND GREYSCALE IMAGES Photographs, scanned images, bitmap images created with paint and photo programs, and images from screen capture programs all fall under this category, and can benefit from downsampling. *Downsampling* means reducing the number of pixels in an image, from a high-resolution dpi to a low-resolution dpi. Downsampling is an effective way to exclude superfluous data from a file, and reduce its file size. It is a particularly important method for PDF files, because most PDF files are viewed on screen at 72 to 96 dpi, and cannot benefit from a greater resolution. Setting the dpi for color and greyscale images close to normal screen resolution (72 dpi) is a good idea, but you cannot ultimately control the exact dpi of the PDF. The degree of downsampling depends on the original resolution of the source document. The Distiller automatically divides the original resolution of the source document by two, regardless of whether you set downsampling options. In fact, the Distiller will continue to divide the resolution by a factor of two until it reaches the dpi that you set in Job Options, so your setting is really the maximum you will allow the Distiller to downsample. If the original dpi cannot be divided by two without going below the specified minimum, the image will not be downsampled at all. If you want to fine-tune the resolution of your color and greyscale images, you can downsample them by exact numbers first in Adobe Photoshop, and then choose not to downsample the image in the Distiller.

COMPRESSING COLOR IMAGES In Distiller Job Options, you can compress color images separately from other kinds of images, which will give you a high degree of control over the quality of your images. JPEG compression is for 16-bit and 24-bit color images, such as photographs. It compresses halftone and continuous-tone images by reducing data in the less-detailed parts of the image. JPEG compression is not recommended for images with large areas of a single color, simple pictures from paint programs, or drawings that have been converted to an image format. Distiller Job Options gives you five levels of JPEG compression to choose from: low, medium-low, medium, medium-high, and high. Low results in the least amount of compression, and the compression will not be visible in the image. High will give you the most amount of compression, and the results will be visible in a slightly blocky image. Of course, the right level of JPEG compression depends on the original resolution of the image. The only way to really know the right level is to do a couple of test runs through the Distiller.

Although it does not decrease file size as much, LZW compression succeeds where JPEG fails. The Distiller automatically uses LZW compression for 8-bit color images, even if you selected JPEG compression in Options. LZW finds patterns in image data and compresses them, without sacrificing color and details. So it is ideal for images with large regions of one color, and simple pictures created from paint programs. LZW should not be used for the kinds of images JPEG is best for—half-tone and continuous-tone images. There are no levels of LZW compression, but there are two options: regular LZW as just described, and LZW 4-bit. LZW 4-bit converts 8-bit image data to 4-bit, and then applies LZW compression of the image. The result is a much smaller image that loads quickly, but which uses only 16 colors. This method is recommended only for simple drawings and charts that did not have much detail to begin with. For complex images, the result of LZW will not be acceptable in the final PDF.

If you are up to it, you can use the AutoFilter option in the setdistillerparams (set distiller parameters) PostScript operator in the Distiller to set the exact compression types and levels for your images. But you have to understand how to read image data, and how to write in the PostScript code to change the defaults. For more on this and other setdistillerparams operations, see the "Setting Distiller Preferences" section later in this chapter.

COMPRESSING GREYSCALE IMAGES You do not have to treat greyscale images differently from color images, but you have the option to select a different downsample dpi and compression method if you need to. You may want to preserve more data for your color images than for greyscale images, for instance. In general, you can rely on the Distiller's defaults to use JPEG for 8-bit greyscale images and LZW for 2-bit and 4-bit greyscale images. LZW 4-bit works quite well with most kinds of greyscale images. You can also hack your way through greyscale image compression in the AutoFilter in setdistillerparams; see the section on setting distiller preferences for more detail.

COMPRESSING MONOCHROME IMAGES Monochrome (black and white only) images that have been scanned in or created in a paint program can benefit from downsampling to screen resolution, as well as from four lossless compression methods. CCITT Group 3 is the method used by fax machines to compress monochrome bitmaps one row at a time. CCITT Group 4 is a more general compression method that works well for most types of monochrome images. LZW is also an option for monochrome images that contain repeating patterns. Finally, Run Length compression is best for monochrome images with large areas of solid black or white.

When you are finished setting Job Options, click OK. These will be the new default settings for subsequent Distiller jobs. You can clear your settings by clicking on the Defaults button in the Job Options box. You can also customize Job Options for each "watched" folder you have specified for the

Distiller. To learn more about watched folders, see the section on setting up watched folders, later in this chapter.

Font Considerations for the Distiller

In order to produce PDF files with fidelity to the original documents, the Distiller needs to have access to all of the fonts used in the document. You may have embedded fonts in the PostScript files that you now want to distill, but that does not mean they will be embedded in the PDF file. The Distiller will just use those fonts as references to reproduce them in the PDF file. If you did not include fonts with your PostScript files, you can give the Distiller access to them either by telling the Distiller the font's location, or by embedding the font in the PDF document. There are certain fonts that the Distiller will always have access to—the basic 13 of the Adobe Type 1 series: Helvetica, Courier, the Times family, Symbol, and Zapf Dingbats. If ATM is loaded on the machine running Distiller, it will also look in that folder. On a Mac, the Distiller will also look for Font Folio, Type on Call, or Suitcase. If the fonts are not available in any of those folders, the Distiller will look for the font in its font database of metrics. If it finds the font there, it will extract the metrics of the font to describe in the PDF file. Failing all of those measures, the Distiller will use the not-too-attractive Courier font.

Setting Font Locations

If you want to ensure that Distiller finds the fonts in your document, but you don't think it's necessary to embed the fonts or use font subsets, you can direct the Distiller to the right font folder in the Font Locations dialog box (Figure 7.15). The folders you list in this box do not need to be specific to the Distiller job at hand; it can be an ongoing resource for the Distiller. So you should list as many font folders as possible in the Font Locations box. Under the Distiller menu, choose Font Locations. The Font Locations box will already contain a list of the "usual suspect" folders we mentioned earlier, but you can add as many as you like by clicking on Add Directory. In the Add Directory box, select a folder/directory on your hard drive or on

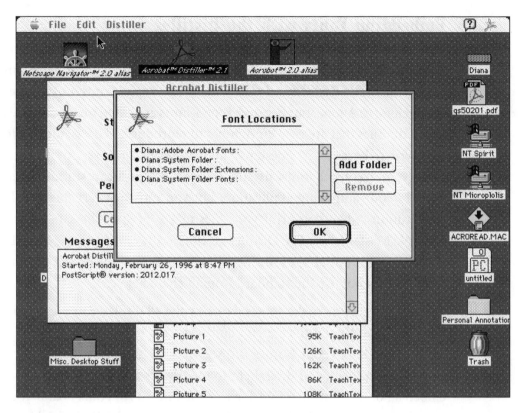

FIGURE 7.15 Setting Distiller Font Locations.

a network that contains fonts. You can repeat this procedure to add all the necessary folders. Be sure to point the Distiller to folders that contain both printer fonts and screen fonts—it needs both to render the fonts in the PDF. On a Mac, screen fonts live in Font folders and have little suitcase icons next to them, and printer fonts are named in the system folder. In Windows, both kinds of fonts are in the \psfonts directory, and have the extensions .PFM and .PFB. You can remove folders from the Font Folders/Directories list by selecting them in the Font Locations box and clicking the Remove button. If a folder in the list does not have a > to its left in Windows, or a little square next to it on a Mac, that means it is not available. To make the folder available you should reinstall it on the hard drive, or reconnect to the network that serves the folder.

Embedding Fonts with the Distiller

To be safe, you can embed Adobe Type 1 fonts into your PDF document, and then choose Font Subsets to reduce the file size before you run a file through the Distiller. The Distiller only lets you embed Type 1 fonts, not just because they belong to Adobe, but because Type 1 fonts are based on descriptive Post-Script outlines that are easy for Acrobat to reproduce. (This is not true for the PDFWriter, because it sidesteps the PostScript process, so if you must preserve non-Type 1 fonts, use the PDFWriter.) You can still use TrueType fonts in your authoring application, but you must convert them to Type 1 substitutions when you print your files to PostScript. The same is true for Multiple Master fonts. The Distiller automatically embeds some Type 1 fonts that Acrobat is not able to substitute, such as symbol or expert typefaces or fonts that do not use the standard Roman character set.

To embed fonts, or make font subsets in the PDF files you create with the Distiller, go to the Distiller menu and select Font Embedding (Figure 7.16). Under Font Lists (Font Names on Mac), locate the fonts that you want to embed, select them, and drag them to the Always Embed List. If you want to embed all of the fonts in a folder, check the Embed All Fonts box. If you want to embed all fonts in a folder except for a certain few, click Embed All Fonts and then drag the fonts you don't want to the Never Embed List. If you want to embed a custom font that is not listed, click the New Font Name button and type the font's name into the Add the Font text field. Choose whether you want to Always Embed or Never Embed it, and then click Add. Click Done, and you are returned to the Font Embedding dialog box. Click OK. These settings will become the default settings for all Distiller jobs until you change them.

Setting Up Watched Folders

Once you have set up your Job Options and font embedding, you can automate the distillation of .PS files by setting up "watched folders," folders or directories on your system that the Distiller monitors and processes when .PS files appear. This is an especially valuable technique when you are running the

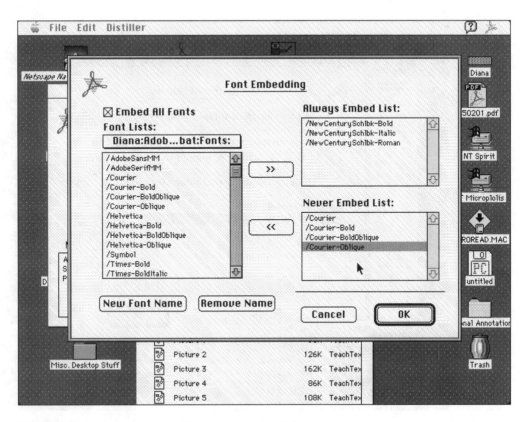

FIGURE 7.16 Setting Distiller Font Embedding.

Distiller on a network, but you can also use it on a local system. To set up watched folders, choose Watched Folders under the Distiller menu (Watched Directories in Windows). (See Figure 7.17.) In the Watched Folders/Directories Options box, you can select as many as 100 folders for the Distiller to watch by clicking Add Folder/Directory and selecting from available folders. For each watched folder you select, the Distiller will create an IN subdirectory and an OUT subdirectory. When you place a .PS file into the IN folder, the Distiller will pick it up and convert it to PDF, and then place it in the OUT folder. At the top of the Watched Folders/Directories Options box, you can check the intervals (in seconds) at which the Distiller checks the watched folders. You should enter in a high number to prevent too much load on your

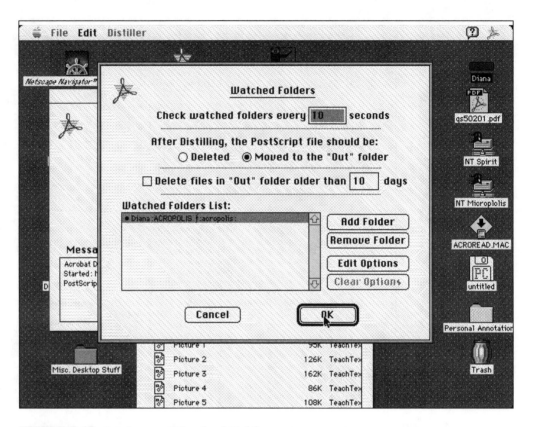

FIGURE 7.17 Setting up Watched Folders.

system. Next, you can choose whether or not the Distiller should delete the .PS file or move it to the OUT folder. Below, you can opt whether to autodelete old files in the OUT folder, and specify the number of days old they must be. While you have IN and OUT folders active, you can still use Distiller in the normal mode by opening .PS files in the Distiller program or dragging them over the Distiller icon (we will describe these techniques later). Priority will be given to .PS files distilled manually over those in watched folders.

You can customize Job Options for each of the watched folders on your system or network. To do this, select the folder from the watched folders list, and click the Edit Options button to the right. The Job Options box will appear, with all of the options we discussed before. Continue by clicking OK, selecting another watched folder, and setting its Job Options. If you do not specify Job Options here, the watched folders will adopt the defaults set in the general Job Options box. To clear custom options for a watched folder, select the folder from the list and click the Clear Options. This will give the folder the Distiller default options. To remove a watched folder from the list, select it and click the Remove Folder/Directory button. This will delete the folder but not the contents of the folder's IN and OUT folders. You can delete the IN and OUT folders directly on your desktop or File Manager.

You can keep track of the activities of your watched folders by checking the DTIME.TXT file, a text-only log that gets placed for every OUT folder. You can open up the DTIME.TXT file in the Notepad, TeachText, or a word processing program, to check the last time the Distiller checked the IN folder for that watched folder, and what the job settings are for that folder. The file will tell you both the settings that you chose in the Watched Folder dialog box and in the Job Options dialog box for that folder.

Setting Up Distiller to Run on a Network

You can configure the Distiller to be a server application on a local network, so that many users can distill files using just one copy of the Distiller. Using watched folders, users can each have IN and OUT folders that the Distiller server will process. Each user can specify the Job Options for his or her Distill jobs. Setting up the Distiller on a network is an excellent way to facilitate Web publishing of PDF documents, because the various authors of documents in a workgroup can easily contribute to the production process. Once the PDF files are in OUT folders, authors can check them and then place them in a general PDF folder for your Webmaster to upload to your site. For detailed instructions on connecting Windows and Macintosh networks to Distiller IN and OUT folders, refer to your online Distiller help guide, accessible under the Help menu in the Distiller program.

There are some issues of which you should be aware when setting up Distiller as a server on a network. First, make sure that none of your users are saving their .PS or PDF files as ASCII—they do have the option to do this in their Distiller Job Options. Some of the data in .PS files are 8-bit binary, and PDF files are completely 8-bit binary, so sending them over a network as ASCII will corrupt the files. Second, there are some limitations on the kinds of platforms that use the Distiller. While the Distiller is very flexible with accepting Mac or Windows-authored .PS files and creating PDFs that can be viewed on either platform, you will run into trouble if you try to make a UNIX machine watch folders residing on Mac and Windows machines. The UNIX machine will not be able to watch non-UNIX folders. You will also have problems distilling .PS files on a Mac or Windows machine that were authored on a UNIX machine, with UNIX-based Type 1 fonts. If your network does not allow setting up the Distiller server any other way, you can convert UNIX-based Type 1 fonts to other platforms with a tool like Fontographer. Third, for security reasons the administrator of the Distiller server must ensure that every machine that has access must be authorized and "trusted." This is because each machine connected to the Distiller must have full read, write, create, and delete access to every watched folder on the network. To date, there are no special password or encryption tools for restricting access to the Distiller or watched folders.

Setting Distiller Preferences

We're almost there, but there are three options in the Distiller Preferences box that you will want to consider before you start Distilling. Go to Preferences under the Distiller menu (Figure 7.18). Your first option is, "Restart [Windows or your Mac] after PostScript fatal error." If you are on a Windows machine, do not select this unless the whole machine is dedicated to the Distiller—otherwise your whole system will reboot, even when the Distiller is working on watched folders in the background, if a Distill job crashes. Distiller jobs crash enough to make this a dangerous option—if you are multitasking while

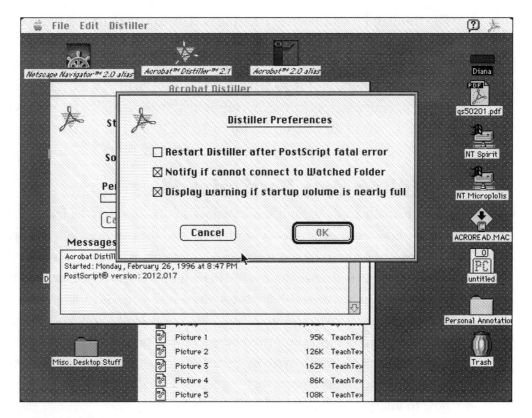

FIGURE 7.18 Setting Distiller Preferences.

the Distiller is doing its thing, your whole system will go down and you may lose unsaved data. The same is also true for Macintosh, although Restarting a Mac is a less dangerous operation. Still, if you are running other programs at the time, you may lose work. You should check this option only if you have a dedicated Distiller machine that is running without human supervision.

The second option in the Preferences box is "Notify if cannot connect to Watched Folder [/Directory]." If checked, the Distiller will show an alert if it cannot find certain watched folders, such as if a server has gone down, or in a worst case, someone has deleted the folder. If you use watched folders, you should check this option.

The third and final Preference setting is "Display warning if startup volume is nearly full." This has nothing to do with .PS waiting in watched folders to be distilled, but rather with PostScript runfiles and setdistillerparams operators residing in the Distiller's Startup folder. Instead of placing multiple PostScript operator scripts in the Startup folder, make a folder for each set and place only one in the Startup file for each job. When you are finished making your selections (these will be the new defaults), click OK.

Distilling Your PostScript Files

You are finally ready to send some PostScript files through the Distiller. Once you see how fast the Distiller accommodates all the compression, font searching, and embedding, and performs the conversion, you will be amazed. In the best case, you will have successful PDF files to which you can then add features in Exchange and launch on your Web site. But there are a lot of things that can go wrong with Distill jobs, because of faulty PostScript files, poorly chosen compression methods, and just plain system crashes (more common on Macintosh systems than Windows). Fortunately, the Distiller keeps logs and status reports that can tell you what went wrong (if you know how to interpret them—we'll teach you how).

There are four ways to Distill .PS files—using the Open file method, the Distiller Assistant for Windows, the drag-and-drop method, and the Watched Folder method. The Open file method is recommended for simple Distill jobs with only one .PS file. The Distiller Assistant is a Windows-only method that acts as a printer driver for the Distiller. The drag-and-drop method is good for distilling large volumes of .PS files that are located on the same system as the Distiller. The Watched Folder method is the one recommended for using the Distiller on a network and for distilling large volumes on one system that has multiple users. Here is how to use each of these methods:

OPEN FILE Simply start the Distiller program by double-clicking on its icon in the Acrobat group on your desktop. Go to the File menu, and select Open. In the Open dialog box, select the .PS file that you want to distill. When you click Open, the Distiller will ask you to choose a .PDF file name for the file. By default, it suggests a name that is the PostScript file name, but replaces the .PS with .PDF. Make sure that the .PDF file is going into the right folder, click Save, and Distiller will start the job. Keep an eye on the Distiller window for helpful status information (Figure 7.19). A bar will estimate the percent of the PS file that has been read, and the Page box next to it will give you a Thumbnail view of each page as it is being distilled. You have the option to Cancel Job, or Pause the Job (pausing the job will give you the option to continue). It is best to let the Distiller run the whole job, however, even if the job is failing. Letting it finish will give you all the messages that will let you know what went wrong. In the Messages window, the Distiller will display

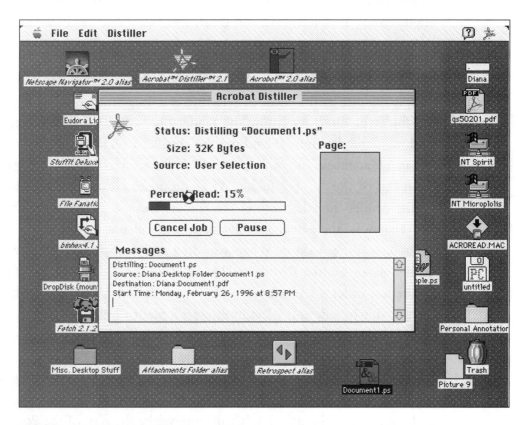

FIGURE 7.19 The Distiller Status window.

status messages that mark each step in its progress. We will explain these status messages and error messages shortly. When the Distiller completes its job, it will place the PDF into the folder you selected. To view it, open it in Acrobat Exchange.

DISTILLER ASSISTANT FOR WINDOWS In the section on printing to Post-Script, you saw how you can use the Distiller Assistant to automate the production of .PS and PDF programs from your applications. To summarize, you simply drag the Distiller Assistant icon to the Startup group in your Program Manager, reboot, and select the "printer" DISTASST.PS in the Print Setup box in your application. You enter the name and destination of the file, and the Assistant prints a .PS file that it then hands off to the Distiller in the background. When all is said and done, you can locate the PDF file in the directory you chose and view it in Acrobat Exchange.

DRAG AND DROP In both Windows and Macintosh systems, you can distill multiple .PS files by the batch by selecting and dragging the file names from their folder or directory (using the Finder on a Mac; the File Manager in Windows), and dropping them onto the Distiller icon sitting on your desktop. On a Macintosh, you can move the Distiller icon to the desktop by dragging it out of the Acrobat folder. We recommend creating an alias for the Distiller (under the File menu in the Finder) and using that as the desktop icon. That way, the actual Distiller program will not be sitting out there vulnerable on the desktop. When you drag and drop the PS files over the Distiller alias icon, the Distiller will launch itself and distill the .PS files in alphabetical order. In Windows, set up the Program Manager and the File Manager side by side and select multiple .PS files by holding down the Shift key and clicking each file once. Then drag them onto the Distiller icon in the Acrobat group in your Program Manager. The Distiller will launch and process the files in the order in which they were created. In the drag-and-drop method, by default the Distiller does not ask you to Save As and choose the destination of the .PS files. It will simply take the root of the PostScript file name, add the .PDF extension, and place them in the same folder as the source .PS files. On a Macintosh, you can make the Distiller prompt you to Save As by holding down the Command key while dragging the .PS files. In Windows, you can prompt a Save As box by holding down the Shift key while you drag the .PS files. While the Distiller processes the files, it will not pause between files, and you must wait until all of them are done to individually deal with problem jobs.

WATCHED FOLDERS Using this method, you will never actually see the Distiller process your files, and you can continue working in another program while your .PS files are being distilled. Once you have printed your files to PostScript, drag or copy the .PS files into the IN folder for the watched folder. The .PS file will be placed in queue for the Distiller, converted to PDF, and dropped in the OUT folder. You can continue working in other applications during this process. You can tell when your PDF is ready by looking in the OUT folder in your watched folder, or by checking the DTIME.TXT file for that folder to see when the Distiller last checked your IN folder. You can check the modification date and time of the DTIME.TXT by selecting its icon and pressing Command-I on a Mac, or viewing the date and time in the File Manager in Windows. You can also open the file in any text reader or word processing program. If it is not within the last few minutes, the Distiller is no longer watching your folder and you must reestablish your connection to the Distiller server. When you check your OUT folder, you should drag the PDF out of it and into another folder from which you can locally access it. Also check the log file that accompanies the PDF to find out what, if anything, went wrong with the Distill.

Understanding Status and Error Messages

While the Distiller is processing a job, it keeps a running tab of its progress in the Message field of the main Distiller window. If you are running a short job using the Open file method, it helps to keep an eye on these messages. If you are running the Distiller in batch-mode or on a network, you won't be able to monitor all of the messages, but you can view them in the message "log files" that are produced with each PDF (and in the event that no PDF is produced). For each PDF file the Distiller attempted to create, it will create a text-only log file with the same file name as the original .PS file, with the .log extension. The log file will be placed in the same destination folder as the PDF file, even if no PDF file was produced. Here is a list of the common messages you will see in these files:

- *Starting Distiller* means that you have started the Distiller program.

- *Ready* means that no job is currently being processed, and the Distiller is ready to receive a .PS file.

- *Distilling [yourfile.ps]* means that it has received your .PS file and is beginning to process it.

- *Building font table* means the Distiller is building a list of Post-Script Font Metrics file names for PostScript Type 1 fonts. This message is always displayed when the Windows version of Distiller starts up, and when you have added a font folder with the Font Locations tool.

- *Paused* means you have clicked the Pause button. The Distiller will remain frozen until you click the Resume button or Cancel Job button.

- *Purging Out folders* means that if you are using Watched Folders, files that have been left in OUT folders for more than the specified number of days are being deleted.

- *Relocating files* means that the Distiller is moving the new PDF file to a folder you have specified, or to an OUT folder.

Of course, status messages and log files will also contain error messages, which are not as easy to understand (and the ones you most want to understand—go figure). Following are discussions of the most common error problems and tips for how to fix them. If your problem is not covered below, check the Support area of Adobe's Web site for a complete archive of technical notes for the Distiller.

"NOT ENOUGH MEMORY TO RUN ACROBAT DISTILLER." If you get this message when you try to start up the Distiller, your system has insufficient RAM available. Insufficient RAM may also cause error messages in log files that include the words "limitcheck" or "vmerror." On a Macintosh, the Distiller requires 6 MB of application RAM to run, and in Windows, the Distiller needs 8 MB of RAM. In Macintosh, first try quitting all other applications, and Restart the machine. If you get the same message, then try increasing the memory available to the Distiller (a few-hundred-K-worth) by editing its Info dialog box. In Windows, increase the virtual memory on your system by editing to the 386 Enhanced box in the Control Panel.

"LIMITCHECK, OFFENDING COMMAND: FINDFONT." This is a common case in a class of errors that contain the word "findfont." They all have to do with fonts, but each targets a different font problem. "Limitcheck" at the beginning of an error message usually means a memory problem, so this one means that there is not enough memory to run the job because of the number of fonts the Distiller is being asked to deal with. You can remedy this problem by reducing the number of fonts folders available to the Distiller, thereby relieving it of having to search through all the available font folders to find the right font. Go to the Font Locations box under the Distiller menu, and remove font folders that you are certain do not contain fonts necessary to produce the PDF document. You may also need to remove font folders from your system because there are folders that the Distiller will automatically search through no matter what you specify in Font Locations. You can do this temporarily by moving unnecessary font folders to a different hard drive or storage medium until the Distiller job is finished.

The Distiller may also have generated this message because one of the required fonts is damaged. This problem is harder to pinpoint—you must remove the fonts and then make them available one by one until you can reproduce the error message. That way you can target the bad font and replace it with a good one in the original application file.

"INVALID FONT: OFFENDING COMMAND: FINDFONT." This error message is usually followed by a few lines of jibberish, which contain the name of the bad font. If the name of the font is one of the base 14 fonts required to run the Distiller (one of the Courier, Times, Helvetica, Symbol, or Zapf Ding-bats), you need to locate the folder for those fonts in the Font Locations box. These base 14 are the Distiller's emergency kit of fonts to use for fonts it cannot find or cannot substitute. The Distiller should automatically look for them in the ATM fonts folder, but if they have been moved around you will need to find them and include their folder in the Font Locations box.

"ERROR: UNDEFINED; OFFENDING COMMAND: @PJL." When you get this message, the Distiller cannot produce a PDF file because the .PS file was targeted to a Hewlett-Packard PostScript printer. This a compatibility problem that you can fix by targeting a LaserWriter or generic PostScript printer when you print your .PS files.

Conclusion

With clean PostScript files, well-chosen job options, and a little luck, your PDF files should come out looking great (Figure 7.20). But your success in creating the PDFs may be cruelly checked by the realization that there is a mistake in the content of the document, which of course you didn't notice back in the original application. Do not fear—it may be possible to fix the problem using the PDF document. Chapter 9 will explain a few methods of editing the content of PDFs using the Touch Up plug-in and Adobe Illustrator.

This chapter has covered the primary ways you can create PDF files with the tools included in your version of Acrobat. These are not the only ways to create PDFs, however. Increasingly, desktop publishing applications (espe-

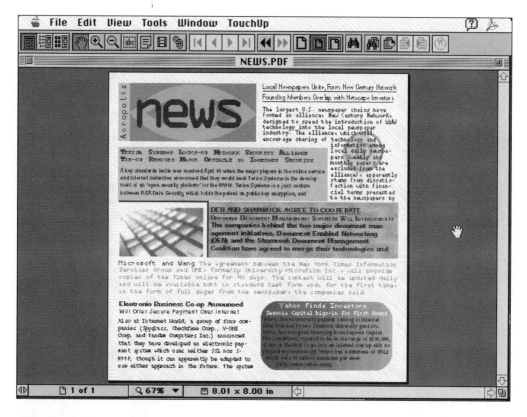

FIGURE 7.20 The finished PDF document.

cially Adobe's) are improving and automating their production of PDFs. Chapter 9 discusses which applications offer streamlined PDF production, and how to make them work for you. We will also provide an introduction to PDFmark, Adobe's markup language for automating the production of certain Acrobat features in your PDF files. The next chapter, "Enhancing your PDF in Acrobat Exchange," will tell you how to manually add these features to your PDF documents.

Notes

1. *Adobe Acrobat Exchange 2.1 Online Guide* (Mountain View: Adobe Systems Inc., 1995).

Chapter 8

Enhancing Your PDF in Acrobat Exchange

Acrobat Exchange provides a number of tools for turning a newborn PDF (which is in effect a picture of the original document) into a dynamic, interactive Web document. These include Bookmarks, Thumbnail views, Hyperlinks, Article Threads, "Sticky Notes," and Weblinks. Unfortunately, many PDF authors are not aware of or don't bother with adding the features Acrobat provides, resulting in some pretty bland PDF documents up on the Web. Taking the time to enhance your PDF will prevent your users' frustrations with navigating the document, and capture their attention for a longer period. It will also make it a better Web document, interlinked with other sites and files on the Web. The following tips are based on Acrobat Exchange 2.1.

Before You Begin

Make sure you are using the most recent version of Exchange so that you'll be able to take full advantage of additional tools and Plug-ins. If you are using Exchange 2.1, you will be able to insert Weblinks and Acrobat Movies into your PDF document. If you are using Exchange 2.0, you can download the Weblink plug-in for free on Adobe's Web site. (Note that the Weblink plug-in will work only in conjunction with these Web browsers: Netscape 1.1 or later, Spyglass Mosaic 2.0 or later, and Quarterdeck Mosaic 2.0 or later. If you do not have one of these browsers, you can download one for free off those companies' Web sites.) As soon as Acrobat 3.0 with Amber is released (circa June 1996), drop everything and immediately upgrade. Only Acrobat 3.0 will let you optimize your PDF files for page-at-a-time downloading and progressive rendering over the Web. Once you are set up with Exchange 3.0 and a Web server with Amber byteserver capability (see Chapter 11), you will be able to "optimize" all of your PDF files, both old and new. Publishing Amberized documents early on will do wonders for your Web site traffic. Trust us. Until then, there is a lot you can do in Exchange 2.1 to make your PDF files look and act like professional Web documents. One thing to remember: It is important to perform certain editing operations before others. For example, you'll want to shuffle pages around before you start setting links, and set Security options the very last. We have presented all of these operations in an order we think will keep you out of trouble. As you add features to your PDF file, Save As the file frequently rather than just doing the Save command. You don't have to rename the file, but Saving As rewrites the file with the new features and often reduces the file size.

You'll recognize the Acrobat Exchange interface from the Acrobat Reader interface—the navigational icons are exactly the same. But Exchange gives you some powerful editing tools that are reserved for you, the author of the PDF document. For example, under the Edit pull-down menu, scroll down to Pages, and follow the arrow with your mouse. You will see the options Crop, Rotate, Insert, Extract, Replace, and Delete. With this artillery of page editing tools, you can make many changes to your PDF document that you might have thought could only be done in the original authoring application. We will walk you through these tools as best we can, but be sure also to check out the Acrobat Exchange help file, accessible under the Help menu.[1] It's actually an online guide in PDF packed with everything you need to know about using Exchange. The Help guide was very helpful to us in understanding the nuances of editing in Exchange, which are not self-evident in the menus or icons.

Editing Pages

Cropping Pages

Is there a white space around a page or all the pages in your document? This is often a holdover from desktop publishing applications. You can get rid of that white space with Acrobat's razor-sharp cropping tool. The Crop Tool will eliminate unwanted margins per your exact specifications, and then blow up the cropped document to fit an 8.5 × 11 page. To crop a page, select Crop under the Edit, Page menu (Figure 8.1). Move your mouse to the border of the Crop Pages box, and move the box to the middle of the screen so that you can see all four sides of the document behind. In the Pages box, select only the page number you are currently working on. Once you've determined the right amount of cropping for the current page, see if all of the other pages in the document have the same amount of white space. If they do, you can go back and enter the right numbers and crop All pages. Then move your mouse to the set of arrows under the words Margins (in inches). Starting at the top, click on the bottom arrow and watch closely as the margin line closes down on the top of your page. You can hold down the mouse button to close in fast, and then move one click at a time to make the line exactly flush with the border you desire. If you go too far, click on the Up arrow to move back. Once you get it right, note the numbered measurement in the Top box to the right. In the future, you can just type in those numbers to crop pages with the same

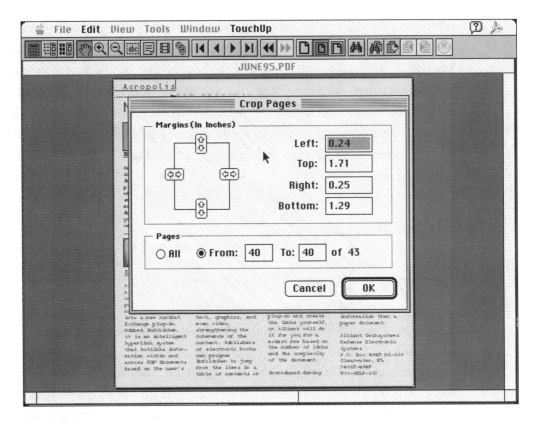

FIGURE 8.1 Cropping a page.

amount of white space. Proceed with the other three sides, noting the measurements for each crop, then click OK. Acrobat will display your new page. Did you crop too much or too little? You can't Undo the crop, but you can go back into the Crop box and reset the margins to 0.00 if you want to restore the original margins, or continue cropping if you cropped too little. Or, you can close out of the document and opt not to Save Changes to it.

Rotating Pages

If your document came through the PDFWriter or Distiller on the wrong axis, you can flip it around using the Rotate Pages command. In the Rotate Pages dialog box, clicking on Left will rotate the page 90 degrees to the left, and clicking on Right will rotate it 90 degrees to the right. To turn the page upside down, just click on Left or Right twice. Select the number of pages you wish to rotate, and click OK.

Extracting, Deleting, Inserting, and Replacing Pages

These page editing tools may be your lifesaver if there are pages with problems in their content or appearance that cannot be fixed within Acrobat. You can remove problem pages with the Extract pages and Delete pages functions. When you Extract a page, you have the option to delete the page or pages after you extract them (Figure 8.2). If you opt not to delete the pages, Acrobat will create a new file called "Pages from [*name of original PDF file*]."

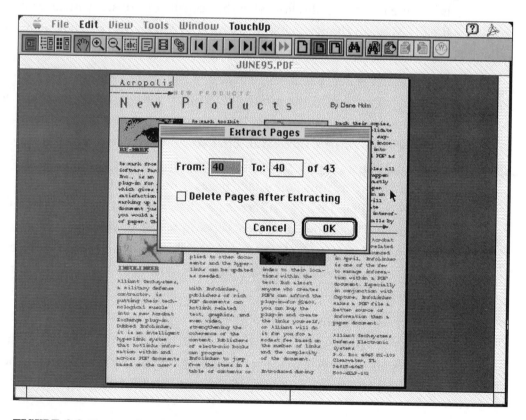

FIGURE 8.2 Extracting a page.

Extracting pages is a good method if you want to remove unwanted pages or parse out a file that is too big. The extracted file will retain links that point to other extracted pages, and sticky notes, but not Bookmarks and article threads. You will have to redo Bookmarks and Articles in the new file. If you want to avoid losing those features, duplicate the whole PDF file and Delete the rest of the pages from the second copy. That way, you'll have two sets of files with their links and other features intact. The Delete Pages option should be reserved for this instance, and in cases where you are sure you do not want to use the pages again. You cannot Undo the Delete Pages command. After you delete pages, Save As the document to remove the pages from the document's cache and reduce its file size.

If you find that you are unable to Extract Pages from a PDF document, that is because it has been disallowed in the Security options. If you have authored the file, you can change the Security for it by Saving As and click on Security. If it is not your file, there's not much you can do about it.

With the Insert Pages tool, you can add in PDF pages without disturbing the links or pagination in the master PDF file. We recommend that you do all page shuffling before you create links, however, because the transfer of such features is not always successful. First you must make a discrete file of the page you want to insert, or multiple pages if they are going to be added in consecutive order. You cannot take pages from one PDF file and insert them into another PDF file. The Insert Pages dialog box asks you to select a PDF file from your hard disk, and then asks you between which pages to put it. If you want to insert several pages that should not be in order in the master PDF file, each one should be a separate file. When you are done inserting the file, choose Save As under the File menu to reduce the new file's size.

You can also combine two PDF files by dragging and dropping with the File Manager in Windows 3.1. First, make sure that Acrobat Exchange and the File Manager are the only applications running on your system. Double-click on the desktop to get the Task List, and choose Tile so that Acrobat and the File

Manager share the screen. In Acrobat, open up the document into which you want to insert a document from the File Manager. In the File Manager window, select the file or files to be inserted, and drag them over to the document area of the open PDF file. You can also drag the file into the Thumbnails column to choose the exact location for the inserted file. The Insert dialog box will appear. Click Before if you want the inserted files to precede the existing pages, or After if you want the files to succeed them. In the Page field, you can specify page numbers between which to insert the file. If you are inserting multiple files using the drag-and-drop method, the Insert dialog box may position only the first file correctly. To avoid this, insert the files separately or move the pages around using Thumbnails.

To replace problem pages with fixed pages, you can use the Replace Pages tool. Unlike the Insert Pages tool, Replace Pages will let you select certain pages from one PDF file and put them in the place of certain pages of the master PDF file. This is probably the best method for correcting problems in a PDF file, since replacing pages does not disturb the links and Bookmarks in the master PDF file. Notes from both files are retained as well. You can also replace pages using Thumbnails—see the following discussion for details.

Using Thumbnails to Edit Pages

Thumbnails, those minipages that appear in a column on the left side of the Acrobat window when you click on the Thumbnail icon (third from left on toolbar), are great for navigating and reorganizing the pages in your PDF document. Most PDF files coming out of the Distiller will have Thumbnails already; if your file does not have them, simply go to Edit menu and choose Thumbnails, Create All. Adding Thumbnails increases the file size of your document, so you may want to Delete All when you are finished working with them (but then users will not be able to use them to navigate the document). Once you have your set of Thumbnails, you can go to certain pages of the document by clicking on that page's Thumbnail picture. You can also extend the size of the Thumbnails window with your mouse to view two rows of Thumbnails or even fill the screen with Thumbnails. Once you set your view of the Thumbnails, you can drag and drop them to different locations in the document. Just click on one of them and move it up or down the column until it is in between the pages you want. The page number of the page that will come before the moved page will be highlighted. You can also delete whole pages of the document by clicking on the page number underneath the Thumbnail for the page, and hitting the Delete key on your keyboard. Beware that you are deleting that actual page from the document, not just the Thumbnail for it.

You can also replace pages of your document with Thumbnails. Open both the source PDF document and master PDF in which you want to replace pages, opening Thumbnail views for each one. (To view two PDF files at once, resize the windows for each so they both fit on the screen.) Select the Thumbnails for the page or pages in the source document you want to insert into the master document. To select multiple continuous page Thumbnails, draw a box around them and move them by clicking on the page number under the first Thumbnail in the set. When you move them, you will see a stacked pages icon. Move the Thumbnails to the Thumbnail column of the master document, placing them over the Thumbnails of the pages you want to replace. You will see the letter "R" appear and the pages to be replaced will have their page numbers highlighted. If you make a mistake replacing pages this way, you cannot Undo it, but you can close out of the document and not Save Changes.

Using Bookmarks

Bookmarks are Acrobat's tool for listing out the contents of a PDF document and allowing users to click on the listing to jump to the correct page (Figure 8.3). They are a very handy tool for users to navigate your document, and they do not add much to your file size, so you should make sure that you add them. The Acrobat PDFWriter and Distiller do not automatically generate them, unless you program the Distiller to write them with PDFmark (see the

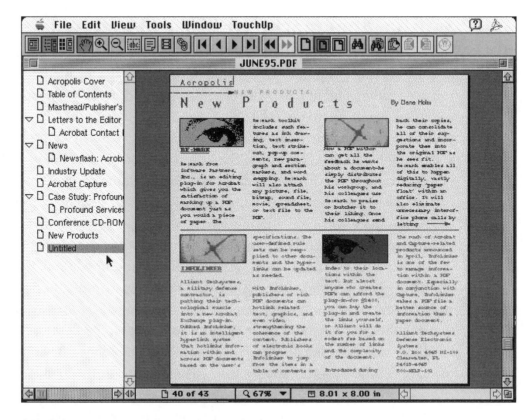

FIGURE 8.3 Editing the Bookmark window.

end of this chapter for more on PDFmark). You can view the Bookmark column by clicking on the second icon from the left of the Acrobat toolbar, or choosing Bookmarks and Page from the View menu. In the PDF file you created, this column will be empty, but you can add Bookmarks and organize them easily. First, decide on how you want your Bookmark table of contents to be structured. In the Bookmark column, you will be able to "nest" the Bookmarks several levels down, so you could structure your chapter like an outline. When you are planning your Bookmarks, keep in mind that the Bookmark column is restricted to one point size, so you should keep the text of your contents brief. And be aware of all your options—you link Bookmarks not only to pages within your document but also to other PDF files, files from other applications, and even to WWW files.

Setting Bookmarks within a Document

When you are creating Bookmarks within a PDF document, it is important to remember that you must be viewing the correct page for the Bookmark you are writing, and at the right magnification, because that Bookmark is going to become an active link to that page. Starting with the first page of your document, choose a legible magnification that you want it to open to, and select Bookmarks, New from the Edit menu, or hit Ctrl/Command-B. Acrobat will give the Bookmark a default name "Untitled," which you can type over with your Bookmark name. You can test your Bookmark by going to another page and then clicking on the Bookmark with the hand icon (move your mouse over the text of the Bookmark for the hand to appear—if you click with the pointer, it will select the Bookmark for editing). Clicking on the Bookmark should bring you back to the page to which it points. If your Bookmark is linked to the wrong page, you can reset its destination by going to the page you do want it to point to, selecting the Bookmark so it highlights, and choosing Bookmarks, Reset Destination under the Edit menu (or Ctrl/Command-R). If you want to change the text of your Bookmark, click on it with the pointer and wait for the text to be highlighted. Then you can click on the text to get the cursor. To delete a Bookmark, select it and hit the Delete key, or choose Clear from the Edit menu.

Before you continue creating Bookmarks, select your first Bookmark by clicking on the little page icon to its left, the choose Properties under the Edit menu (you can also hit Ctrl/Command-I on your keyboard) (Figure 8.4). There, you can set the default magnification for all subsequent Bookmarks. In the Bookmark Properties box, make sure the Action Type is Go to View, then click on the Edit Destination button. Under the Magnification pull-down menu, select the zoom type that you chose for your first Bookmark. If it was a specific zoom percentage, select Inherit Zoom, and all other Bookmarks will inherit the zoom level. To continue creating Bookmarks, page through your document and hit Ctrl/Command-B for each important page. You can paste titles and headers from the document into the Bookmark zone with the standard Copy and Paste commands located under the Edit menu.

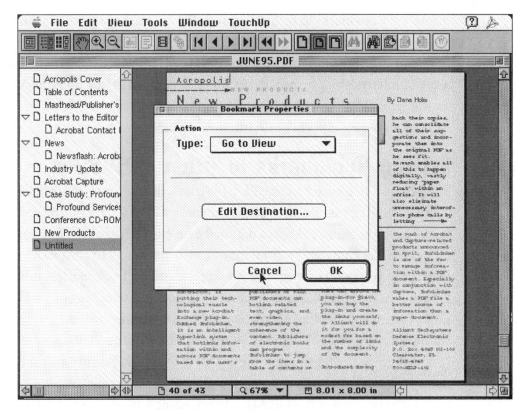

FIGURE 8.4 The Bookmark Properties box.

Once you've created all your Bookmarks, you can move them around by selecting the page icons next to each one and moving them up and down the column. To select a number of Bookmarks, select one by clicking on it, then hold down the Shift key and press the down arrow key for as many Bookmarks as you want (they must be in order). Moving Bookmarks changes the place of the Bookmark, but does not move the actual pages within the document. Moved Bookmarks will still link to the correct destinations. You can also "nest" Bookmarks to create a hierarchy like an outline. To indent one Bookmark under another one, select the Bookmark and move it to the right. A black bar will appear showing you where the Bookmark will drop. You can do this for several levels. Once a Bookmark has other Bookmarks nested under it, it will have a triangle next to it. Clicking on the triangle will cause the nested Bookmarks to be hidden, and clicking on it again will unfurl them. Beware that once you nest Bookmarks, anything you do to change the destination or magnification of the topmost Bookmark will also be done to those nested underneath it. If you are planning to do a variety of Bookmark destination types, like launching other files and Web sites, save the nesting for last so you can separately set the destination for each Bookmark.

Setting Bookmarks to Other PDF Files

You can set a Bookmark in one PDF file that will link off to another PDF file. This is a good option in cases where the master PDF is only one piece, like an index, in a number of PDF files that make up one "document." To create such a Bookmark, simply add a Bookmark to the master PDF (it doesn't matter what page you're on). Select the Bookmark and go to Properties under the Edit menu. In the Bookmark Properties dialog box select Go to View in the pull-down menu next to Action Type. Then, with the Edit Destination box still open, go to the File menu in Acrobat and Open the PDF document that you wish to be the destination file for the Bookmark. Be sure that the destination file is named according to the DOS eight-letter file-naming convention, with the extension .PDF. Also, do not name a file that is not on the same hard drive as the master PDF—if your destination document is on another medium, copy it over to the same directory or folder as the master. When you open the destination file, the name of the file will appear in the Edit Destinations box. Go to the page of the destination file to which you want the Bookmark to go and set the desired magnification in the Edit Destinations box. Click Set Action. Acrobat will take you back to the master PDF so you can test out the Bookmark. If you want to change the destination again, just follow the same steps.

Setting Bookmarks to Other Application Files

You can set a Bookmark to launch a file in another application. Using this tool, you can make a virtually seamless compilation of different kinds of electronic documents—spreadsheets, presentations, multimedia files—with a PDF "front-end." We do not recommend this operation for the Web, however, since each of the other file types would require its own viewer. It is a good method for CD-ROMs and other local media. To set this kind of Bookmark, make a new Bookmark like you normally would, select it, and go to Properties under the Edit menu. In the Bookmark Properties box, change the Action Type to Open File. Then click on the Select File button and Select the destination file you want in the Open dialog box. Then click Set Action in the Bookmark Properties box. When you test the link, Acrobat may not switch to the other application if it is already up; you will find it has opened the document when you go to the other application.

Setting Bookmarks to WWW Files

With the Weblink plug-in, standard in Acrobat 2.1 and later, you have the option to set a Bookmark to launch a URL on the Web. For you, as a Web publisher, this is a more appropriate tool than the Open File option. Using Weblinked Bookmarks, you can mirror the Weblinks within your document or create a compendium of Weblinked PDFs and HTML pages that are individually updated. The procedure is the same as setting Bookmarks to launch other files—make the Bookmark, select it, then go to Properties under the Edit menu. In the Action Type menu, you will find the option World Wide Web link. Select it, and then click the Edit URL button. Enter the destination URL, making sure you are entering the full and correct file name, with the "http://www" prefix. If the URL points to a coordinate on an image map, click the Mapped Coordinates Link box. Then click OK, and Set Action in the Properties box. When you test the Bookmark it should attempt to launch your Web browser and your connectivity software. Make sure that you have specified a browser for your Weblink plug-in (you can set the browser type in Weblink Preferences, under the Edit menu), and that your data line is connected. Once you have successfully set Weblinked Bookmarks, make sure you update their URLs in the event that the names of sites and documents change. To learn how to set Preferences and Base URLs for your Weblink plug-in, refer to the section on hyperlink Weblinks later in this chapter.

Setting Bookmarks to Do Nothing

There are some instances where you may want to write text in the Bookmark column but do not want it to link anywhere. For example, you may want to write "Table of Contents" at the top so that users know what it is. To do this, make the Bookmark, select it, and then go to Properties under the Edit menu. In the Action Type menu select None, and then click Set Action. You now have your ineffectual Bookmark.

Using Hyperlinks

Hyperlinks behave like Bookmarks in that they can be made to launch other pages, files, and Web pages by clicking on them. But hyperlinks reside inside the PDF document and can look any way you like. Acrobat Exchange will let you draw links, visible or invisible, around any words, pictures, or regions of the document you like. They are infinitely more flexible than the links possible with HTML and much easier to create. Setting links in Exchange, like setting Bookmarks, is entirely a visual operation (except for entering in URL addresses). And they are easily tested, so you don't have to worry about your PDF document's links like you would the links in an HTML file.

Drawing Links

Go to the page where you want to make a word or picture a link. Go up to the toolbar, and select the Link tool (represented by two chain links, to the right of the Note tool). Now you are in link mode, and your mouse pointer has turned into a cross-hair. Go to the item to be linked and draw a square or rectangle around it. When you release your mouse button, the Create Link dialog box will appear (Figure 8.5). There you have the option to make the link visible or invisible, as well as choices for the appearance of a visible link. If your design

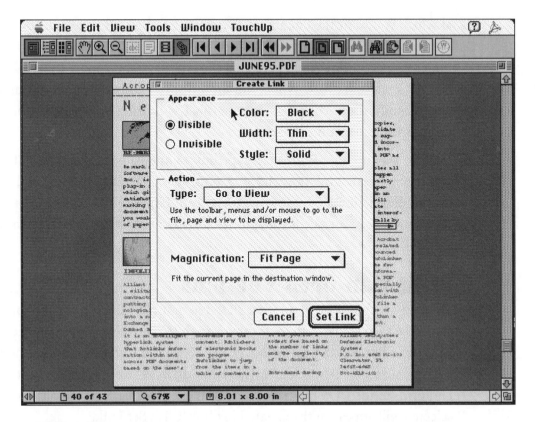

FIGURE 8.5 Creating links.

includes link attributes already, such as a box around the word or a button-like appearance, you probably want to leave the link invisible. But make sure that the item is obviously a link in your design, or else all users will have to go on is the little hand icon, which points its finger when it is moved over a link. If you want to make the link visible with Exchange's features, click visible and choose a color, line width, and style (solid or dashed) for the link box.

Setting a Go to View Link

Now you can set the type of link you want. If the destination for the link is a page in the same PDF document, select Go to View from the Action Type pull-down menu. Then, *with the Create Link box still open,* go to the destination page of the document. Once you are there, determine the magnification at which you want the document to open—Fit View, Fit Page, Fit Width, Fit Height, Fit Visible, or Inherit Zoom. Choose one of the standard magnifications, or set a specific zoom percentage for the page and choose Inherit Zoom in the Create Link box. When you are finished modifying link appearance and magnification, click Set Link. Acrobat will bring you back to the link page so you can test it out.

You can also use the Go to View type link to open a page in a different PDF file. In the Create Link box, choose Go to View as the action type, and open up the destination PDF file with the Create Link box still open. Go to the destination page, and set the magnification in the Create Link box. Then click Set Link.

Setting an Open File Link

To open the first page of another PDF file or a file from a different application, select Open File as the action type in the Create Link box. Then click the Select File button, and the Select File to Open box appears. Choose the file, making sure that it resides on the same drive as the master PDF file and conforms to the DOS file-naming convention. The name of the file you have selected will appear in the Create Link box. Click Set Link.

Setting a Weblink

Weblinks are vital for the PDF files you intend to put on your Web site. As with Bookmarks, you will want to use Weblinks to open other files instead of the Open File link option for Web-based PDFs. Using Weblinks, you can make your PDF document interact with other PDF documents on your server and with remote HTML files. As a rule, you should always use Weblinks when you mention Web sites and URLs in your document and to link back to your site's home page and Help files. If you are publishing a magazine or journal, you can take advantage of Weblinks to point to sponsors' sites.

To set a Weblink, draw a link as you normally would, with the Link tool. When the Create Link box pops up, choose the appearance of the link, and then choose World Wide Web link for the Action Type. Click on the Edit URL button to enter the WWW address, starting with http://www and the rest (Figure 8.6). If you have entered in a Weblink somewhere else in the document, that URL will appear in a pull-down menu under the URL field. If you want this link to go to the same place, just select it from the menu. If the URL you are entering refers to a point on an image map, click in the Mapped Coordinates Link box. Then click OK, and Set Link in the Create Link box. Now, when you move the hand icon over the Weblink, a *W* should appear inside the hand. When you click on it, Acrobat should attempt to launch your Internet connectivity software and your Web browser. If it doesn't work, make sure your data line is connected and you have selected a browser for your Weblink plug-in (you can do this in the Weblink Preferences box,

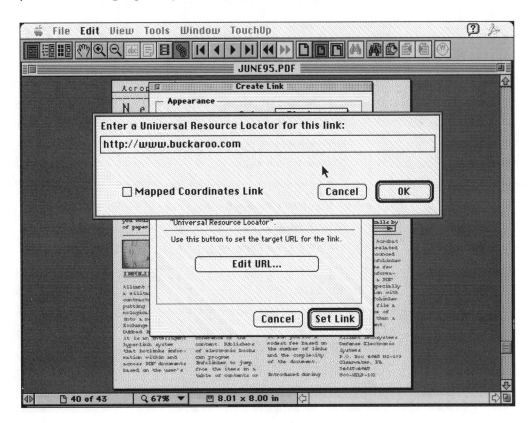

FIGURE 8.6 Entering a URL for a Weblink.

discussed below). Make sure you keep track of the Weblinks in your document and keep their URLs up-to-date. You can change the destination URL for a Weblink by following the link editing procedure described later.

You can set Preferences for your Weblink plug-in to control the display of the Weblink icon in the toolbar, to display the destination of a URL in the document status bar, and to set the Web browser to be launched by Acrobat when you click a Weblink on your system. These preference settings will apply only to your version of Exchange, and will not be passed down to the user of your document. But they may help you with testing your Weblinks. In the Edit menu, select Preferences, Weblink (Figure 8.7). In the Link Information pull-down menu, select Always Show if you want the destination URL for a Weblink to display in the status bar (when the pointer passes over the

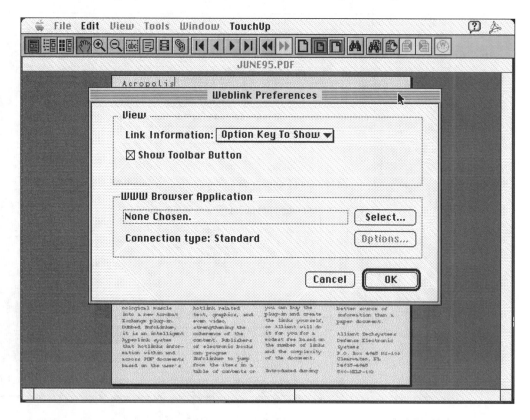

FIGURE 8.7 Editing Weblink Preferences.

Weblink). Choose Control Key to Show if you want to see the destination URL only when you hold down the Control Key, and Never Show if you never want to see the destination URL. Click in the Show Toolbar Button box if you want the Weblink icon to appear in your Exchange toolbar. Click in the Show Progress Dialog if you want to see the rate of a document being downloaded after you have clicked a Weblink. Underneath WWW Browser Application, Click Browse (or Select on Macintosh) to locate the Web browser on your system. Select the Weblink-capable browser on your system (Netscape Navigator, Spyglass Mosaic, or Quarterdeck Mosaic), and click OK. If you do not have one of these browsers resident on your system, you can download any of them for free from their respective Web sites: http://www.netscape.com, http://www.spyglass.com, and http://www.quarterdeck.com.

If your document contains many Weblinks to documents located on your server, you can sidestep the tedious process of typing in complete URL addresses for those documents by setting a Base URL for the files. For instructions on how to set a Base URL, see the section on Setting Document Info later in this chapter.

Editing Your Links

You can edit your link by clicking on the Link icon again, and clicking on the link box that comes into view (in Link mode, all links are temporarily visible). When you click on it once, the link box becomes selected and you can move it or resize it. When you double-click on the link box, the Link Properties box pops up. In it you can change the settings you originally made, including the link type and destination. When you are done making changes, click OK and the new link setting will be in effect.

Using Article Threads

Article threads are Acrobat's tool for guiding readers through multicolumn documents that may not readily be legible onscreen. Also called "text flows," they are an important feature that resolves the problem of magnification and screen size when navigating through a document. You can tell when you are navigating through a PDF document that is threaded, because there is an arrow inside the hand icon. If you click on an area of text that is threaded, that area will automatically magnify to the Maximum Fit Visible Magnification (set in the General Preferences dialog box—the default is 200%). When you are finished reading that section, instead of scrolling down just click again with the hand at the bottom of the text you have just read. The next portion of text will pop up, even if it is on the next page. You can use article threads to guide readers through any kind of text-heavy document, although the text should be organized in columns of some sort. The article thread feature is designed to accommodate multiple "articles" per document. Your text does not have to be organized as articles per se, but if your content can be divided into subsections, you should create article threads separately for each section.

Creating Article Threads

To create a series of article threads, go to the page in the document you want them to start on. Choose Article under the Tools menu (the Article tool does not have an icon in the toolbar). Your mouse pointer will turn into a crosshair. Starting at the top-left corner of the first text column, press your mouse button and draw out a box around the column (Figure 8.8). When you release the mouse button, the article box will appear with the number 1-1 at the top, meaning "Article 1, Box 1." Your pointer turns into the article icon, so you can go ahead and create the second article box with the next column, which will be 1-2. Continue to draw article boxes until you come to the end of the article or section. When you are finished, click on the words "End Article" on the status bar at the bottom of the screen or press Return on your keyboard. The Article Properties box will pop up. Enter the Title, Subject, and Author of the article or section (this will be helpful in keeping track of the articles in the document). Enter a few keywords that appear in the text, to aid

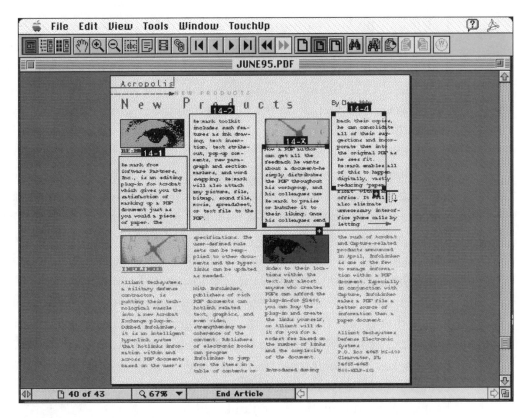

FIGURE 8.8 Drawing an article thread.

searching for the article. Click OK. You are still in Article mode, so you can start the next article thread set, beginning with Article 2-1. Or you can click on the hand icon to go back to normal browsing mode. When you pass the hand over the article you created, an arrow should appear inside the hand. Click your way through the article to test it.

Deleting, Adding, Resizing, and Moving Article Boxes

If you want to delete the article or certain boxes in the article, go back to Article under Tools, click once inside the box to be deleted, and press

Delete on your keyboard (or Clear under the Edit menu). Acrobat will ask you if you want to delete just that box, or all the boxes in the Article. To add an article box to an article you've already created, select the Article tool and click in the article box after which you want to add a box. When the box is selected, click on the plus sign in the bottom-right corner of the box with the article icon. The next article box you draw will be inserted in the right order into the article, and boxes following it will be automatically renumbered. To resize an article box, wait until you have finished creating all the boxes in the article and click End Article. Click once in the article box you want to resize, and click and drag in or out the corners of the box. To move an entire article box, select it and drag it to the new location holding down the mouse button, and release it once it is positioned. The article box will move, but not the text inside it. To combine articles, select Article from the Tools menu and click once inside one of the boxes in the article that comes first. Click the plus sign in the bottom-right corner of the box. Then hold down the Control key if you are in Windows, or the Option key in Macintosh, and click any article box in the article that comes after. The two articles will be combined in the right order, and the boxes will be automatically renumbered.

Viewing and Editing Article Properties

To view a list of the articles in your document, go to Articles under the View menu. The Articles box will appear, naming all the article titles that you have entered in the Article Properties box (Figure 8.9). If you did not enter a title, articles will be named "Untitled Article 1," and so on. To view the article in its place in the document, click View. To edit Article Properties, click Info and enter new information to the Article Properties box, and click OK. The new information will be saved the next time you save the file.

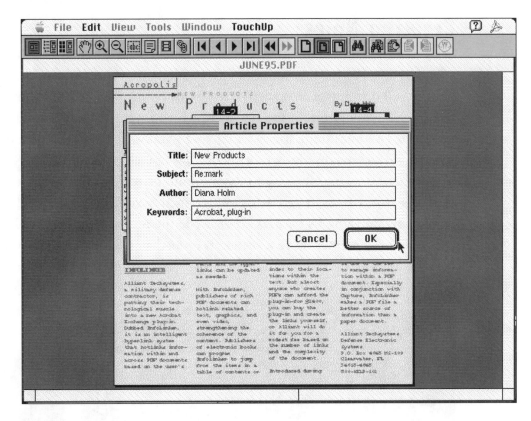

FIGURE 8.9 Editing Article Properties.

Annotating Your Document with "Sticky Notes"

Not to be confused with Lotus Notes, Acrobat Notes are the Post-It notes of PDF's digital paper. They can be used to add last-minute corrections to the content of a document, to explain to users how to use the document, and for review of a document within your workgroup. Notes look like little page icons, and open up to a text window when you double-click on them. Notes can be personalized by several different authors, by changing the name that appears in the top bar of the Notes window. You can make as many Notes as you want on a page, for the whole document. Notes can be imported from other PDF files and exported to be PDF files of their own.

Creating Notes

Select the Note tool in the Acrobat toolbar (small page icon between the text selection tool and the link tool), or choose Note from the Tools menu. Your pointer will turn into a cross-hair. Draw a box on the page where you would like the Note to appear, in the size to which you want the Note window to open up. The minimum size for the Note window is two inches by three inches, and the maximum is four inches by six inches (Figure 8.10). Don't worry about drawing a box up to the minimum size; just clicking once with the cross-hair will result in a two-by-three-inch box. You can resize the Note window by dragging its corners. Then write the text of the Note inside the window. You can enter more text than is immediately visible in the window, because there is a scroll bar. You can also paste text into the Note window.

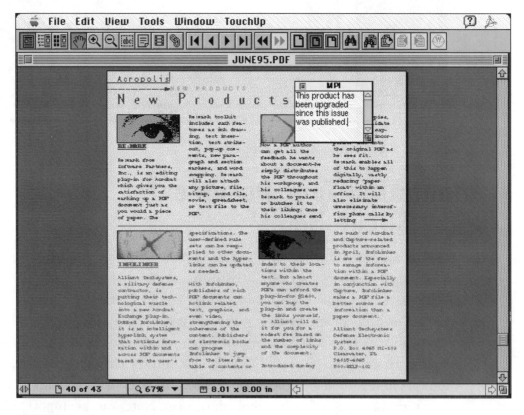

FIGURE 8.10 Creating a Note.

The font and point size will be fixed for the Note window, however. In general, Note text should be brief. When you are finished, close the Note window to view the Note icon on the page. To move the icon on the page, just drag it to a new position. To delete a Note, click once on its icon and hit the Delete key, or choose Clear from the Edit menu. To view a summary of all the Note text in your document, select Summarize Notes from the Tools menu. A new document called "Notes from [*PDF file name*]" will open up with a summary of Notes in the order in which they appear in the document. You can Save As this summary if you like. Back in the document, you can search on Notes by choosing Find Next Note under the Tools menu.

Editing Note Properties

To change the name label on the Note window, or the color of the Note icon, click once inside the Note window and go to Properties under the Edit menu. The Note Properties box will appear. You can enter a new name for the Note label, and change the color of the Note icon by selecting one from the pull-down menu. A date/time stamp is provided so the user can know when the Note was added. Click OK when you are done. The Note you selected will show its changed properties. If you want to change the default properties for all Notes, go to Preferences, Notes under the Edit menu. The Note Preferences box will appear, in which you can change the default name label, color, font, and point size for all Note windows. If you change the font and point size, all existing Notes will be affected with the new font and point size. The name labels and colors of existing Notes will remain the same, however. Click OK when you are finished.

Importing and Exporting Notes between PDF Documents

If there are a number of copies of one PDF document floating around, such as in a group review situation, you may want to copy Notes to all of the versions of the document. To import Notes into a PDF document, open the receiving document and choose Notes, Import from the Edit menu.

The Open dialog box will pop up. Select the PDF file that contains the Notes you want to import. Click Select, and the Notes will be copied into their exact places in the receiving file. Notes that were already in the receiving file will not be affected. To export Notes out of a PDF document, choose Notes, Export from the Edit menu. The Export Notes As dialog box appears. Enter a file name for the destination file, and click OK. The resulting file is a blank PDF that contains the Notes, placed on the same positions on the page of the original document.

Adding Links to Acrobat Movies

Acrobat Exchange 2.1 and later features the Movie Tool, Acrobat's plug-in for linking to Apple Quicktime or Windows AVI format movie files. To prepare the movie files, you must use a separate application to create the movie file, such as Adobe Premiere or any digital video software that can save movie files as Quicktime or AVI. Quicktime movies in PDFs can be played back on both Windows and Macs if they are saved in the "flattened" cross-platform format in your movie-creating application. AVI movie files can be played back only on Windows machines. You can also add sound files to PDFs with the Movie Tool—Macintosh System 7, AIFF, Sound Mover (FSSD) files, and Windows AIF and WAV files. Your users must have movie and sound playback capabilities on their systems to be able to view your Movie Files. Using Adding Acrobat movie files is a great way to add a multimedia element to your PDF files, but they are not a viable option for your PDF Web documents. The Movie Tool is capable only of linking off to separate movie files, not of embedding the movies within the actual PDF. The linked movie file must be separate from but residing on the same disk as the PDF file. You could instruct users to download both a PDF file and the movie file, and place them in the same folder or directory, but few may have the patience. You are better off reserving your Acrobat movies for PDF files that you publish on CD-ROM or on another local medium.

We will digress from Web publishing for a moment to explain how you can use the Movie Tool to link your PDFs to movie files and sound files for local media. First, load the movie file on the same disk where your Acrobat Exchange resides. Then, in the PDF document, select the Movie Tool icon in the toolbar, represented by a film symbol (to the left of the link tool). Your pointer will turn into a cross-hair for drawing the box for the movie play area. Or just click once with the cross-hair, and the movie will play at its original size. When you release the mouse, the Open dialog box will appear, looking for a file name with the extension .MOV for a Quicktime movie file. Select the movie or sound file you want to link to, and click Yes to convert the file if it is not in a cross-platform format. Click OK in the Open box.

The Movie Properties box appears. Enter a name for the movie or sound clip in the Title field if you want the clip to be named something different from the file name. In the Player Options box, click Show Controller if you want the user to have controls to pause or stop a movie playback. If you opt not to give users a controller, you have a few options to set the playback in the Mode menu—Play Once Then Stop, Play Once Stay Open, Repeat Play, and Back and Forth. Below, you have the option to play back the movie in a Floating Window above the PDF document. If you check this option, you have a number of window dimensions to choose from from a pull-down menu. If you do not choose Floating Window, the movie will play as an inline clip within the PDF page. In the Movie Poster area of the Movie Properties box, you can choose whether to display the first frame of the movie as a poster (or preview still), and how many colors to include in the poster. Your other options are Don't Show Poster or Retrieve Poster from Movie. Finally, you can set the width, style, and color of the border that surrounds the playback window. When you are finished, click Save Preferences if these will be the settings for all your movie links, and click OK. The movie link will be inserted into the PDF file. To edit Movie Properties, click on the Movie icon again and select Properties from the Edit menu. To change the placement of the movie clip in the PDF, select the Movie tool, click on the clip to select it, and drag it to the desired location. To move it only slightly, hold down the Option key in Macintosh, or the Control key in Windows while you drag it to slow down the drag.

For more on using the Acrobat Movie Tool, refer to the Acrobat Exchange Online help guide. If you are planning on creating a PDF CD-ROM with Movies, be sure to see Chapter 13, "PDF on CD-ROM," for special CD-ROM production tips.

Setting Document Info

Filling in the Document Info fields in Exchange is important for professional-quality PDF documents. Using Document Info fields, you can give credit to the authors of the document, insert keywords to streamline searching for the document, control how the PDF document opens up on the user's screen, set a Base URL for the Weblinks in the document, and view the Security settings for the document. When Document Info fields are thoroughly filled in, they can provide a wealth of information about the document for users' reference and your own.

General Document Info

In the General Document Info field, you can fill in the Title, Subject, Author, Creator, and Producer of the document, as well as give keywords that are found in the document (Figure 8.11). To edit this field, go to Document Info, General under the File menu, or hit Ctrl/Command-D on your keyboard. By default the file name of the document is entered as the Title, and the licensee of that particular copy of Acrobat Exchange is entered as the Author. You can change either of these fields. Enter the Subject of the document and type in a few keywords that express the subject and are found within the text of the document. This information will help users searching on Document Info fields locate your document. The Creator of the document is the authoring application with which the document was originally created, and will have been automatically added to the Doc Info field in the conversion process.

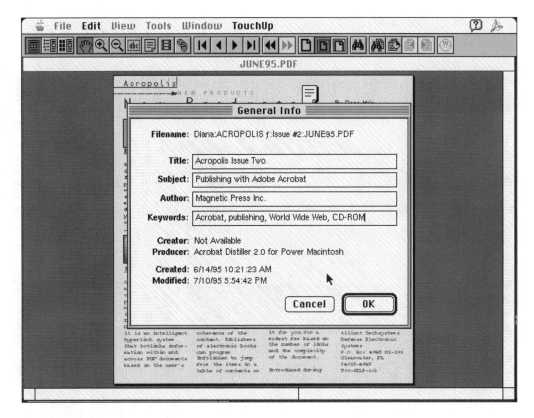

FIGURE 8.11 Editing the General Document Info field.

The Producer of the document signifies which Acrobat tool was used to do the conversion to PDF. The Document Info also gives the date and time when the PDF was produced, and the date and time of the file's most recent modification. The accuracy of these times depends on the clock within the system that generated the PDF. When you are finished editing the General Doc Info field, click OK. That information will be saved with the document and visible to users of the document using Exchange or the Reader.

Fonts Info

The Fonts field, accessible under Document Info, Fonts, under the File menu, tells you which fonts were used in the original application, and which fonts were used in the PDF document (Figure 8.12). It is valuable for both authors

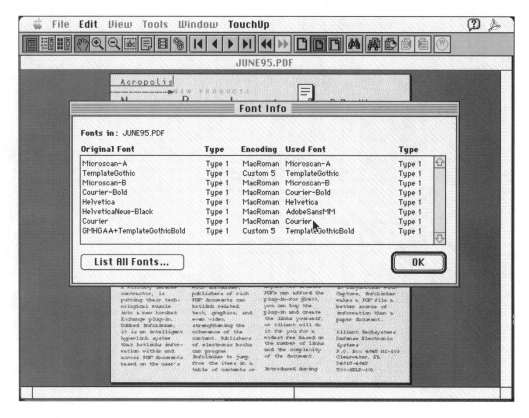

FIGURE 8.12 Viewing Fonts Info.

and users of a PDF document to find out if Acrobat has substituted a font in the document. This field is not editable and is visible to users of the document.

Open Info

Using the Open Info field, you can determine the way your PDF document will open and display on the user's screen (the user does not have access to these settings) (Figure 8.13). Go to Document Info, Open under the File menu. You have four options for the page display—Page Only (no Bookmarks or Thumbnails), Bookmarks and Page, Thumbnails and Page, and Full Screen. Full Screen mode means that no Acrobat toolbar or menus are displayed with the document; the document fills the entire screen in presentation mode. To navigate the document this way, users must use the arrow

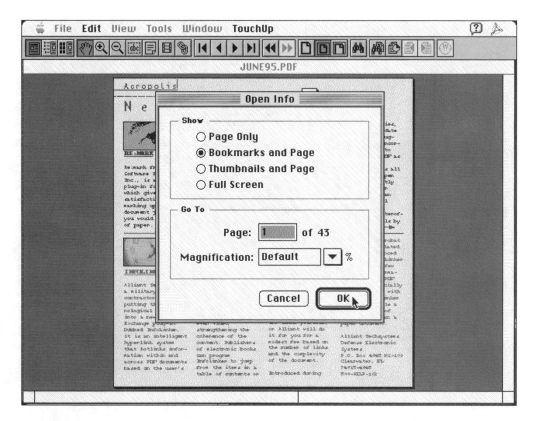

FIGURE 8.13 Entering Open Info.

keys on their keyboard, or press Escape to show the Acrobat window (the mouse pointer is still available for clicking on links and notes). Full Screen is an impressive and dramatic way to set a document to open, but you should let users know how they can navigate and exit Full Screen mode. Perhaps you could do this with a "sticky note" on the first page. In the Open Info field, you can also set the page number on which the document should open and at which level of magnification.

Security Info

Rather than being set in the Document Info fields, Security Information is displayed here for users of the document (Figure 8.14). The author of the document has the option to set Security for the document in the Save As dialog

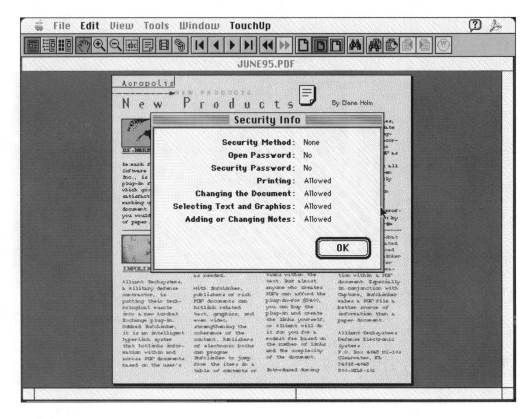

FIGURE 8.14 Viewing Security Info.

box (to be discussed in the next section). To view the Security settings for a given PDF document, go to Document Info, Security under the File menu. The Document Security box will tell you if a Security Method has been applied to the document, if a password is required, if printing is allowed, and if certain editing features are enabled—Changing the document, Selecting Text and Graphics, and Adding or Changing Notes. By default, no security method is applied and no passwords are required; printing and all editing is allowed.

Base URL

This is a handy tool for the author of a PDF to use in conjunction with the Weblink plug-in. It is not accessible to users of the document. Setting a Base

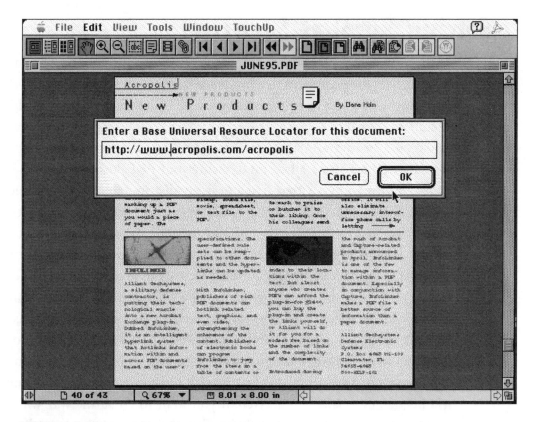

FIGURE 8.15 Entering the Base URL.

URL means that you can sidestep the first part of the URL addresses for Weblinks that are all located in the same directory on your server, by entering in the information that is common to every URL (Figure 8.15). For example, if every PDF document on your server can be found in the directory http://www.mysite.com/docs/, you could set that as the Base URL and then just fill in document names for your Weblinks, such as "report.pdf" and "map.pdf." When the user clicks on the Weblink, Acrobat will refer back to the Base URL, piece the parts of the URL together, and call up the document. If you want to use a Base URL for documents on your server, but also link off to remote Web sites, simply type in the complete URL for the remote sites.

Setting Acrobat Security

As the author of a PDF document, you have the option to set a certain level of security in the document that limits the user's ability to tamper with it and distribute it. The security you set for your PDF files will come down with the document over the Web. But before you start setting security with Acrobat, you should be aware of the limitations of Acrobat's security method, and consider whether you really want to secure your PDF documents on the Web (where information is either free and freely distributable, or of commercial value and sold online using a sophisticated encryption system). The level of security offered by Acrobat can prevent individuals without the right password from opening the PDF file, and it can disallow printing and editing of text, graphics, and sticky notes. Acrobat security may curtail the user's distribution of the document, but remember that if an authorized user wants to pass along a document, she or he can very easily pass on the password as well. There is no special link between the authorized user and the specific copy of the document. And while you may want to protect your document from editing, Acrobat security cannot guarantee that the copyright of your document will be safe, especially on the Web. If you want to go all the way with PDF document security, to the point of selling the document online, there are third-party PDF encryption programs that offer a more sophisticated security level. For more information on these, see Chapter 12, "Securing Commercial PDF Files from Unauthorized Access." If you are not planning on selling your PDFs on the Web, you may want to sidestep the security process altogether. You do not want to alienate enthusiastic readers of your content by not letting them print out or reference your PDF documents any way they like.

If a PDF document that will go up on your Web site is making the rounds within your workgroup for review, or you are circulating a confidential internal document inside your organization, you may want to set standard Acrobat security. Setting security should be the very last stage in working with your

PDF document in Exchange. Once you have enhanced your PDF to its maximum potential, choose Save As from the File menu and click the Security button. If you want to set a password, without which users cannot open the document, go to the field next to the words Open the Document in the Security box (Figure 8.16). Enter a combination of letters, numbers, and keyboard symbols between six and twenty characters long, which bears no logical relationship to the author, file name, or content of the document. To require a password to change the Security settings for the document, enter in a completely different password where it says Change Security Options. Below, you can choose which functions will not be allowed for the user—Printing, Changing the Document, Selecting Text and Graphics, and Adding or Changing Notes. When you are finished, make careful note of the passwords you

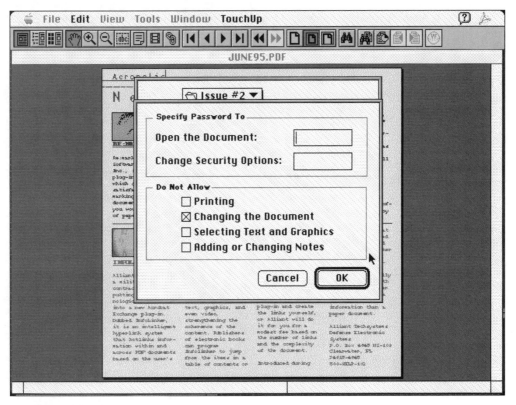

FIGURE 8.16 Setting Security Info.

have chosen, *especially* if you chose one for changing the security settings. Note them outside of the system you are working on. When you click OK, Acrobat will prompt you to confirm the password by retyping it, and then clicking Save. To change a password, go back to the File menu and choose Save As, and click the Security button. In the Security box, type over the bullets with the new password, confirm it, and Save it. To delete a password, delete the password bullets in the Security box and click OK, then click Save in the Save As dialog box. If you delete the owner's Change Security Options password, all security settings for the document will be deleted as well.

Notes

1. *Adobe Acrobat Exchange 2.1 Online Guide* (Mountain View: Adobe Systems Inc., 1995).

Chapter 9

Special-Purpose PDF Production Tools

Since the release of Acrobat 2.0 in 1994, Adobe has been working hard to intro-

duce PDF compatibility and output devices in its own desktop publishing

programs, to make the transition to PDF publishing easier for their current

customers, and also to add value to upgrades of the products. Until Acrobat, all

of Adobe's products were geared toward prepress design, and not toward Inter-

net publishing. Now Adobe has introduced compelling features into their

applications that make them high-quality creation programs for both print

and digital media. In this chapter, we will discuss ways you can streamline your

PDF production by taking advantage of features in Adobe Illustrator 6.0,

Adobe PageMaker 6.0, and Adobe FrameMaker (the acquired version of Frame's FrameMaker 5.0). We will also tell you how you can use the Adobe Touch-Up plug-in to correct mistakes in the content of your PDFs, and how you can open up a PDF in Adobe Illustrator and make changes to text and graphics.

Adobe isn't the only one that has been scurrying to integrate their applications with Acrobat. Corel Ventura 5.0 also offers integrated support for Acrobat features, as well as Cascade's set of QuarkXtensions for PDF output. Other third-party Acrobat developers have created PDF production tools that automate conversion, markup tasks, editing and management of .PS and PDF files. We will describe these tools and tell you how to get them. Finally, we will give an introduction to Adobe's PDFmark operator, a set of PostScript programming commands that you can use to customize your PDFs. Unlike the software tools discussed in this chapter, PDFmark is complicated and difficult to implement, but if you can master it you can count yourself among the noble few.

Desktop Publishing Programs that Feature PDF Integration

Adobe PageMaker 6.0

PageMaker 6.0 is the first major upgrade to the page composition software since Adobe acquired it from Aldus in September 1994. Among the major improvements Adobe introduced is a plug-in called Create Adobe PDF, which lets users Save PageMaker documents directly into PDF. The Acrobat Distiller is installed along with PageMaker 6.0 on the deluxe CD-ROM version, and performs its conversions in the background. Acrobat hyperlinks and Bookmarks are automatically created from properly marked index and table of contents text in the PageMaker document (use the Create Index and Create TOC commands). Multiple PageMaker files can be collated into one

PDF document by selecting Book from the File command and selecting the files to be combined, and then using the Create Adobe PDF command. To use the Create PDF command on documents created with earlier versions of PageMaker, you can open those files up in PageMaker 6.0.

The Create Adobe PDF can be found under the File menu (Figure 9.1). In the Create Adobe PDF dialog box you have the option to Distill Now or generate a PostScript file to distill later. If you choose to Distill Now, you can opt to view the PDF file in Acrobat by checking the box and selecting your version of Acrobat. At the bottom of the box, you can choose to include downloadable fonts and edit Distiller job options. PageMaker can launch the distiller with default job options or you can specify all the options you normally would in the Distiller program. You can set options for hyperlinks, Bookmarks, and

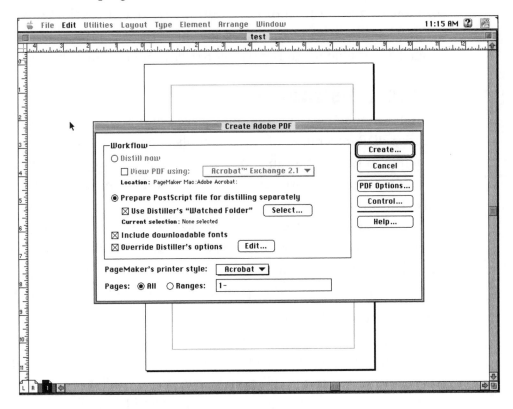

FIGURE 9.1 PageMaker's Create Adobe PDF box.

article threads by clicking on the PDF Options button. Your choices are to link PageMaker TOC and index entries, to create Bookmarks and edit their names, to create article threads and define them, to set the magnification of pages, to generate document info, and to create Notes. When you are finished setting options, click Create and specify a name and destination for the file. The distilling should happen in the background and place the file in the right folder. To generate a .PS file to be distilled later, click "Prepare PostScript File for Distilling Separately." You can place that .PS file in a Distiller watched folder by checking that option and clicking the Select button to specify the folder. If you do not opt to put the .PS folder in a watched folder, you can save it elsewhere and manually distill it later on. Click Create to generate the .PS file.

For more detailed instructions on creating PDF out of PageMaker 6.0, refer to the *User Guide* that accompanied the software.[1] For information on how to purchase or upgrade to PageMaker 6.0, visit Adobe's Web site.

Adobe Illustrator 6.0

Illustrator, Adobe's art creation and image editing program, has the most extensive PDF integration of Adobe's applications. Not only can Illustrator 6.0 output to PDF, but it can also serve as an editing program for PDF files. With a new import/export feature, you can edit single pages of PDF files and reinsert them into the whole file without disturbing links, Bookmarks, or Notes. You can change text characters, alter curves, add color or gradients, and even add new vector-based artwork to PDF files. What's more, Illustrator will automatically launch Adobe Photoshop and the Photoshop toolbar within Illustrator for editing of photographs in PDF files.

Illustrator creates PDF out of EPS files with a simple Save As PDF option (Figure 9.2). The export to PDF function, which is implemented as a Plug-In to Illustrator, is quite new and not yet perfect. In some cases, PDF files exported from Illustrator will contain artifacts or exhibit font problems. If this happens, the best workaround is to open the PDF in Illustrator 6.0 and

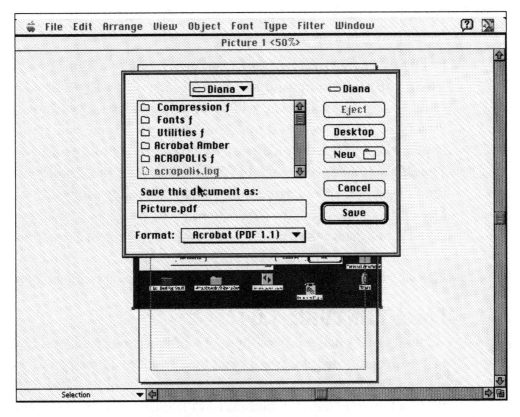

FIGURE 9.2 Illustrator's Save As PDF box.

print it to a PostScript file, then Distill that PostScript file with the Acrobat Distiller. If the PDF in question was one page of many, you can use Acrobat Exchange's Replace Pages feature to reinsert the page into the PDF file.

Adobe FrameMaker 5.0

FrameMaker, the large-scale business document software, has demonstrated high-quality, smooth output to PDF since Adobe acquired it from Frame, Inc. FrameMaker automatically maps paragraph tags to create Acrobat Bookmarks, creates hypertext links, translates FrameMaker "alerts" to Acrobat sticky notes, and generates article threads from FrameMaker "flows."

FrameMaker passes these features down to the Acrobat Distiller by creating "enhanced" PostScript files.

If you have FrameMaker 5.0, you can create PDF out of a Frame document by selecting the Print command and then clicking on Generate Acrobat Data. Click Acrobat Setup, and you will see several options for generating Bookmarks. Select the types of text from which you want to automatically generate Bookmarks, organize their hierarchy with the arrows, and click Set. Then you are ready to print to PostScript. In Windows, turn on Print Only to File in the Print dialog box, enter a name and destination directory, and click Print. On Macintosh, choose File in the Destination area of the Print dialog box and click Save. Do not change the default .PS file name that FrameMaker provides; this will ensure proper linking between files. To generate your Frame-enhanced PDF, simply run the .PS files through the Distiller as you normally would.

Corel VENTURA 5.0

Ventura, Corel's desktop publishing program, features enhanced output to PDF with automated Bookmarks and links from Ventura tables of contents and indexes. Ventura creates PDFmark syntax for links created within the Ventura Publisher file, then outputs this PDFmark in the PostScript stream.

To take advantage of this feature, then, you will have to have both the Acrobat Distiller—as links cannot be automatically made using PDFWriter—and a printer driver capable of creating PostScript files.

Cascade QuarkXtensions

Quark, one of Adobe's major competitors in the applications market, does not provide output to PDF in their popular desktop publishing software, QuarkXPress. But Cascade Systems has developed a series of Plug-ins that transfer Quark features to PDF excellently. Called QuarkXtensions, it is a series of five tools for use within the QuarkXPress program. ThreadMarker XT lets you set up article threads for PDF automatically within Quark. OptionMarker XT replaces Quark's print options with Acrobat Distiller's job options. NoteMarker XT lets you set up annotations in Quark that will auto-matically be translated into Acrobat notes. Bookmarker XT allows you to set up Bookmarks in Quark that will become Acrobat bookmarks in the PDF. Finally, LineMarkerXT allows you to set links in Quark documents that will become links in the PDF file. For more information, call Cascade Systems at (508) 794-8000, or email info@cascadenet.com.

Making Last-Minute Changes to Your PDF

There aren't many ways to get yourself out of the jam when you notice a typo in your otherwise perfect PDF, or wish you could recompress a graphic and replace it the PDF. But these two tools can be real lifesavers if you know how to use them correctly, and if you are tolerant of buggy results.

Editing with Touch-Up

Touch-Up is an Adobe Plug-in for Acrobat Exchange that has not yet been released at the time of this writing, but will probably be a feature in Acrobat Exchange 3.0. It installs as a menu item with options to correct suspect words generated by Acrobat Capture, to alter or relocate text, to white out a graphics selection, and to edit images using Adobe Photoshop (Figure 9.3). The text altering feature is the most radical for Acrobat, since font information is buried pretty deep in the structure of the PDF file. It works, but the spacing of the letters often gets jumbled in the beta version. You can also alter the style of the text, changing font and size, or you can relocate the text to a different part of the document or even on top of a graphic. Whiting out graphics is an intriguing tool for covering up unwanted graphics without actually deleting them from the file. To edit, export, or replace EPS graphics, you can use the Photoshop editing tool. This is a great way to improve the quality of your graphics without having to redistill. We look forward to seeing what the fledg-ling Touch-Up Plug-in will do once it is officially released.

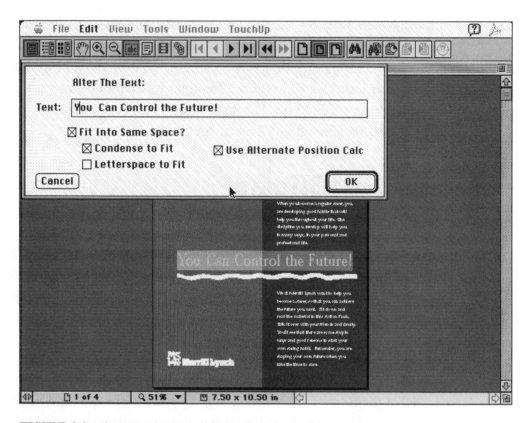

FIGURE 9.3 The Touch-Up Plug-in's Alter Text feature.

Editing with Illustrator

The Touch-Up Plug-in provides a subset of the editing functionality available from Adobe Illustrator 6.0, which is Adobe's premier PostScript editing and drawing tool. The difference is that Touch-Up works directly on PDF files, while Illustrator performs a file conversion first: A PDF file opened in Illustrator 6.0 is converted to the Illustrator .AI format on input and exported back to PDF on output. Because PDF files brought into Illustrator are still effectively Illustrator files, they can be edited in almost any way that Illustrator permits, which includes sizing and scaling, moving elements from front to back or vice versa, adding vector drawings, new typographic effects, shading and radial fills, and using the whole assortment of illustrator special effects.

The only things to watch out for are that text cannot typically be reflowed in Illustrator the way it can in PageMaker. Illustrator tends to treat a line of text as an object, so changing a word at the end of a line can often result in a great deal of hand-manipulation to rekern the type or move a word onto the next line. In many cases, you will find it more efficient to go back to the document's original authoring application, if it is available, and use that to recreate the page than to edit the PDF in Illustrator.

Third-Party PDF Production Tools

The following tools, available from Acrobat software developers, are intended to ease many of the labor-intensive and tedious aspects of large-scale PDF production. Some of them provide the kind of automated bookmarking and linking that the above-mentioned desktop publishing programs offer, but these tools can apply the automation to any kind of source document during or after the distill process. Others aid the production of PDF out of Acrobat Capture, or help you organize PDF documents once they have been made. All of the following products are made by official Adobe developers, from whom you can look for advanced PDF manipulation tools with each Acrobat release.

XMAN xToolsOne

The xTools line of Plug-ins for Acrobat Exchange 2.1 will help you manipulate and add features to your PDF files once they have been created. There are ten of them:

1. *xMarker,* a customizable electronic pen that lets you mark up PDF documents.

2. *xPrint Selection* lets you select an area of a PDF page and print out just that section.

3. *xSelect* solves one of the problems of the Acrobat text selection tool, which is that it selects across columns horizontally. xSelect

lets you draw a rectangle around a portion of a page and select it for copying to the clipboard.

4. *xAnnotations Window* builds upon the Acrobat Notes report, telling you the title, location, modification date of Acrobat Notes and xMarker notations. This window also summarizes the locations and destinations of all the links in a document.

5. *xShowLinks* enhances the Acrobat link display mode by allowing you to view links while you work with other tools.

6. *xDogEar* is an electronic "dog ear" tool for bookmarking pages of a PDF. The page corner actually looks folded down, and its location is added to the xAnnotations window.

7. *xFootnote* lets you create footnotes for PDF documents by turning selected text into footnotes, and cutting it to the clipboard for use in other applications.

8. *xDateIt* tracks the modification dates of all the links, marks, and Notes in a PDF document.

9. *xMakeLinks* processes selected text, tables of contents, indexes, and number tables and turns them into hyperlinks per your specifications, drastically reducing link production time.

10. *xMakeBookmarks* takes selected text and automatically generates Bookmarks for the items in the text. You set destinations in an options box.

For more information, visit XMAN at http://www.xman.com, or call (415) 986-1773.

Handmade Image Alchemy

Handmade makes magic with Image Alchemy, which will take an image in any—we mean *any*—format (70 varieties are currently supported), and convert it to PDF. In fact, Handmade guarantees that all 70 of those formats, of which PDF is one, can be converted to each other, or they will do the conversion for you free. Image Alchemy generates high-quality images from its conversions by using color management tools like under-cover removal, gamma correction, and spiffing. It will match your image to your existing palette, or create one for you along the Heckbert Quantization or Uniform Palette algorithms. Image Alchemy can apply JPEG, CCITT Group 3 or Group 4, Run-Length Encoded, or LZW compression to converted images. You can resize the images as much as you like, due to Image Alchemy's unlimited scaling algorithms. You can increase the screen loading speed of your images by using any one of Image Alchemy's trade-off controls—Nearest Neighbor, Pixel Averaging, Linear Interpolation, and Lanczos 2 or 3. Furthermore, you can employ a wide range of dithering techniques to optimize them for printing.

If you want to make a PDF out of an image in a unique format, or want to convert images into formats that your desktop publishing application can work with, Image Alchemy is a headache- and time-saving tool. For information on how to get it, call (800) 358-3588, or email sales@hand-madesw.com.

Software Partners' Re:mark and Compose

Re:mark was the first markup plug-in for Acrobat. It gives you the satisfaction of marking up a PDF document just as you would a piece of paper. The Re:mark toolkit includes such features as ink drawing, text insertion, text strikeout, pop-up comments, new paragraph and section markers, and word swapping. Re:mark will also attach any picture, file, bitmap, sound file, movie, spreadsheet, or text file to the PDF. Now you can get all the feedback you want about your PDF document—simply distribute the PDF throughout your workgroup, and your colleagues will use Re:mark to praise or butcher it to their liking. Once your colleagues send back their copies, you can consolidate all of their suggestions and incorporate them into the original PDF. Using Re:mark, you can send PDF documents for your Web site around for review, ensuring that your Web documents reflect the collective wishes of your organization. Re:mark has a suggested retail price of $129.95.

Compose is a production toolkit for the power PDF publisher that automates several of the most odious production and markup tasks. The first item in the toolkit is Bookmarks By Example, which scans a PDF document for headings (in a certain font and style that the user has told it to look out for) and creates hierarchically organized bookmarks from them. Second, Compose lets you duplicate frequently used hyperlinks such as Next Page and Main Menu throughout a long document with the Copy Link tool. Third, the toolkit includes a Document Composer, which compiles several individual PDF documents into a single document, and accordingly repaginates it. If the source file for one of the documents shows a page number that has changed, Document Composer will actually white out that number and replace it with the correct one. Finally, Compose features the PDF Navigator, an alternate interface for launching PDF files by selecting them by title and author, instead of by their eight-letter DOS file name. This tool is particularly valuable for CD-ROMs in PDF, which may contain hundreds of those inscrutable file names. On the Web, your users won't be able to view your PDF file names this way, but PDF Navigator may be a helpful internal archiving tool. The Compose suite of tools runs on both Windows and Macintosh, and sells for $795. The PDF Navigator tool can be purchased separately for distributing on CD-ROMs with Acrobat Reader and Exchange.

For more information on these and other PDF Plug-ins in development, contact Software Partners at (415) 428-0160, or visit their Web site at http://www.buckaroo.com.

Vertec Solutions' Verzions and Tranzform

Verzions is a workflow software program which integrates Acrobat Capture with Acrobat Distiller in a batch-oriented production-level environment. The Verzions workflow guides you through the page-scanning process, breaking down documents and checking ACD files for errors with their own *Reviewz* screen. Verzions adds value to Capture by automatically converting Capture files (ACDs) into PDF, and tracking the documents for easy searching and retrieval. The tracking function features job tickets, a queue manager, and page numbering that is consistent with the hard copy. Verzions also automates indexing, linking, and archiving of PDF documents created with Capture. Verzions makes large-volume PDF conversions of legacy and word-processed documents a no-hands operation, making the journey from paper to the Web much quicker and less painful.

Tranzform is a tool for creating PDF forms that can be distributed to be filled out by other Acrobat users. Tranzform is not yet a Web application, but a Web version for Windows NT servers running the Netscape server is under way. When Vertec does release this version of Tranzform (probably 2.0), it will make dynamic PDF CGI forms possible. Imagine actually filling out the PDF tax forms that the IRS currently publishes on their Web site for people to print out! PDF forms capable of communicating with Web servers would be a vast improvement on HTML forms, allowing for a custom appearance and greater security options.

Here's how Tranzform currently works for local networks. The application has two modes, Definer and Fill-Out. Fields can be created and characterized in Definer, and many standard fields such as CheckBox and Currency are already included as options. In Fill-Out, users can work from templates and tab through the fields as they fill in the information. The standardization of the field names, as defined in a global file, is an important feature of Tranzform for users who want to ensure consistency in the data being collected. If a change in a field name is necessary, the change will be globally made so that all relevant forms are affected. Another interesting feature stores the data separately from forms in an ASCII Trailer Document so that existing data can be exported to new forms. Finally, managers won't have to furnish the Tranzform software for every forms user—Acrobat Reader enables non-Tranzform users to view and print the PDF forms.

For more information on Verzions and Tranzform, call (910) 855-1766 or visit http://www.vertec.com.

Advanced PDF Production with the PDFmark Operator

PDFmark is an operator of the PostScript programming language that can automatically add features such as Bookmarks, article threads, document information fields, and links to PDF files when you run them through the Distiller. PDFmark syntax can be given to the Distiller in one of two ways, either as part of the PostScript file itself (as is done by FrameMaker and other programs) or as a separate PostScript file to be added to the PostScript by Distiller. The latter case requires a third file known as a "runfile" which tells the Distiller where to look for the PDFmark and PostScript elements.

PDFmark is the most direct way to customize your PDF documents and speed the production process, but it is also the most difficult to learn if you are not already a PostScript programmer. Adobe offers a guide called the *PDFmark Reference Manual* on their Web site that gives examples of how to write commands to automate the production of Notes, links, Bookmarks, article threads, page cropping, and dictionaries for indexing. But much can go wrong when you substitute your information for theirs. One space or typo in a PDFmark file or runfile will crash your whole distill job, and the cause of the crash is rarely obvious.

A set of examples of PDFmark syntax are provided along with the Acrobat Distiller as a file called pdfmrkex.ps, which is contained in the Xtras subdirectory or folder of the Distiller directory or folder. This document gives examples of almost every type of PDFmark syntax, and you should start by distilling it to see what happens.

For example, one of the sections of the file gives the following example of the PDFmark for a Bookmark:

```
[/Count 2 /Page 1 /View [/XYZ 44 730 1.0] /Title (Open Actions) /OUT pdfmark
[/Action /Launch /File (test.doc) /Title (Open test.doc) /OUT pdfmark
[/Action /GoToR /File (test.pdf) /Page 2 /View [/FitR 30 648 209 761]
/Title (Open test.pdf on page 2) /OUT pdfmark
```

If you examine this statement, you'll see that it contains the content of three Bookmarks, each with a title (defined by the phrase "/Title") that will appear in the Bookmark window, and a set of instructions defining the name of the file to be opened (these happen to be cross-document Bookmarks; if they were Bookmarks within a document there would be no "/File" statement), and the zoom level to which it should be opened (defined by the "/View" statement). The "/Count" statement defines how many secondary Bookmarks will be contained under the main Bookmark and whether they will appear as expanded or contracted Bookmarks when the document is opened.

PDFmark is a very useful tool for automatically generating PDF documents with links, threads, Bookmarks, and document information fields all in place. For large document sets, setting up PDFmark scripts can be much more efficient than opening the documents and adding markup elements by hand or with Plug-ins. With a properly created set of PDFmark scripts, you can create a directory with thousands of documents and drop them all on the Distiller at once, then come back to pick up the finished documents.

Notes

1. *Adobe PageMaker Version 6.0 User Guide* (Mountain View: Adobe Systems Inc., 1993–1995).

Part Three

Chapter 10

Launching PDF Files on Your Web Site

So much planning and production has brought you to this momentous stage in your Web publishing project that the technical tasks of actually launching your PDFs on your server will be a breeze. You have already configured your Web server to support the PDF file type by adding it as a MIME type to the list of file type extensions in the Server Root directory (you can go over the instructions for this in Chapter 5). In Acrobat Exchange, you implemented a Base URL for the PDF documents on your server in the Document Info field, and added Weblinks to documents both on and outside your server (see Chapter 8 to refresh your memory). This chapter will tell you in further detail how to plan the file architecture of your PDF files on your server so that your Base URLs will work properly. We will tell you, as far as we can at this point, how you will be able to use the Amber version of Exchange to optimize your PDFs for page-at-a-time downloading, and how to implement the Amber CGI script so that your server can byteserve your Amberized files. Finally, we will tell you how you can connect your HTML home page and navigational pages to your PDF files using the standard PDF GIF icons as links. Once all these pieces are in place, your Web site is ready to go live! Chapters 11 and 12 will tell you how to implement searching and security technologies on your Web site.

Planning the Document Root Directory

A Web site is made up of two main sections, the Document Root and the Server Root (Figure 10.1). The document root contains the directories and folders that contain your Web documents that are available to the public. The main directory names of the Document Root and the Server Root vary depending on your server type. This is a general description of Web server structure as it probably exists on your system. In general, your HTML and PDF documents should be placed in folders in the Document Root, in a tree-like structure roughly according to their hierarchy in the site. The Server Root contains the server software, log and configuration files, the CGI bin, and other executable scripts. It is the active part of the host machine that handles the communication between the server and the client browser. Its files are not viewable by the public, and are usually protected at some level by your server software.

Where do your PDF documents fit into all this? The first step is simply to make a sketch document root tree, allocating folders to the different types and levels of documents you want on your site. You could start with a folder for the top-level documents, like the home page, navigational pages, the Help file, and the FAQ file. Then you could group the rest of the documents,

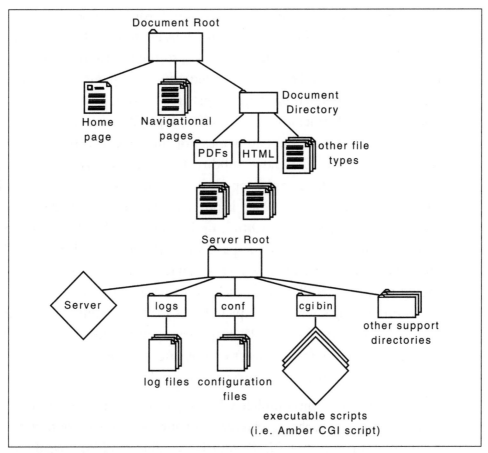

FIGURE 10.1 The Document Root and the Server Root: How to organize your documents and scripts.

HTML and PDF, and folders according to their category on the site. For example, if you categorize your site by Our Company, Our Products, Our Research, Our Database, and Our Partners, you could make five subdirectories under the top level of documents, and place the relevant documents in each folder. Or you can divide the subdocuments according to file types, reserving a folder called PDFDOCS. This may carry some advantages if you want to implement the Amber CGI script, so that all of the PDF files are easily located by the script.

Once you have designed the Document Root, you must determine the URL pathnames for all the folders and documents. First, write down the file names of all the documents on your server next to their place in your Document Root tree. They should all have eight-letter long file names, with three-letter file type extensions that have been registered as MIME types in your Server Root, such as welcome.html, report.pdf, or logo.gif. Then, moving up the file hierarchy, determine the pathnames for the documents. For example, report.pdf in the Company subdirectory would have the pathname company/report.pdf. Give the top-level folder the same name as your hostname in your main URL, which is probably your organization's name. Call the home page file welcome.html, or index.html, and Web browsers will automatically launch the home page when the main URL is entered. The other files in the top directory, such as navigational pages and the Help file, should have normal file names such as mainmenu.html or help.html. Now you can piece together the complete URLs for the documents on your site. Simply combine the home URL, http://www.ourname.com, with the folder and document name paths to construct complete URLs, such as http://www.ourname.com/company/report.pdf.

Although constructing complete URLs for the documents on your site helps you establish a consistent structure to your Document Root, you do not need to enter complete URLs in your HTML links and PDF Weblinks. Since all the documents you will be linking together inhabit the same general directory under your home URL, you can enter "relative" URLs when you create links among them. For example, if you were linking from the home page to the help file in the same top-level directory, your link could point just to help.html. Or if you were pointing from the home page to a PDF in one of the subdirectories, you could point the link to the subdirectory and document names, as in company/report.pdf. Within PDF documents, Base URLs work in the same way for Acrobat Weblinks, by allowing you to enter just the information that expands on the main Document Root directory. For example, you would enter in http://www.ourname.com/ as the Base

URL for all the PDF documents on your server, and then just enter directory and file names in your Weblinks. If all your PDF documents reside in a directory called PDFDOCS, all Weblinks between PDF documents could contain just the individual file names. For links to remote Web sites in both HTML and PDF pages, you must enter complete URLs.

Optimizing PDF Files for Amber with Exchange 3.0

With Acrobat Amber Exchange 3.0, you will be able to optimize both new and existing PDF files for downloading off the Web. The final version of Amber Exchange will not be released until summer 1996, but we can give you some information about how optimization will work and what it will do. Exchange, and not the Distiller, will be the first Acrobat tool to perform Amber optimization, in a Save As function. Adobe is also developing a plug-in for optimizing existing PDF files for Amber by the batch. Optimization actually goes in and changes the file structure of a PDF, reordering the data elements for progressive downloading and rendering. The result is that elements common to every page of a PDF are downloaded once and held constant on the screen; then text, images, and embedded fonts appear one after the other. (The elements that take the longest to load are downloaded last.) Optimized PDF files, when served with the Amber Byteserver CGI script, are able to be downloaded one page at a time, allowing for very quick browsing of PDF files online. Another benefit is that when optimized PDF files are byteserved, they can be as long and as large as the author likes, because the user will not have to wait to download the entire file. Furthermore, if your users are browsing with the Netscape Navigator 2.0, they will be able to view your optimized PDFs right within the Acrobat toolbar, and even view embedded PDFs within HTML pages.

For all of this to work smoothly, however, you must implement the byteserver script correctly, and your users must be equipped with the Amber Reader. You should make it clear to your users on your home page that they need this new version of the Acrobat Reader, and that they should be using Netscape 2.0 for optimal performance (this is not too much to ask, since the majority of Web users browse with Netscape). Be sure to include a link to the area on Adobe's Web site where users can download the Amber Reader, which is currently http://www.adobe.com/Amber/Download.html (Figure 10.2). The Amber Byteserver CGI script will also be available for free on Adobe's site when it is finalized during spring 1996. In the next section, we will tell you how to implement CGI scripts on your server so that you can install the Amber script when it is available.

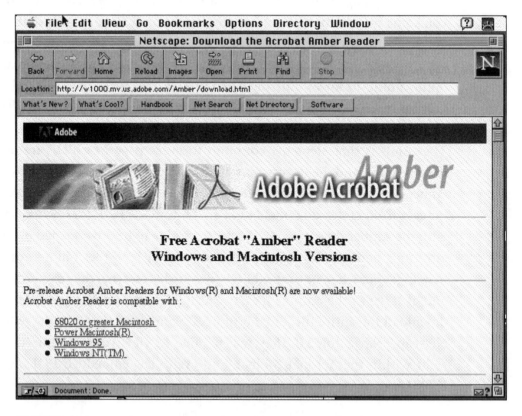

FIGURE 10.2 The Amber Reader download page on Adobe's Web site.

Implementing the Amber Byteserver CGI Script

Before we get into how to use the Amber script to byteserve your PDF files, let's go over what server scripts are and what kinds of scripts may add value to your Web site. An executable script is a series of commands written in a programming language like C or Perl that perform an operation when activated by the Web browser. Most CGI programs involve a direct exchange of information between the browser user and the host server, resulting in a transaction or a custom document generated on the fly, as in the case of a fill-out form. The script resides in the Server Root of your server in a directory called cgi-bin, and often has the filename extension .CGI. Reserving a special directory for executable scripts is important, because you can configure the server to treat every document in that directory as an executable, not as a document to be delivered and displayed. CGI stands for Common Gateway Interface, and is the protocol for Web server scripts. For a CGI script to work, both the server and the client browser software must be CGI-compatible, but this is true of practically all servers and browsers today.

You do not have to be a programmer to use CGI scripts on your server. It is possible to write your own custom scripts, but this is usually the province of experienced programmers. There are a host of ready-made CGI scripts out there that you can use to create fill-in forms, database search interfaces, or even advanced online payment systems. Your server software probably comes with a few basic CGI scripts for creating forms or email fields. Until the technology for PDF forms becomes Web-compatible, the interfaces for CGI programs are always going to be in HTML. Fortunately, most servers come with HTML templates that you can easily customize for your interface. Activating existing scripts is also pretty easy. Just copy them to the cgi-bin directory in your Server Root. (Most server software comes with a directory for scripts; if you don't have one just create one called "cgi-bin.") If the CGI script is for a fill-out form, place a link to the CGI script's file name on one of the HTML pages of your site. The text of the link could read something like "Fill out our subscription form." When the user clicks on that link, the CGI script generates a blank form that the user types into. On the form, there needs to be some sort of Submit button the user can click when he or she is finished. The browser then takes the content of the form and compiles a complex query string URL for it, which it sends back to the server. The server script then takes the submitted information and uses it to synthesize a new document, which can be a confirmation or a search results page. That synthesized document could indeed be a PDF, as is demonstrated by David Glazer on his site, "Dynamic PDF" (http://www.best.com/~dglazer/adobe/). Visit the Dynamic PDF site to see demos of CGI scripts that return synthesized PDF documents, and to read about how you can customize a script to do that on your site.

The Amber Byteserver Script

Not all CGI scripts involve forms, however. A CGI script can orchestrate any kind of request and response communication between the server and the browser client. In the case of the Amber script, the browser using the Amber Reader is requesting a PDF document (which must be optimized for Amber), and activating the byteserver script on the host server (Figure 10.3). The byteserver script communicates to the browser the byte count of the whole PDF file, and then determines whether the browser (Amber Reader) is able to accept byte ranges. If so, the script byteserves only enough data to display the first page of the requested PDF document, or whichever page of the PDF the client requested. When users click the next page tool to continue browsing the PDF, the byteserver script is activated again and serves up the necessary bytes to display the next page. The requests and responses between the browser and script are extremely fast, and the pages display quickly because they are optimized for page-at-a-time downloading. Of course, users will also have the option to download the entire PDF file using the Save As function in their browser.

At the time of this writing, only a few pieces of the Amber architecture are in place. A working beta version of the Amber Reader is available for Windows 95,

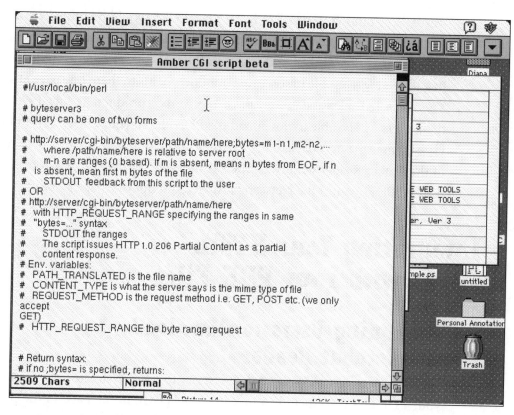

FIGURE 10.3 Extract of the Amber Byteserver CGI script (beta).

Windows NT, and Macintosh for use within the Netscape Navigator release 2.0 (currently the only Amber-compatible browser that lets the user view PDFs within the browser interface). The Amber version of Exchange is in a very early beta stage, and the optimization function has not yet been fully ironed out. There is a beta of the Amber byteserver script being used to serve Amber demos off the Adobe site, but none is publicly available. We do know that for the script to work it must be serving a PDF file that was created with Amber Exchange 3.0 or Distiller 3.02. When the script is finalized, it will be available for free downloading from Adobe's site. To use it, all you will have to do is place it in your cgi-bin directory, and the URL pointing to the script must have the words "/cgi-bin/byteserver/" in it. So a legal URL would be http://www.acropolis.com/cgi-bin/byteserver/amber.cgi. If the PDF files in your Document Root are optimized for Amber, and users on the browser end are using the Amber Reader, you will be able to serve up your documents to them one page at a time. The projected release date for all of the Amber products is July 1996. Until then, users will be able to download the PDF files in your Document Root and view them using Acrobat as a helper application. If they are using a beta version of the Amber Reader with Netscape 2.0, users will be able to view your nonoptimized PDFs within the Netscape browser, but not one page at a time.

Integrating Your HTML Pages with Your PDF Files

Prompting Users to Download the Acrobat Reader

The first step in making sure that visitors to your Web site are able to view your PDF files is to include a link in your HTML home page to the page on Adobe's site where they can download the Acrobat Reader. If you do not make this explicit on your home page, non-Acrobat users will become frustrated and leave your site. You should add text to your home page such as, "Many of the documents on our site are in the Adobe Acrobat PDF format. To view these, you must have the Acrobat Reader configured as a helper application to your Web browser. To download the free Acrobat Reader, Bookmark our site and click here to go to Adobe's Web site." Make the words "click here to go to Adobe's Web site" a link, for which the HTML should read:

```
<A HREF="http://www.adobe.com/Acrobat/freeread.html">click here to go to
Adobe's Web site</A>
```

You can also distribute the Acrobat Reader from your own server, for all the platforms for which the Reader is available. First download all the different versions of the Reader from Adobe's site. Then all you have to do is comply with the Electronic End User License Agreement that comes with the installer for each version of the Acrobat Reader. Once you accept those agreements and install the Readers, you can make unlimited copies of them and distribute them off your Web site. For more information, see the distribution information posted on Adobe's site at http://www.adobe.com/Acrobat/AcroDist.html.

Setting HTML Links to PDF Files

To make your PDF files accessible to your users, you will need to include links to them in your HTML file. These links can be relative within the Document Root of your server, just pointing to the directory and file names of the PDFs. For example, to link the words "Annual Report in PDF" to the actual PDF file report.pdf in the directory pdfdocs, the HTML would read:

```
<A HREF="pdfdocs/report.pdf">Annual Report in PDF</A>
```

Clicking on "Annual Report in PDF" would cause the browser to start downloading the PDF file and launch the Acrobat Reader to view it. It is good form to warn users of the file size of your PDF documents, even in the case where you have optimized the file for Amber. If users do not have the Amber Reader, they will have to download the whole file, so it is best to give them an idea of how long they will have to wait by giving them the byte count.

It is also a good idea to place one of the standard PDF GIF icons next to the HTML links to your PDF files and link the GIF to the PDF file as well. You can download the PDF GIF icons from Adobe's site, on the "Serving PDF Documents on the Web" page (Figure 10.4). They come in two sizes, big and small. Adobe also makes available a "Get Acrobat" GIF button, which you can link to the Reader download area on Adobe's site. Which ones you use on your site is purely a matter of preference. To download them, click on the icon you want from the Adobe page and the actual GIF for the icon will appear. To download it, use the function in your Web browser to save images, such as "Load to Disk," "Retrieve to Disk," or "Save Next Link as." Once you have downloaded the icon, you will need to embed it in your HTML file as an inline image next to the text that links to the PDF document. To embed the GIF next to the words "Annual Report in PDF" *and* make it a link to the PDF file, the HTML command for a GIF called pdficon.gif in a directory called images, and a PDF document called report.pdf in the directory pdfdocs would read:

```
<A HREF="pdfdocs/report.pdf"><IMG SRC="images/pdficon.gif">Annual Report in
PDF</A>
```

A mouthful of HTML, but it should work, and it is the classy way to link to a PDF file. Just substitute the directory name and file name for the destina-

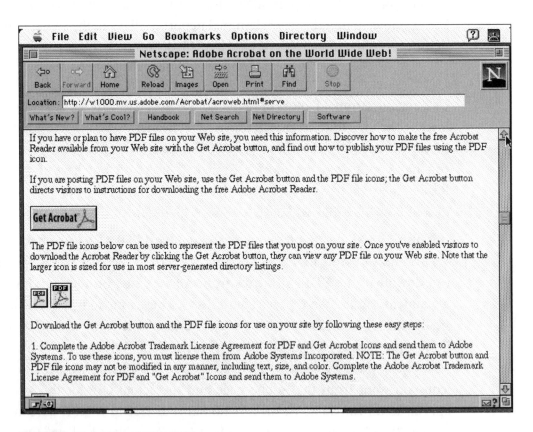

FIGURE 10.4 The PDF GIF icons.

tion PDF file, and the directory name and file name of your GIF file, and the text of your link for the examples we've used, and fill them in between the HTML commands.

You can also configure your server to generate the PDF GIF icon next to PDF document listings in server-generated directory listings. On the NCSA HTTPD server or similar servers, open the ServerRoot/icons/ directory and enter:

```
AddIcon /icons/PDFmid.gif .pdf .PDF
```

in the ServerRoot/conf/srm.conf file. To include a text notice that the file is a PDF, add these two entries to the ServerRoot/conf/srm.conf file:

```
AddDescription "PDF document" .pdf
AddDescription "PDF document" .PDF
```

On the CERN HTTPD or similar server, place the GIF file in the server_root/icons/ directory and add the line:

```
AddIcon /icons/PDFmid.gif PDF application/pdf
to your configuration file in server_root/config/.
```

One of Adobe's claims about Amber is that it will be possible to embed thumbnail-size PDF files into HTML pages and make them links to full-size PDF files. We have not seen or heard of this feature since one of the original Amber prototype demonstrations, but keep a look out for instructions on how to do it once the final Amber Exchange product is released. Embedding PDFs into HTML pages would let you sidestep inserting GIFs, and let you make much more interesting home pages since PDF image sizes are smaller than GIFs and JPEGs. Perhaps this feature will be enabled by Adobe's PageMill, so that a publisher could just drag a PDF image into the HTML page template. We expect the interaction between HTML and PDF to become more seamless as Adobe improves Acrobat's performance on the Internet, making the decision to use either format on your Web site purely a matter of preference. And as Web browsers become more integrated with Acrobat Amber, we may see Web sites that are 100 percent PDF from the home page down.

Chapter 11

Making Your Web Site Searchable

You can add tremendous value to your Web site by giving full-text search capability to the documents on your server. You won't see many Search buttons on Web sites today, but we predict that searchability will be standard on Web sites that host volumes of documents, particularly documents in PDF. This is because as the volume of information on the Web increases, and the excitement of "surfing" wears off, users in search of particular tidbits of information will want to get online, perform a tailored search, and quickly get offline.

Unfortunately, Acrobat's tool for full-text indexing of PDF files, Acrobat Catalog, cannot create indexes that can be accessed via the Web. When you create an index for a PDF using Catalog, a separate index file with a special extension, .PDX, is generated. That file cannot be embedded in the main PDF document, nor can it reside on a disk more remote than a local network. Furthermore, the Acrobat Reader is not equipped with the Search tool necessary to access Catalog's .PDX files; only users with Acrobat Exchange can use Search. Catalog is, however, an excellent tool for indexing your PDF documents on your own system or local network, to keep a searchable archive of all your PDF files. You can also make Catalog indexes available on CD-ROMs that you publish using Acrobat Reader with Search (for more on publishing PDFs on CD-ROM, see Chapter 13). We will explain how you can use Catalog to generate indexes for your local PDF files.

The good news for PDF Web publishers is that a number of software tools have cropped up that not only index PDF files for the Web, but all of your HTML files as well as other file formats. These search and retrieval tools for the Web are capable of communicating between Web servers and clients to accept search queries and process them as CGI operations. Search engines that support PDF can receive queries via HTML forms and return the documents to your users in their native PDF format. The cost of these Web indexers ranges from free (a beta release) to tens of thousands of dollars. Later in this chapter we will give you a roundup of these tools, with contact information if you would like to find out more.

About Acrobat Search

There are two ways of locating information in PDF documents: the Find tool, and the Search tool. The Find tool, represented by binocular icons in the Acrobat toolbar, is included with the Acrobat Reader and Exchange. When a PDF document is open, users can click on the Find tool and enter a keyword to search for. Acrobat will then page through the document and highlight occurrences of the word. The Find tool is okay for locating a word in a short document, but quite limited when it comes to long documents. It is a slow and rather unsophisticated search mechanism. Search, on the other hand, is a full-text search engine that Acrobat licensed from Verity Corporation for inclusion in Acrobat Exchange and Reader with Search for CD-ROMs. It is not available to users of the free Acrobat Reader. Represented by a binocular icon with a page behind it, Search is able to whip through volumes of PDF files, even when they're not open. It allows users to perform highly specific searches using key words and phrases and Boolean operators (and, or, etc.), or more open searches using wildcard symbols, word stemming, and "sounds like" commands. The flip-side of this great Search tool is that you, the author, must use Acrobat Catalog to index your PDF documents. Search will work only on PDF documents that have been properly indexed. The Catalog product is a higher-end part of the Acrobat product line, packaged with the $1,595 Acrobat for Workgroups, or selling alone for $500. Once you have acquired Catalog, the indexing part is easy and will ultimately enhance the value of your PDFs for your local users and your own PDF document archive. For detailed instructions on how to use Acrobat Search at the user end, refer to the Acrobat Exchange online help guide.

Indexing PDF Files with Acrobat Catalog

Catalog is available with the Windows and Mac versions of Acrobat for Workgroups, and is also sold as a separate package. The software will index your PDF documents, building a list of all the words found within it and keeping track of the file name and page number on which they are found. Exchange users (the Acrobat Reader does not support Search unless it is the Reader with Search for CD-ROMs) can perform keyword, phrase, Boolean, and other flexible searching techniques to locate information in an indexed PDF document.

To use Catalog, you must install the Catalog disks that came in your Acrobat package. You will need to have cleared an extra 6 MB of RAM for Catalog to run on a Macintosh, and 8 MB of RAM to run it in Windows. When you start Catalog, it should be the only program running. Memory problems are the number one reason index builds fail, so take those RAM requirements seriously, tweaking the virtual memory on your system if you need to.

Once you have installed Catalog, there are a few things you should check in the PDF files that you want to index. First, is the PDF file the final, perfect version you want to publish? It had better be, because tampering with the file after you index it will cause problems and inconsistencies with searching. Second, remove all document security you have applied to the PDFs; the document must be totally accessible to the Catalog software. You can reestablish security once the indexing is finished. Third, make sure that the Document Info fields for the PDF have been filled in and the information within them is consistent (do not use variations on the document's title, for example). Be sure to enter keywords in particular, because once indexed, users can search on Document Info fields alone to narrow a search. Fourth, have a look at the file size of the PDF—if it is a particularly long document, the indexing will go more smoothly if you break it up into smaller pieces. In fact, if the file size is so large that it limits the amount of RAM available to Catalog to perform the index, Catalog may automatically break up the file. You are better off breaking it up yourself along logical lines. But you will also have to publish the document in parts; you cannot recompile the parts because they will have separate document indexes. Fifth and last, place the PDF files that you want to index in one folder or directory on your system. If you want to index your documents one at a time, place them in individual folders. Catalog does not index PDFs by the file, but by the folder. It will index all of the PDF files in the folder you specify, and all of the subfolders and subdirectories, so make sure you accordingly organize your documents.

Setting Catalog Preferences

The next step is to open up the Catalog program by double-clicking on its icon in the program group. You can set parameters for your indexing jobs by editing Catalog Preferences, accessible under the Edit menu. Click on the *Index* button. You will see a series of options that you will not know what to do with (Figure 11.1). The first is the rather ominous "Time Before Purge (seconds)." Purging (deleting) the contents of an index is important when you make changes to a document and rebuild the index, because it removes all the old data from the

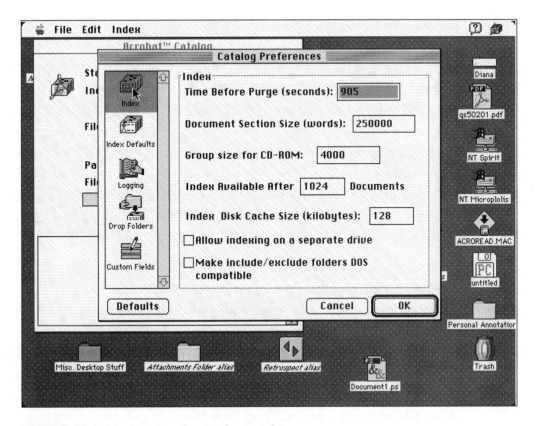

FIGURE 11.1 Setting Catalog Index Preferences.

index in preparation for the new one. In the case where Catalog is running on a network and indexes are available to multiple users, the index you want to purge may be in use. The "Time Before Purge" option means that after a given time Catalog will go and purge that index regardless of whether it is in use. The default time setting is 905 seconds, which equals 15 minutes. You may want to increase this time to avoid alarming consequences for the user of the index.

The next option is "Document Section Size (words)," which governs how long a document has to be before Catalog automatically breaks it up into smaller pieces. Since we advise breaking up large files yourself and not allowing Catalog to break it up willy-nilly, we suggest you increase the word count by whatever the word count of your largest document is, adding a few thousand words to be safe. "Group Size for CD-ROM" is relevant only if you are indexing a PDF to be stored on a CD-ROM. "Index available after [#] Documents" is based on the same function, but is for PDFs going to other media such as online. "Group size" means a batch of files that Catalog has grouped together for the process of incremental indexing. Normally, Catalog will index all of the documents in a collection and not make the indexes available until it is finished. With the Group Size options, you can make indexes available as Catalog continues indexing a collection by setting the number of documents (group size) after which it must make their indexes available. If you are publishing your PDFs on the Web, their indexes will not be available until you launch the documents on your site anyway, so these options may not be relevant. But if you are also serving the documents on a local network it may be a good idea to tinker with group sizes.

"Allowing indexing on a separate drive" means that Catalog will be able to locate and index PDF files that do not reside on the same drive on which Catalog is running. We do not recommend clicking this option, because PDF files that are remotely indexed are difficult to move around and redistribute (which you inevitably will be doing with Web-destined documents). Locally indexing PDF files makes the resulting document much more portable. The only instance in which you should allow remote indexing is if your PDF production infrastructure is engraved in stone and you do not need to redistribute the files. In the Macintosh version of Catalog, there is one more option in Index Preferences—"Make include/exclude folders DOS compatible." This option will automatically give an eight-letter file name with the .PDF extension to all document folders indexed by Catalog. This is an important option to check, because it will allow non-Macintosh users to locate your documents using Acrobat Search.

Moving on to the next item in Index Preferences, *Index Defaults*, you can set default Index Options (these can also be set on a per-job basis by clicking the Options button in the Index Definitions box, which we cover later). (See Figure 11.2.) The first option is "Do Not Include Numbers." Check this box if you want to enable users to search on numbers. This is recommended if numbers play a meaningful but not dominant role in the document. If the document has thousands of numbers in it, search results for numbers will not be meaningful. The "Word Options" offer three types of searches to

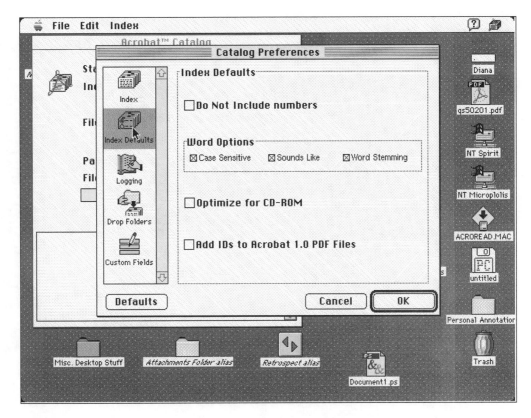

FIGURE 11.2 Setting Catalog Index Options Defaults.

allow—Case Sensitive, Sounds Like, and Word Stemming. These are flexible search options that you should enable for the user. Beware, however, that including numbers and those three search options in the index will increase the PDF document's file size by about 20 percent. "Optimize for CD-ROM" means that Catalog will assume that the index is not going to be updated for that document, removing some data and reducing the index file size. "Add IDs to Acrobat 1.0 Files" will make Catalog compatible with PDF files that were created with Acrobat 1.0.

The third item in Catalog Preferences is *Logging* (Figure 11.3). As with the Acrobat Distiller, Catalog keeps log files of its progress on indexing jobs. Logging options allows you to enable or disable logging, determine which

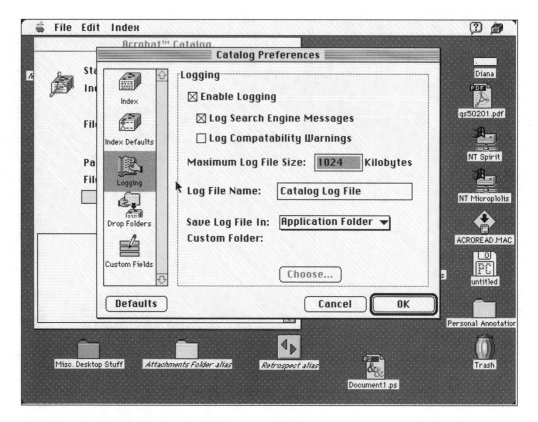

FIGURE 11.3 Setting Catalog Logging Preferences.

kind of messages are included in log files, set the maximum log file size, name the file, and save it to a folder or directory. Click the Log Search Engine Messages if you are interested in messages coming from the Verity search engine. Check Log Compatibility warnings if you are worried about conflicts coming from different platforms on your network. Change the Maximum Log File Size if you want to decrease it from the default 1 MB (any larger, and it's going to take up too much space on your system).

The fourth option in the Preferences box is *Drop Folders*, which would allow dragging and dropping entire PDF document folders or directories and dropping them onto the Catalog icon on the desktop (Figure 11.4). If you do allow it, you can set default indexing options for folders treated this way. You can give indexes a default name with the .pdx extension, choose a destination

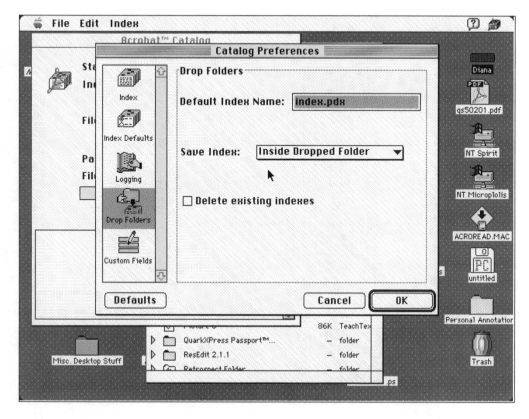

FIGURE 11.4 Drop Folders options.

folder, and choose to delete existing indexes for those documents. Finally, the fifth option is *Custom Fields* (Figure 11.5). This option will make Catalog recognize and index any custom Document Info fields you may have created for your PDFs. For information on how to use PDFmark to create custom Document Info fields, see the section on PDFmark in Chapter 9.

Creating an Index

Once you have set Catalog Preferences, you can begin the process of creating an index for your PDF file (or collection of files). The first step is to create an index parameter file, which has the file type .PDX. This will be the skeleton of the index, which will fill up with data from the document when you build the index. Select New from the Index menu (File menu in the Mac version),

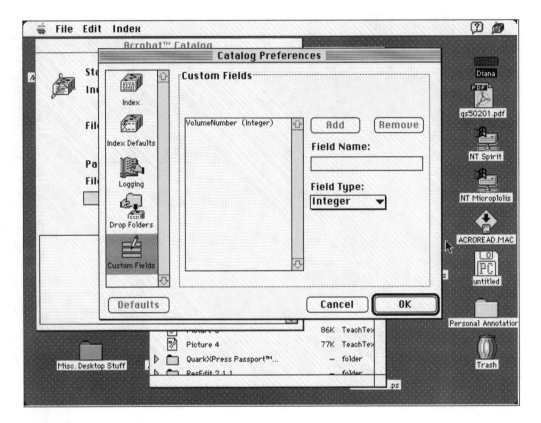

FIGURE 11.5 Custom Fields options.

and the New Index Definition box will appear (Figure 11.6). First, specify a title for the index, which does not have to be a short file name. The title will be the reference for the user to choose from in a list of available indexes. In the Index Description field, enter the names of the specific documents in the collection, the types of searching you have enabled, and any other information that might be helpful to the user. Next, click the Save As button to name the actual index file. The index name must be eight letters long and have the .PDX extension. This name will also be the name of the subdirectory in which the search database is stored. Take care to choose an appropriate location for the index. It must be on the same drive as the documents you are going to index, and that drive must have plenty of room. Next, Add the folders or directories you want Catalog to index by selecting them. When they

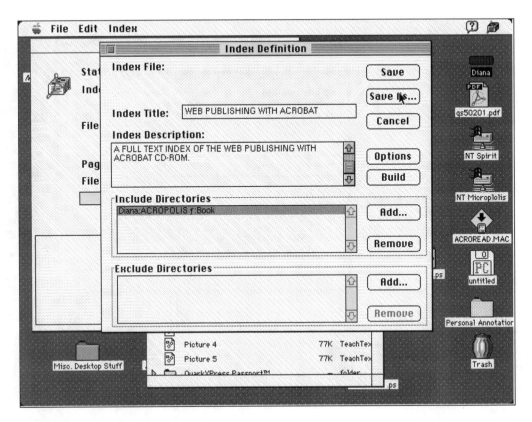

FIGURE 11.6 Defining a New Index.

appear in the Include Directories/Folders field, they will be indexed. You can exclude certain subdirectories or folders from indexing by adding them to the Exclude Directories/Folders field.

The final step before you build your indexes is to set Index Options, which you can do by clicking the Options button in the New Index Definition box (Figure 11.7). The first option is "Words Not to Include in Index." Here you can select among a list of "stopwords" such as *the, an*, and so forth and add stopwords of your own by typing into the Word field and clicking the Add button. You can remove a stopword by selecting it and clicking the Remove button. Adding stopwords helps to reduce file size, but beware of using too many because they could limit natural language phrase searches. You also have the option not to include numbers; this option should reflect what you chose

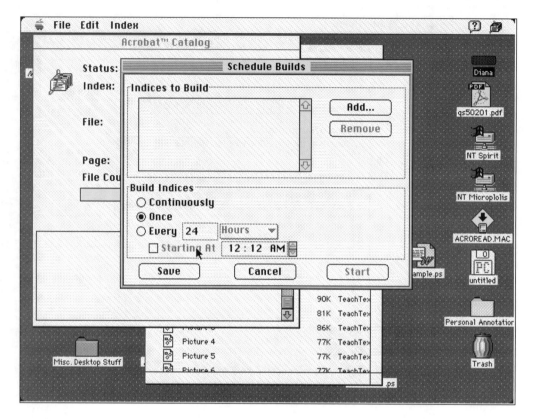

FIGURE 11.7 Setting a Schedule for Index Builds.

in Catalog Preferences. The rest of the options listed, Word Options, Optimize for CD-ROM, and Add IDs to Acrobat 1.0 PDF Files, are repeated from the Index Defaults box from Catalog Preferences, and can be changed here.

Building the Index

Now you are ready to build the index(es) for your PDF files. With the New Index Definition box still open, click the Build button. Or you can drag the PDF document folder onto the Catalog icon on the desktop if you have enabled Drop Folders in Preferences. The process is not unlike Distilling— Catalog will begin whirring away in the background, displaying its progress as it goes along. To stop the build, click the Stop button. When Catalog is finished building the indexes, the last line in the status messages will read

"Index Build Successful." To test out your new indexes, open up one of the PDFs in Exchange and click on the Search tool. Click Indexes in the Search dialog box. The titles of your new indexes should be listed; if not, you can add them by clicking Add and locating the indexes. Then, select the right index and perform any kind of search that you enabled (using words and phrases you know are there). If Catalog was able to successfully build an index for the document, searching should be 100 percent accurate. If your index build crashed and you did not get an "Index Build Successful" message, check the log file "Acrocat.log" for error messages. Probably there was not enough system memory to run the job. Try quitting out of other applications, increasing available memory, and rebooting your system. You may also want to limit some of the search options by adding stopwords and disallowing number searches, for example. To redo the Build, simply repeat the process.

Rebuilding and Purging Indexes

You can update the indexes for a document collection by putting new or changed PDFs into the target folder, and choosing Build under the Index menu (under the File menu in the Mac version). Catalog will update the indexes for all of the new documents, as well as documents that have been modified since the date of the last index build. If you want to change the index Options for an index, you will have to purge the existing index and build a new one with the new options in effect. This sounds like a drastic procedure, but it is really a routine part of the indexing process. Purging indexes prevents the existence of multiple indexes for one file and other conflicting data in PDF files. Purging is also a good way to "clean up" index files that have been incrementally updated a few times. To purge an index, select Purge under the Index/File menu. Select the index you want to purge and wait while Catalog deletes the indexes contents. When it is finished, select Build and build a new index for the document.

You can maintain healthy indexes by setting Catalog to automatically rebuild a set of indexes on a regular basis. This is a great way to update indexes whose documents have changed, or to rebuild indexes from scratch to keep them compact. You have to purge indexes yourself, however, before Catalog is scheduled to rebuild them. To set a schedule for Catalog, select Schedule under the Index/File menu (Figure 11.8). In the Schedule Builds dialog box, click Add and select the indexes you want regularly rebuilt. You can choose to build the indices Continuously, Once, or at scheduled intervals. Choosing Continuously will make Catalog constantly watch the specified directories for new PDF files. Selecting Once will build all of the selected indexes one time. If you choose the Every option, specify a time at night or whenever the system Catalog is running on is likely to be free. The computer on which Catalog is loaded must be on 24 hours a day for the schedule to work, and Catalog must always be running. Click Start to put the schedule into effect, or Save if you want to save the schedule and start it later. Once you start the

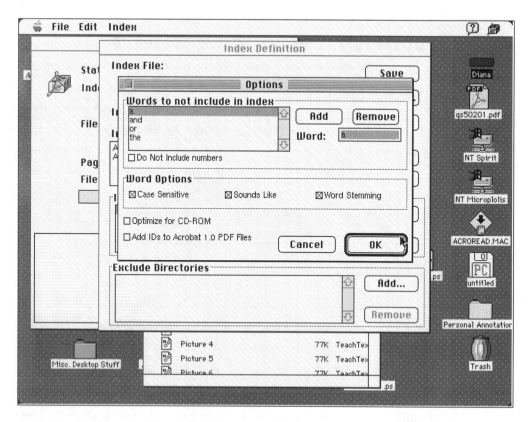

FIGURE 11.8 Setting Index Options.

schedule you will not be able to build indexes the manual way; you must stop the schedule before you can manually build. In the event that someone turns off the system running Catalog, or there is a power failure, you must go into the Schedule box and restart it once Catalog is running again.

Once you have indexed your PDF documents with Catalog, it is time to think about the other content on your Web site. How can you provide a full-text index for your HTML content as well as your PDF content? Is there a way to index both kinds of documents at once? Read on to learn about special tools that can do just that.

PDF-Compatible Web Site Indexing Tools

These indexing tools feature close integration with the PDF format, from extracting ASCII text from PDFs and creating full-text indexes to retrieving PDF documents and displaying them in Acrobat. They are also capable of indexing the HTML documents on your site, and a variety of additional file formats.

Verity Topic Internet Server

Brought to you by the same people responsible for Acrobat's internal search engine, Verity's Topic Internet Server is software that communicates with your Web server to index your site and search document collections on behalf of your users. Available for Windows NT and UNIX-based servers only, and at a significant $10,000, the Topic Server is a powerful tool that could turn your Web site into a fully searchable library of diverse document formats. Topic performs full-text indexing not only of HTML documents, but also of PDF documents, 50 standard word processing formats, TIFF, and spreadsheet formats. Topic will maintain the integrity of PDF indexes generated with Catalog, while it takes the ASCII text out of PDF files and includes it in its Topic library. Topic is also capable of retrieving PDF files in their original format and serving them one page at a time using an embedded version of the Amber technology. Topic has a scalable architecture that can support millions of documents for thousands of users. You can even use Topic to index the same variety of document formats residing outside of your Web server, on CD-ROM, a local network, or a database. It features a customizable CGI interface in which you can tailor the appearance and wording of HTML query forms and results lists.

Once you have indexed the documents on your site using the Topic File Indexer, your users will be able to perform a wide range of searching techniques based on Boolean operators, proximity, field operators, fuzzy logic, term weighing, zones, and selected sections of documents. The results of their searches are displayed according to your specifications and are ranked by degree of relevancy to the search terms. Webmasters can monitor the activity of the search engine with detailed activity reports generated by the Topic server.

Other interesting Verity products, both of which feature close integration with PDF, are the Topic Agent Server, which constantly searches the Web for information according to the user's interest, and the CD Publisher, which integrates CD-ROM documents with Web documents. To find out more about the Topic Internet Server and other Verity products, visit their Web site at http://www.verity.com.

AppleSearch

AppleSearch is Apple's offering to users of the MacHTTP Web Server Solution, although they originally licensed it from PLS (Personal Library Search) for users of AppleTalk local networks. In its Web iteration, AppleSearch provides most of the capabilities of other Web indexers at a fraction of the cost. In fact, it comes bundled with the Internet Server Solution, which all together is a fraction of the cost of the Verity Topic Server.

AppleSearch's ease of use suggests that it may have been the inspiration for the Acrobat Catalog interface. Indexing documents is a matter of clicking an Index button, or it can be a scheduled automatic procedure. Making the indexes available to your Web server is as easy as dragging them to the right folders. Users will be able to do keyword searching on all the document types you have on your server, including PDF. (But to allow sophisticated searching techniques on PDF documents, you should index them using Catalog.) The Web version of AppleSearch features AppleSearch CGI, a point-and-click program for creating query forms and generating search results for users. It also comes with AppleSearch Reporters, search agents that will troll your server for certain words and produce a relevancy-ranked list of results. For more information on AppleSearch and the Apple Internet Server Solution, go to Apple's site at http://www.apple.com.

Odyssey ISYS

Available for Windows and DOS, the ISYS line of indexing and search tools includes a special version for Acrobat and one for the Web. ISYS for Acrobat features a special interface for search and retrieval of PDF files on a LAN, WAN, CD-ROM, or Web server. Users can employ a wide variety of query options, such as plain English, menu-based queries, and advanced Boolean and proximity searching techniques. A special query technique of ISYS is Fuzzy Searching, which accounts for misspelled words or errors in OCR scans when it searches a PDF. Fuzzy Searching would be an especially useful technique for PDF documents that were scanned in with Capture. To index PDF files with ISYS for Acrobat, you do not have to prepare the files in any way; ISYS automatically recognizes the PDF format. The ISYS indexer can handle up to one million documents or two billion different words in a database. Once a user's query hits on a document, the user can select it and ISYS will display the PDF in Acrobat. ISYS returns the document in a read-only format, but will allow certain enhancements such as adding text notes, graphics, and links on top of the retrieved file.

ISYS Web is the indexing and search product that will index up to 40 file formats and automatically convert them to HTML. Users can employ the same variety of query techniques, and view the results within their Web browser. All search results are relevancy-ranked and linked to the documents' URLs. To find out more about ISYS, call (303) 689-9998.

Cascade MediaSphere

Cascade's MediaSphere is a unique "digital library system" that not only extracts and indexes ASCII text from a variety of document formats, but can index and search any binary object, such as PDF and picture, sound, and video files. MediaSphere also features extended Acrobat integration, using PDF as the primary display format for search results. Instead of just retrieving the title of a document or multimedia file, MediaSphere will retrieve the original file and display it in PDF or in a video playback program. Users can search with natural-language queries, and view relevancy-ranked results in an easy-to-use Info View interface. On the server, files are stored in a Sybase relational database that tracks the activity of all objects within it. Media-Sphere runs on Sun Microsystems' SPARC servers, and the client software is available for both Mac and PC. Originally developed for local and wide-area networks, Cascade recently announced the Web extension to MediaSphere, called the W3 extension. W3 extends its support to Amber on the Web, and also incorporates the MUSCAT Web explorer and Sun Microsystems' Java. Search results are displayed as thumbnail pictures within Java-encoded "light boxes." When a PDF thumbnail is clicked on, MediaSphere proceeds to byte-serve the PDF file using the Amber technology. W3 is based on Netscape's Web-server technology and is compatible with all HTML Web browsers.

For pricing and other information on MediaSphere, call (508) 794-8000 or visit their Web site at http://www.cascadenet.com.

Fulcrum Surfboard

Surfboard is the Web-optimized version of Fulcrum's heavy-duty full-text search engine, SearchServer, which is widely used on corporate LAN servers. It is compatible with HTML, PDF, and a host of other Web standards and common document formats. Surfboard's indexes are searchable not only by Web browsers, but also by other Internet clients like Gopher, AOL, and Delphi, because it complies with the WAIS and Z39.50 Internet protocols for search queries. At the client end, Surfboard offers users Intuitive Searching, a kind of query that will retrieve documents similar in content to the one the user is viewing. Surfboard also allows a wide range of standard search techniques and produces relevancy-ranked results. Uniquely, Fulcrum is able to search and retrieve text in European languages other than English.

Surfboard adds value to its search engine by giving you security options to restrict users' access to certain search databases and keeping careful track of who comes into your site and what they do there. The price is dear, however, starting at U.S. $15,000. Surfboard is compatible with UNIX systems and Windows NT.

Architext Excite

One of the most compelling new Web search engines is Architext's Excite, a concept-based indexing and retrieval tool with several features that challenge their competition. Most significantly, they are offering version 1.0 of Excite for free on their Web site—reason enough to go with their product, given the hefty price tag of other search engines. Another unique feature is that their engine is able to garner the core concepts of documents and even summarize their subject matter in relevancy-ranked search results. Indexing with Excite is as easy as filling out a few forms, and your documents will be indexed at a high rate of over 300 MB per hour. Excite can handle a wide variety of file formats, including PDF, using a flexible file filtering scheme. What's more, the file size of Excite's indexes is much smaller than average, about 15 percent of the size of the original document collection. Excite automatically generates CGI scripts, HTML forms, and results pages for search queries. Users can search using the standard set of search techniques, as well as with concepts and query-by-example (finding documents similar in subject matter to the current one). For more information on Excite, visit the Architext site at http://www.architext.com.

Chapter 12

Securing Commercial PDF Files from Unauthorized Access

Once you have established your Web site and published your public documents, you may want to consider the possibilities of publishing certain documents to a select audience, such as paying subscribers, customers, or your employees. Or if you are a publisher of original content, you probably want to protect your copyright more securely than simply adding copyright statements to your documents. All of these scenarios involve different levels of security that different technologies are emerging to provide. The first level is server-based security that protects your host machine from unauthorized hacking, such as firewalls. The second level is public- and private-key encryption to protect credit card transactions and other exchanges of valuable information between users and servers. The third level is document-based encryption, which comes with a downloaded document to require a password from users or to prevent the document from being passed along to unauthorized or nonpaying users. We will discuss document-based security in detail in this chapter, particularly as it pertains to your PDF documents.

Copyright Issues Involved with Web Publishing

The Web, unlike traditional publishing avenues, is a free-for-all for document providers and document users. Web publishers can launch just about anything they want (at least until the Communications Decency Act cracks down on "obscene" content on the Web), and Web users are free to read and redistribute other people's Web documents at will. In the case of HTML documents, users can view your source HTML code right in their browser, edit it, and create an unflattering or incendiary version of your document. There is nothing to prevent someone from taking all of the documents from a WWW site and placing them on another site. Indeed, copying documents or groups of documents—known as "caching"—is a common practice on the Web, since documents can usually be retrieved more rapidly from the cache than from the original site. Indeed, both WWW browsers and the Acrobat products cache pages locally. Most Web publishers do not have the army of lawyers that major print publishers keep to control misuse of their content, and at first Web content was not compelling or valuable enough to worry about misuse. But Internet publishing tools like Acrobat have made it possible to reproduce previously published printed matter for the Web, and to create documents in which the publisher has invested significant resources in design and development. Whether you are an established publisher of printed content or your Web site is your first-ever publishing venture, you need to be aware of the anarchy of copyright on the Web and what you can do to control the distribution of your Web documents.

The following guidelines for establishing copyright of your Web documents are just that—guidelines. There is no copyright enforcement body on the Web that will chase you or your users down for not complying with traditional copyright law on the Web. But until Internet-based copyright laws are established and enforced, you can help foster a community of mutual respect among quality Web publishers, which most PDF publishers are. Assigning copyright notices to your Web documents may also protect you in the event you are challenged in a lawsuit or want to pursue misuse of your content in court. By law you have the right to copyright protection regardless of whether you post a notice, but you should include one as a statement of ownership of a document in the event that you are challenged to prove it. A copyright notice can read simply © [*Your Name*] 1996. It may help your users to outline what you consider reasonable use of the material, such as quoting it properly. If you are reprinting other authors' materials on your site, take care to obtain permission from the original author unless your reproduction of their content falls under the "fair use" exceptions to copyright law, such as for academic or nonprofit purposes. Be aware that images as well as text can benefit from copyright notice, and you should obtain permission before using somebody else's image on your site. For more detailed copyright guidelines and discussion of developing copyright laws for the Internet, visit these Web sites:[1]

- *The Copyright FAQ*, at http://www.cis.ohio-state.edu/hypertext /faq/usenet/Copyright-FAQ/top.html. Moderated by Terry Carroll, this FAQ has extensive discussion of U.S. copyright laws and their application to the Internet.

- *Copyright Clearance Center Online*, at http://www.openmarket. com/copyright/. This site provides collective copyright licensing services to obtain permissions.

- *Fair Use in the Electronic Age: Serving the Public Interest*, at http://arl.cni.org/scomm/copyright/users.html. This is a report from the Association of Research Libraries which outlines "fair use" of copyrighted materials on the Internet by individuals, libraries, and educational institutions.

- *Intellectual Property and the National Information Infrastructure*, at http://www.uspto.gov/niiip.html. This is a report by the Working Group on Intellectual Property Rights, a subgroup of the Information Infrastructure Task Force.

Is WWW Commerce Ready for Prime-Time?

Your desire to maintain control over your intellectual property notwithstanding, nowhere is the importance of controlling the distribution of your documents greater than when you are selling them online. The solutions for this lie not in publishing copyright notices and crossing your fingers, but in security technologies, many of which are now available in commercial Web servers. But there is another hurdle for establishing a commercial publishing venture, which is a distrust on the part of vendors and consumers alike of the vulnerability of online money transactions. Despite almost universal acceptance among information industry insiders of the premise that the WWW will develop in three stages—first communications, then publishing, then commerce—the Web has been a hard sell, commercially speaking. Consumers may or may not ever buy tangible goods over the Web, but they will—indeed already do—buy information. The reason for this is simple. Unlike goods that must be transported via some non-Internet channel, information products can flow back to their purchaser along the very same channel over which they were purchased. The result is that electronic information products can be immediately delivered, in real time. Consumers of such information goods get what economists call *place utility*—they can get it delivered to where they are—and *time utility*—they can get it right now. So it is likely that once people's perceptions of the security of Web transactions rise in confidence, the convenience to customers and informational value to vendors will make the Web a viable commercial space.

Secure Web Technologies

Consumer confidence in secure transactions on the Web may take a while to gain strength, but the technology to protect your Web site and implement secure commercial programs is here today. This section describes tools that secure commercial transactions, tools for protecting Web documents, and encryption tools for PDF in particular. We also tell the story of Dial-A-Book, the first service to sell books in PDF on the Web.

Tools for Web Commerce

There are already a number of products designed to work with security programs to enable money transactions on the Web. Many commerce programs rely on the submission of the user's credit card number, while others avoid the problems associated with submitting real credit card numbers with what is called *digital cash*. Digital cash works by encrypting users' credit card numbers in denominations of digital cash equal to the cost of the online product, and submitting the "cash" to the vendor who has the software to deencrypt the credit card number. There are a number of companies competing to establish their version of digital cash as a standard, such as Digicash' "ecash," CyberCash, NetCheque, and NetCash, among others. Payment services that don't use the cash metaphor offer credit-card-owner-anonymity, described in one AT&T blueprint, or provide virtual bank accounts for users, as in First Virtual Holdings, Inc. (http://www.fv.com).[2] Early in 1996, Visa and MasterCard struck an agreement to set a standard for transmitting credit card information over the Internet, called Secure Electronic Transactions. Still under development, the system will allow Web browsers to accept credit card numbers using a standard piece of software. Both Microsoft and Netscape Communications Corporation were involved in the development of the software, which promises to guarantee safe transmission of credit card numbers.

Protecting Web Documents

WWW servers can be configured to limit access in a number of ways. The most common are to limit access to users who enter a valid name and password pair, or who arrive from a particular group of IP addresses. Using the software built in to most major server packages, a publisher can with reasonable degree of confidence restrict access to a WWW site. Netscape's publishing server and Open Market's server will both allow publishers to manage subscription lists of online customers, turning away subscribers who have not paid their bills, sorting subscribers by level of service and routing them to the appropriate part of the site, and so forth. However, to the extent that these server packages are serving HTML documents, they do not provide security against the passalong of copyrighted material. The server cannot control the use of documents once they have been downloaded by a user, and HTML documents are almost always unencrypted.

PDF documents, by contrast, can be encrypted and password protected. Acrobat Exchange includes encryption software licensed from RSA Data Security, the company that holds the patents on Public Key Cryptography, and Acrobat Reader includes decryption software of the same sort. The Acrobat encryption software is based on RC4—one of RSA's symmetric stream ciphers, so called because they encrypt and decrypt using the same key—unlike Public Key encryption, which uses two different keys for encryption and decryption. RC4 encryption can be performed quickly and is quite reliable.

From the perspective of a publisher, however, the fact that a document may be encrypted is not by itself a solution to the problem of copyright violation. If the user must be given the password in order to open the document, the document is not really secure: Once that user is in possession of the document and its password, he or she could pass both to another user. An encrypted document with a known password might as well not be encrypted. This is an instance of the difficulty well known to cryptographers as the "Key Exchange" problem: How should the secret code, or key, needed to unlock a message be protected, and what will protect the key used to protect the first key, and so on? Public Key cryptography was developed to solve this problem by eliminating the need for a key to be passed from sender to recipient along with the document.

Third-Party PDF Encryption Tools

Adobe has not built a solution to the key exchange problem into Acrobat— a publisher can protect a document using Acrobat, but cannot also protect the password to that document. At the present time, two types of third-party software have been developed to protect PDF documents from redistribution. The first type replaces the Acrobat standard encryption with other encryption using a different password mechanism; the other type retains the Acrobat standard encryption and adds an additional layer for managing passwords.

The first type of security takes advantage of the fact that the Acrobat API allows for other encryption systems to be used in place of the RSA RC4 cipher. PDF documents can be encrypted by a plug-in effectively implementing any encryption system, and decrypted by another plug-in using the same system. One such product available today from SoftLock Services, Inc. uses that company's proprietary encryption technology implemented in a pair of Plug-ins to lock documents on a CD-ROM or an Internet site. Documents protected by the SoftLock system cannot be opened except in the presence of a software key, which is itself protected from passalong by being tied to some unique feature of the user's computer. Another such system is under development by Software Partners, Inc., the leading developer of Plug-ins for Acrobat, but details of its functionality have not been released.

The second type of third-party software acts as a preprocessor, or front-end to the Acrobat standard encryption. Such systems store a copy of the document's password outside of the PDF file and retrieve it when the document is being opened. Passwords are stored in encrypted form, then decrypted and presented to the Acrobat standard encryption system to open the document. One such system, KeyChain from Magnetic Press, Inc., is being used to protect books delivered by the Dial-A-Book system.

Case Study: Dial-A-Book

Dial-A-Book Inc., based in New York City, offers PDF versions of in-print trade books over the Internet, either as standalone products or in conjunction with a paper copy of the same book. The service operates as a bookseller, offering books at list price and taking the bookseller's commission of 40 percent, which is enough to cover the cost of providing the service and creating the PDF copies of the books, according to its founder, Stanley R. Greenfield, a former Ziff-Davis executive (Figure 12.1).

The first Dial-A-Book project is currently offering books published by the Institute of Electronic and Electrical Engineers (IEEE) from the IEEE WWW site (http://www.ieee.org) (Figure 12.2). Anyone may purchase a book from the WWW site and download the electronic version immediately; the paper

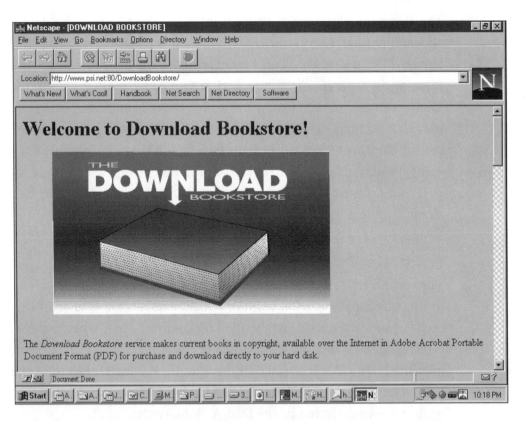

FIGURE 12.1 Dial-A-Book's Download Bookstore page on the PSI site, at http://www.psi.net:80/DownloadBookstore/. Go here to download IEEE books in PDF.

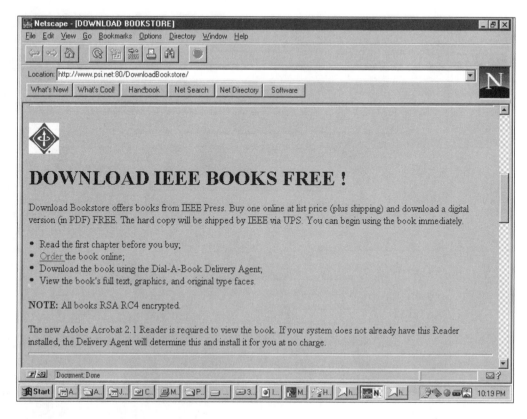

FIGURE 12.2 IEEE books in PDF are available to download for free, and the hard copy you purchase will be sent to you via UPS.

version is sent from IEEE the next day. According to Anthony Ferrara, IEEE's director of publications, this service provides a significant added value to IEEE, as many of the organization's 300,000 members live outside of the United States and must wait 30 days or more for a book to arrive in the mail.

Users order a book from Dial-A-Book by filling in an HTML form on the IEEE WWW site (Figure 12.3). The contents of this form are passed to a server maintained by Performance Systems International (PSI) in Herndon, Virginia, which validates the credit card transaction and logs the buyer's name and the name of the book ordered into a database. Acknowledgment of the transaction is then sent back to the IEEE site, where the

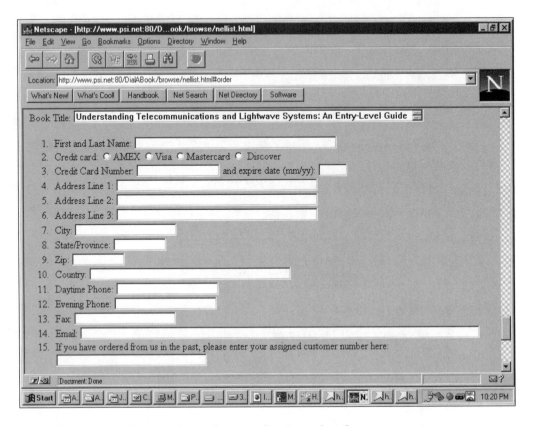

FIGURE 12.3 The HTML form for purchasing a book.

user is invited to download a software agent that will complete the transaction (Figure 12.4).

This 280-Kbyte agent program, produced by Digital Delivery, Inc., of New York City, expands itself onto the user's hard drive and checks to see whether that computer already has Acrobat Reader 2.1 or Exchange (Figure 12.5). During this process, the user is asked to enter the name on the credit card that was used to purchase the book (Figure 12.6). The Delivery Agent then makes a connection to the PSI server database to check whether the book has already been installed, proceeding only if it has not.

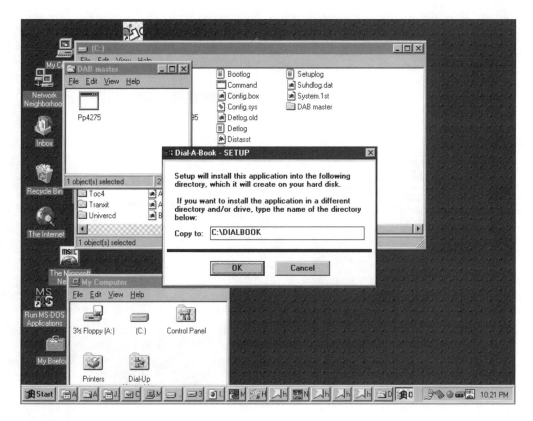

FIGURE 12.4 The Dial-A-Book Setup box.

Once the validation has been completed, the Delivery Agent downloads the book from the Digital Delivery WWW site. The Agent operates in the background, allowing the user to do other things while the process is under way (and will continue to operate even if the user reboots the computer). When the Agent has finished downloading the book it runs the installation programs for Acrobat (if necessary) and for the Magnetic Press KeyChain document security system (Figure 12.7).

The KeyChain system places an encrypted version of the password needed to open the book onto the user's hard disk. Whenever the user attempts to open that book, the KeyChain client plug-in retrieves the password from the user's hard drive and uses it to open the PDF.

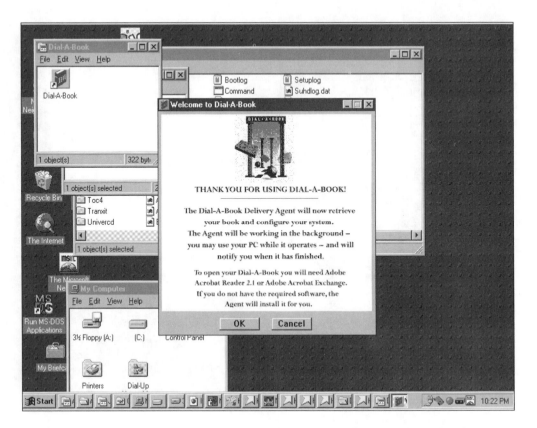

FIGURE 12.5 When you see this screen, the agent is about to download your book in the background. You can continue working on other things and even reboot while the download is in process.

As you can garner from the Dial-A-Book example, launching a commercial Web publishing enterprise requires the integration of several unique technologies and the expertise to implement each of them. Since many of the technologies, such as Digital Delivery's agents and Magnetic Press's KeyChain software, are brand new and proprietary to their developers, you should enter into your commercial Web enterprise in the spirit of cooperation. This means that as a publisher you will need to seek out partners who can carry out the transmission and security of your commercial documents using the

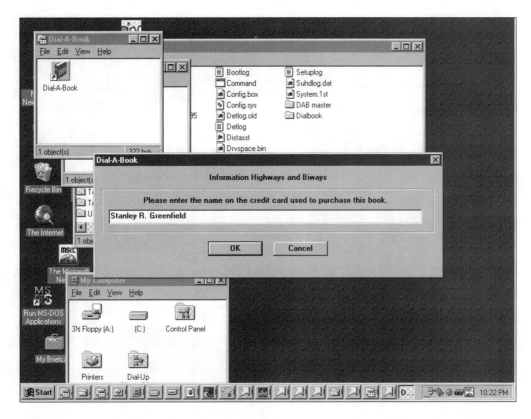

FIGURE 12.6 Confirming the title of the book and your credit card number to complete the download.

latest technology. That leaves you to worry about producing your content and marketing it, which are full-time jobs in themselves. A good way to keep on top of Web developers who may be able to help you is to attend the many Internet industry conferences and expos, such as Internet World, Seybold, and Multimedia Expo. Also, Adobe publishes *Adobe Acrobat Software: A Guide to Related Services* as a free booklet in every Acrobat package and also as a PDF on their Web site. The guide is a resource of all of Adobe's third-party developers, with descriptions of their products and services and contact information.

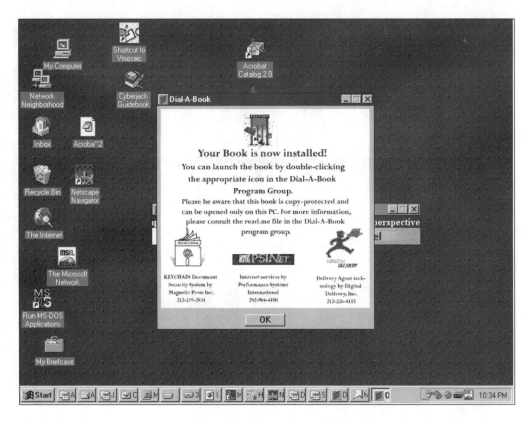

FIGURE 12.7 Confirmation that your copy-protected PDF book has been installed, with the logos of all the companies that collaborated to make it happen: Magnetic Press, PSINet, and Digital Delivery.

Conclusion

This concludes our discussion of publishing PDF on your Web site. We wish you the best of luck in putting all the different technological pieces together in a successful PDF publishing venture. The frontier for making original and technologically advanced use of PDF on the Web is wide open, so follow your instincts and challenge your organization to keep up with all of the new possibilities that arise in the next few years. And don't forget to publicize your site, not only for your market but also to the Acrobat and Web communities. Your site may do something new with PDF that will impress and inspire your fellow Web publishers. Once your site is ready, be sure to send mail to Adobe's Webmaster (webmaster@adobe.com) and ask to have your site put on the "Web Sites with Cool PDF" page. Having a link posted on Adobe's Web site is a great way to increase traffic on your site.

Part Four, "Beyond the Web," will tell you how you can extend your PDF publishing to other communications channels—CD-ROM, Lotus Notes, and offline publishing systems. After all, your PDF documents are inherently portable, and should be repurposed on as many different media as possible to reach the widest possible audience.

Notes

1. Mike Franks (*The Internet Publishing Handbook*, Reading, MA: Addison-Wesley, 1995) did the surfing for these sites.

2. Franks, 231.

Part Four

Beyond the Web

Chapter 13

PDF on CD-ROM

PDF and Other Electronic Media

One of the great advantages of the Portable Document Format is that it lends itself to distribution on a variety of media. So far, this book has concentrated on techniques for publishing PDF on the World Wide Web. And that is certainly an attractive distribution mechanism for publishing electronically.

But it is not the only one. In the following chapters we'll take a look at some of the other main ways of packaging PDF documents and distributing them.

First, in this chapter we'll look at how to produce CD-ROMs quickly and easily. Available today for under a thousand dollars, the CD writer is within the budget of any professional publishing operation. With so many potential advantages to the CD-ROM medium for publishing, archiving, or even simply data transport, a CD writer belongs in every Web publisher's production shop.

Another way of distributing PDF is using Lotus Notes, the communicating document database software. Notes is used by a growing number of businesses to unify workgroups within the organization by giving them shared access to the same set of critical organizational data. Even better for those with a publishing bent, Notes also can be used to deliver information to a closed user group, like a private network. If your target audience uses a lot of Notes (as is often the case in financial companies and in very large organizations), you might have a look at Chapter 14 for some ideas as to how Notes can help you leverage your investment in creating PDF documents.

Finally, in Chapter 15 we'll look at some of the other ways you can distribute PDF documents—today and in the future.

These may be the final chapters in our book, but they are far from the final chapters on distributing PDF, a format that will live long and prosper as the universal electronic publishing format for digital documents. For ongoing coverage of the exciting evolution of the PDF publishing industry, tune in to our *Acropolis* Web site at http://www.acropolis.com/acropolis. Now, on to our discussion of CD-ROM.

PDF and CD-ROM

Compact, shiny, a marvel of modern technology holding up to 680 megabytes of computer data...the *Compact Disc–Read-Only Memory*, more commonly known as *CD-ROM*, has a lot going for it. Thanks to the ISO 9660 format (a standard way of writing data onto the disk's surface), CD-ROMs are in most cases multiplatform data storage media. That is to say, you can put the same CD-ROM disk into a PC, a Mac, or a UNIX machine, and the disk will be readable. That's quite an achievement when you think about it— each type of machine uses floppy diskettes that are written to differently, and that therefore are unreadable on other systems.

The development of the multiplatform CD-ROM format gave rise to a question, however: It's one thing to be able to read the CD-ROM disk, but quite another to be able to use the programs or information contained on it. For a time, this led to serious research and development into things like universal operating systems or abstract system code that would permit machines with different hardware and operating systems to run the same piece of program code. IBM, Apple, Sun—virtually all the big names had their go at one or another "universal software" code scheme that would level the differences between hardware platforms and operating systems. Well, all of those efforts have come and gone—all except the noble SuperDrive floppy disk drive that Apple has been delivering with all its Macintosh systems since the Mac Plus; and the SoftWindows software for Macintosh (by Insignia Solutions), which lets you run Windows programs relatively well on your PowerMac.

At the same time IBM and Apple were pouring massive R&D into their joint venture Taligent, and Sun was touting Wabi (an interpreter that would let Windows applications run on Sun workstations), Adobe was developing Acrobat. At the time, it wasn't clear to many people what Acrobat (then named Carousel) was for. It was clear that PostScript had the lion's share of the desktop publishing market, but the big guys and the smart money were concentrating on developing the info highway via a universal software environment. If all machines could run the same programs, data exchange would be trivial.

The big guys and the smart money were wrong. John Warnock and Adobe rightly recognized that word processors and operating systems may come and go, but the information that we create with our computers ought to stay—whatever the word processor *du jour* happens to be. Warnock had it right on that golden day in May 1993 at the original Acrobat introduction when he asked us how many times in the last five years we'd switched word processors—and in so doing lost access to all that information we'd been creating. Starting a new word processor is kind of like beginning a new intellectual history. Well, according to Warnock, that's not good enough in an age that's supposed to be the dawn of the Information Revolution. If we were really with it, we'd be able to change operating systems and authoring programs the way we change clothes, *and* still have access to all the information we or anybody else ever made. If we were really with it, we'd be using something like Acrobat.

What a breath of fresh air that was! How utterly odd is the concept of your *information* taking precedence over your *operating system*! We all gave John a standing ovation and have been Acrobat groupies ever since. The general market has taken a little longer to come around but the essential *rightness* of the Acrobat idea remains. What many of us today don't appreciate was how far outside the prevailing thinking about *everything* Warnock and Adobe were when they brought PDF and Acrobat into the world.

On that fine day, the original multiplatform vision of the ISO committees was realized. Finally, you could publish one set of data for all platforms. The era of media-independent electronic publishing had begun. Now all people had to do was to use Acrobat tools and publish in PDF.

CD-ROM Market Overview

Everybody knows that you can hardly buy a computer any more without a CD-ROM drive in it. In 1995, for example, according to Infotech, a CD-ROM consultancy in Woodstock, Vermont, about 95 percent of all desktop computer systems sold from the factory were supplied with CD-ROM drives. Even laptops can have CD-ROM drives. My little Toshiba here, for example, has a double-speed CD-ROM drive right in it, and it's no bigger, no heavier, and no more expensive than the rest.

For publishers, this is good news. During the lean years, in the mid- and late 1980s when CD-ROM was just getting established, information publishers would count the number of CD-ROM drives installed (one million, four million, ten million...) as against the total installed base of PCs (25 million, 40 million, 60 million...), and conclude that somewhere between 2 and 16 percent of their potential market (i.e., all PC users) had CD-ROM drives. In most cases, this was not enough to make CD-ROM a serious distribution option. So in order to meet the maximum number of potential buyers, publishers used diskettes. This meant that all they could afford to put onto the diskettes was ASCII text—because that was all the diskette could hold and ASCII was the only format they could be sure to deliver to all different types of computer users.

Thank goodness those days are gone. In 1995 alone, more than 40 million CD-ROM drives were shipped, bringing the installed base of CD-ROM systems to over 65 million worldwide. For reference, there are about 90 million households in the United States. We're not yet at the penetration rate of television sets, but we're on the way: In 1995 there were more PCs sold in the United States than there were TVs. So publishers: It's okay to publish on CD-ROM now, because the demographic of CD-ROM users is pretty much the same as that of PC users. And that, by the way, is a pretty strong demographic.

When to Use CD-ROM versus the Web

Being a Web publisher, you already appreciate the speed and convenience—and above all the cost-effectiveness—of publishing on the World Wide Web. But you can't hand a Web site to somebody. You can't put a fancy package on it. You can't hold it up in front of a group of potential buyers. It has one major problem that is also its biggest advantage: It exists only in cyberspace. Because publishers often need to have a tangible product to sell (if only to make the bean-counters happy), CD-ROM is a great way of creating that tangible something. You can make a CD for any number of reasons:

- As a product to sell through traditional physical distribution channels like bookstores, software stores, mail order, and so on;

- As an adjunct to your existing paper documents—a kind of "paper plus" electronic publishing strategy;

- As a giveaway or promotional item, to hand out at trade shows, to put into company information packages, to hand out to clients, and so on;

- To preserve your Web site at various stages in its evolution, for archival value (and who knows, maybe one day to revert to your original design as a Web Site Classic Edition just to keep your audience on their feet); or

- To package your Web site itself on a CD-ROM (easier to fit in your pocket than a pocket cellular phone and modem—and less expensive to consult for hours at a time).

You can even say that your Web site is defined as a CD-ROM (for all the information up until publication date, or for a baseline database of information that is static and unchanging) integrated with the online resource of the Web (for all the latest information, news, e-mail, and so on). This is also a strategy for reducing the number of "hits" on your server, for those for whom too many hits is a problem.

For all of these reasons, you should consider making a CD-ROM. But how do you decide when to use the Web and when to use the CD? The scenarios listed in Table 13.1 will help.

TABLE 13.1 When to Use CD-ROM versus the Web

For this kind of information or application...	Use this distribution medium or combination
A giveaway or promotional item	CD-ROM
Applications requiring user input, feedback, or communication	Web or Web plus CD-ROM
Big document databases that people will want to search through again and again	CD-ROM
Information that doesn't appreciably change over time	CD-ROM
Something you want people to *access*	Web
Something you want to *deliver*	CD-ROM

CD-ROM Production Tips

In this section we'll look at how you can take the PDF publishing expertise you've developed and put it to use in a new way: by publishing a CD-ROM. As with publishing on the Web, making a CD-ROM is a craft. The first time out can be rough going, but once you get the hang of it you'll find you can get the job done with style.

It used to be that CD-ROM publishing involved creating a big multimedia program. In fact, many CD-ROMs are still conceived as big databases or simply as giant executable programs. CD-ROMs made with Macromedia Director, for example, follow this model. What you have on the disk is a program that integrates words, pictures, sounds, animations, and video sequences.

Because of the complicated nature of multimedia programming—Mac or Windows—traditional CD-ROMs are relatively difficult and expensive to make. For starters, there's always a significant cost for *data conversion*, simply to get the information into the right format for programming. Then there's an elaborate *scripting* process that is the essence of the multimedia programmer's art. To make multimedia programs function, they must first be "storyboarded" or designed as a sequence, and then programmed so that the program takes the required elements and displays them in the required fashion. There's a fair degree of classical computer *programming* involved also, as the program must be told to constantly watch for "states" of the action on the screen, and to behave differently depending on the "state" the program is in.

In addition to all of this, most traditional CD-ROM titles will require two separate instances of the program file on the disk—one for Macintosh users, and one for Windows users. This conversion process, which most multimedia authoring tool vendors will deem self-evident, more often than not represents a significant amount of reworking of the original program code—sometimes up to 80 percent. It's no surprise, then, that so many traditional CD-ROM titles are losers: They simply cost too much to develop.

CD-ROM publishing with PDF differs in many ways from the traditional mold. For example, there's no such thing as "programming" in the PDF world (at least not necessarily: You can create custom CD-ROM Plug-ins for your Acrobat publishing project if you want to). You can therefore spend your development time making the information in your CD-ROM title, rather than making the program to run your CD-ROM. This is probably the biggest single advantage of choosing Acrobat and PDF for your CD-ROM publishing project, and it's one that makes Acrobat CD-ROM titles primarily *informative* rather than *entertaining*.

A second advantage of PDF is that there's rarely any data *conversion* to worry about. Of course, there's a conversion of source files to PDF from the original Quark, PageMaker, or other authoring format. But if you've already done that, either as a part of your normal production process or as a part of your Web publishing effort, the PDF files you have on hand will go onto CD with only minor modifications—and if you're smart in the way you construct them, with no modifications at all.

Finally, if you choose to present your data in PDF you have only one set of data files—the same for Mac and Windows. Just slap the Acrobat Reader programs for Windows, Macintosh, UNIX systems, and DOS users (yes, there are still some of those out there) onto the disk for users to install, and you're golden. Among electronic publishing media, only Acrobat offers you this cross-platform compatibility right out of the box. But as a seasoned Acrobat Web Publisher, you know that already.

Setting Up the Disk Hierarchy

The first trick to producing a successful CD-ROM is to understand the architecture of files on the disk—and understand how to leverage that architecture when you're creating your PDFs. Like a Web application, a PDF CD-ROM has a main menu or home page, and links from that page to other pages, which themselves link to further pages, and so on. The design of the link structure and of the ways in which the eventual user will use the PDF files is called the *navigation design.* The navigation design that you will create for your CD-ROM should be based on the information that you're going to provide. You can describe this in many different possible ways, but the way that matters for this work is to describe the *documents* that you'll be delivering on your CD-ROM. This leads to the trusty three-step approach to CD-ROM building.

Acrobat CD-ROM Architecture in Three Easy Steps

STEP ONE: MAKE A DOCUMENT INVENTORY FOR YOUR APPLICATION Take out all the documents you plan to deliver on your CD-ROM. Identify each one by its file name and by the role it will fill for your application. If you don't have all the documents you need, make up a file name for each new file that you'll need to create.

STEP TWO: CREATE THE DISK'S NAVIGATION DESIGN The main links on your disk are links from document to document. Within a single document, you might have links to multimedia objects, but the overall rhythm and impact of the information you're delivering will depend on how you choose to make your documents accessible. Key idea: Make it simple. Let the documents speak for themselves.

STEP THREE: PROGRAM YOUR PDFMARK Step One and Step Two have provided the information you need to develop a PDFmark script. PDFmark is the programming language for the Acrobat Distiller program, and it provides instructions to the Distiller as to how to create PDF documents. It is a simple yet powerful way to add value to your PDF, and represents the bricks and mortar of the PDF publisher's craft. For more on PDFmark, refer back to Chapter 9, "Special-Purpose PDF Production Tools."

PDF Navigation Pages

Now it's time to plan the tree structure of your links—the "arborescence" that is the heart of your navigation design. Because much of the benefit of PDF comes from its ability to use both new and preexisting data files, much of the information on a CD-ROM that you build may come in the form of "ignorant" PDF files, that is, PDFs which in their on-screen design are blind to the fact that they're part of a CD-ROM or Web site.

As a result, it's common practice to create a number of *navigation pages* for the CD-ROM application that help guide the user to the document he or she needs. We often use a three-tier structure of a Home or Welcome page, which links to a small number (usually not more than five) of second-tier or "department" pages, which then link down into the real document "stuff" of the CD or Web site. Whether and how much you choose to follow a hierarchical directory tree structure on your CD-ROM or your Web site is up to you. There are those who prefer a flatter kind of organization, arguing that such designs are truer to the *true* nature of hypertext.

That may be so, but at the end of the day all publishing, whether it be CD-ROM or Web or paper, is about communicating. "Form ever follows function," said the great Chicago architect Louis Sullivan, and CD-ROMs are no different. You can make your CD-ROM's tree structure a towering hierarchical redwood or a tangle of hypertext vines, as long as you make it work for what you're trying to say. By the way, just because we've done most of our CD-ROM and Web publishing with a bunch of PDFs made from preexisiting documents doesn't mean that you can't or shouldn't use PDF to construct a disk or a Web site from scratch. If you're going to do that, you can really work some exciting stuff into your navigation design, by knowledge-engineering your application up front.

In this conception, Acrobat becomes a simple yet robust multimedia authoring tool. Using traditional page-design programs and Acrobat's capability to link in other media types (such as audio, animation, or video objects), you can create multimedia applications quickly and easily—much more easily, in fact, than traditional multimedia programming tools, which require "hard" programming skills. To borrow from Apple's advertising campaign from a few years back, Acrobat is in many ways "multimedia for the rest of us."

Principles of Creating PDF Navigation Pages

If You're Building a CD-ROM that Reuses Existing Documents:

- Make a home page with the necessary number of "department" choices on it. Remember that your visual design may suffer if you clutter your menu page with too many choices, while your navigation will suffer if you offer too few. If you can let your users get where they're going with three menu choices or less, you've successfully avoided "menuitis." More than that, and your customers will spend more time in menus than they will with your information.

- Department pages should link directly to some of the most popular documents you expect users to be accessing. It's okay to have some more menu selections on your department pages, but if you don't have a few documents right there for the asking, you're tending toward menuitis. If you're having trouble deciding how many departments you want, or what they should be, look at your Document Inventory and pick out the top ten best and most important documents on your disk. Classify them into however many departments seem right, then fit the rest of the lesser-important information into those categories.

- Duplicate your home-page/department structure in Acrobat Bookmarks inside of each document. This gives users more than one way to get from place to place on the disk. It's easy to create a standard Bookmark file containing links to all of the documents you'll be publishing using the PDFmark operator. Send this file to the Distiller along with your documents, and presto! All of your documents contain links to every other document on the disk.

- Try to "foreshadow" menu choices by including a little more information about where a specific link will take your user. For example, on a home page, you might have choices such as Products, Services, Support, and Customer Service. If you also provide a bit of editorial next to your menu buttons and corresponding links, you can give users a chance to bypass an entire menu level and go directly to an information item of interest. Foreshadow a couple of the most popular menu items in a given department. Your users will thank you.

- Don't try to add any navigation aids onto the pages themselves of the documents you're reusing. If you do, it amounts to reauthoring them (which negates the great advantage of using PDF for republishing: the ability to use what you already have). If you do want to add navigation from those documents, do it by adding Bookmarks or by adding visible links—which lets you modify the visual appearance of the pages.

If You're Building a CD-ROM from Scratch Using PDF as Your Publishing Format:

- Build navigation "buttons" into your pages by pasting a bitmap into your page, then using Acrobat Exchange to make that button link to the desired endpoint. Better yet, use PageMaker or FrameMaker to create master pages that contain dedicated links—for example, Next Page, Previous Page, Home Page.

- Develop a visual language of button types. Using shape, size, and color, you can build navigation into the information you're authoring, as you're authoring it. In effect, this forces you into creating a qualitatively different type of information. On balance, your information will be better as a result of this reflection.

- Build hypertext links into the text as it's being developed. As your writers are writing they can make references to other parts of the document—or to other documents. This leads to powerful capabilities for information access: because hypertext makes any part of a document—or any document—available at just a click of a button, effective authoring demands an awareness of just what this can add to the user's experience. In essence, hypertext is the footnoting of the electronic publishing age. But of course, it offers so much more.

- Finally, remember that even though you may be starting to make a CD-ROM from scratch, you can *still* use some existing documents to buttress your presentation or to bulk up your disk. It's an advantage that authors of other multimedia works don't have—so take advantage of it.

At this point, nothing is especially different for your Web or CD-ROM design. The two media share the same general principles, as in both cases the fundamental unit of application development is the intelligent communicating document, the PDF. CD-ROMs begin to diverge from the Web on a few different levels. First, at the level of the media themselves, CD-ROMs are static and standalone information carriers while the Web is a dynamic and communicating environment. Second, CD-ROMs have no practical limits in terms of the size of PDF file you can put onto one. You can make a single 600-megabyte PDF and put it onto a CD-ROM; with the Web, even with Acrobat Amber and byteserver CGIs, you'd hesitate to do so. Finally, CD-ROMs are *the* multimedia medium, combining text, graphics, audio, and video with impunity while the Web remains largely a text-and-graphics affair, with the emphasis on good old 14.4 Kbps–friendly text.

Consequently, you'll have a great deal more freedom publishing your PDF on CD-ROMs than you do on the Web. Go for that rich color by selecting JPEG Low in the Distiller Job Options. Forget about downsampling and keep that image at 300 dpi. Treat yourself to full CD-quality audio in your sound tracks. In most cases you'll have plenty of room for all of this, and more.

CD-ROM Link Syntax

You will probably want to create a variety of different folders (directories and subdirectories to Windows users) on your CD-ROM for file management purposes. When you do, you'll need to apply the correct *link syntax* in order to link one PDF to another on the disk. By link syntax, we mean the nomenclature you use to direct the Acrobat Reader program to a specific PDF file, even though that file may be in another folder or another disk. This isn't a problem when you create links for yourself to use; you simply open up the Link tool, draw your button, then use the Select File button to navigate to the proper PDF, hit the Set Link button, and you're done.

But things change when you need to create links that other people are going to use on other machines that may not even be the same type of machine as yours. Acrobat, being a universal file viewer for the PDF file format, has handled this problem intelligently—with a universal file-linking syntax. We've seen one of these before in the form of the Universal Resource Locator (URL) syntax used in Web publishing. Well, guess what Acrobat uses? The same basic syntax. Even though Acrobat's interdocument linking architecture was invented before most of us even knew there *was* an Internet, the good folks at Adobe managed to make their link syntax Internet-compatible. Coincidence?—perhaps not; here's how it works:

1. Navigation up and down the folder/directory structure is achieved through a system of double dots (..) and slashes (/), just like in URLs.

2. Slashes (/) indicate motion "down" (deeper) into the folder/directory tree; double dots (..) indicate a movement "up" the tree closer to the root.

Let's say there's a CD-ROM disk with a folder called Folder1, then inside Folder1 there's another folder called Folder2, and inside Folder2 there are two folders, one called Folder3 and another called Folder4. Now in each directory there's a PDF file with the corresponding number. So in Folder1 we have 1.PDF, in Folder2 there's 2.PDF, and so forth. To round things off, let's put a file called 0.PDF in the root directory.

In this way, you can plan the syntax your links are going to have once you've designed the directory structure your disk will feature. It's very important to know the syntax of all your links in advance, and to keep track of them on a piece of paper (or better yet, a database). If you know all your links in advance, you can build PDFmark statements so you can automatically create a set of links while you Distill your documents. Even better, you can go back and change your links simply by changing your PDFmark statements—a great feature for debugging or for recycling old PDF into new products.

There are some cases when you'll want or need to specify a drive letter in addition to a directory in order to specify the location of a certain PDF file (or attached multimedia object). This is trickier because Acrobat reads the operating system's drive designations, which differ radically from platform to platform. On the other hand, Acrobat superimposes its own directory navigation syntax onto that of the operating system in order to offer a universal navigation capability.

Here's what Acrobat will do if I build a link that crosses over from the current drive to drive C: on my Windows machine: the resulting syntax is /C/PDF/AMBER.PDF. This is an unresolvable link for users who don't have a drive C: on their machine, with a directory called PDF. You see where this is leading: Don't jump drives when you're creating an Acrobat CD-ROM. Stick with navigation links that go from one place to another on the same CD, follow the rules given above, and you'll be fine (Table 13.2).

TABLE 13.2 CD-ROM Link Syntax

To get from here...	To here...	Here's your syntax:
0.PDF	1.PDF	Folder1/1.PDF
0.PDF	2.PDF	Folder1/Folder2/2.PDF
1.PDF	0.PDF	../0.PDF
3.PDF	0.PDF	../ ../ ../0.PDF
3.PDF	4.PDF	../Folder4/4.PDF
2.PDF	3.PDF	Folder3/3.PDF

A Single PDF File for Both CD-ROM and Web?

You bet: Because Acrobat's link syntax mirrors that for Web URLs, you can create an entire application on CD-ROM, then use the exact same PDF files for your Web site. Just be sure you mirror the CD-ROM's directory structure on the Web server, and place all the PDF files in the same directories on the Web machine as they're in on the CD-ROM, and all the links that you made for your CD-ROM will still work perfectly. As long as you can get your users to the root directory on the CD, or the home page of your Web site, the rest will work just fine. This is really quite amazing when you consider the amount of time and energy that it can save.

Remember that the directories declared on the CD-ROM must mirror the server's directory structure *as seen from the Web*, not the physical directories on the machine itself. Often, Web directories are "mapped" to physical machine directories with quite different names, so if this is the case on your server, remember to create directory mappings or aliases that match those on your CD-ROM.

Publishing CD-ROMs Using Acrobat Reader with Search

Late in 1995, Adobe introduced a new product, Acrobat Reader with Search, to address the growing market for Acrobat CD-ROM publishing. Before Reader with Search, publishers had trouble adding full-text search functionality to CD-ROMs, because the native search mechanism of Acrobat, Acrobat Search, was only available as a plug-in, and plug-ins could work only with Acrobat Exchange. So in order to get search capability, publishers had to fork over real money (about $10 per disk pressed) in order to license a copy of something called Acrobat Exchange LE, which was essentially the Exchange product without the ability to create or save new files. Needless to say, this was a big limiting factor for Acrobat in the CD-ROM marketplace.

Then the Adobe folks found a way to permit the Acrobat Reader program to accept Plug-ins—not all Plug-ins, mind you, but only the Plug-ins that had been sprinkled with magic dust, making them Reader-enabled. (In fact, any developer can enable a plug-in to work with Reader by licensing a special developers' kit from the Adobe Developers' Association.) So, with the release of Acrobat 2.1, we found a Reader program that integrated the Weblink and Movielink Plug-ins. And we found a new product on the market for publishers, called Acrobat Reader with Search.

The way Reader with Search works is that you, as a publisher, buy a box for $800 or so, which permits you to create a single CD-ROM master containing PDF files, an Acrobat Catalog full-text index, and the Windows and Macintosh versions of the Reader with Search program. Your license permits you to press as many CD-ROMs as you want, but only while you're at the well. Later, if you go back to the CD-ROM pressing factory, even with the exact same CD-ROM master, you must buy another copy of Reader with Search.

When you're creating CD-ROM applications along with a search module, you proceed in roughly the same way as if you were making a CD-ROM without an index: Create your files, make a home page, make links, watch out for link syntax, and so forth. But when you're done, you set the Acrobat Catalog program loose on the mass of PDF files that you mean to publish and create a new index. From the Catalog main screen, choose Index-New. Fill in the name and description. Call the index something that has to do with your project—All Web Publishing Project Files, for instance. Now select the directories that contain the PDF files you're going to publish by clicking the Add button. Before you build your index, be sure to click the Options button in order to instruct Catalog to build an index that is optimized for CD-ROM (Figure 13.1).

Now you can build your index. During the indexing process, Catalog will create a new index file, the name of which is determined when you Save As your new index. The new index file itself will have the extension .PDF (Webpub.pdx, for example). In addition, Catalog will create a directory/folder on your disk that has the same name as the file (for example,

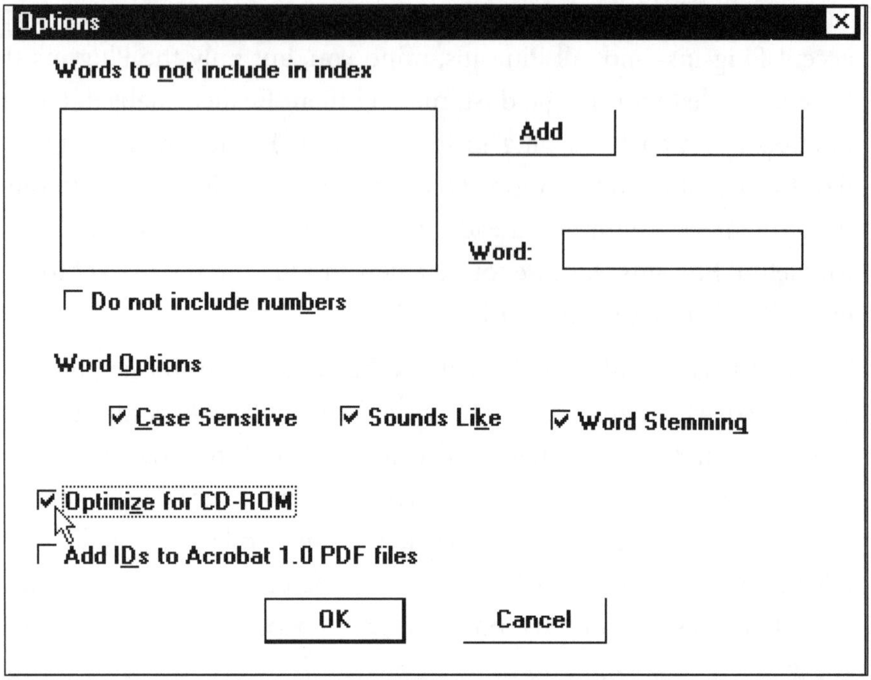

FIGURE 13.1 Optimize your index for CD-ROM for best performance.

Webpub). In this directory will be a number of subdirectories that contain the "stuff" that the Acrobat Search Plug-in uses to navigate the disk and find the right PDF files (Figure 13.2).

When your index is complete, you'll need to copy the .PDX file (Webpub.pdx, for example), and the entire index directory (Webpub) and all its subdirectories, onto your master CD-ROM along with your PDF source directories and files. By the way, be sure that you have the same directory/folder names on your CD-ROM as you do on your source hard disk when preparing your CD-ROM image. If, for example, you have PDF files in directories called Winter, Spring, Summer, and Fall, be sure that your CD-ROM also has directories/folders with the same names and that the same PDF files are inside them. Catalog stores pointers to the PDF file locations—and if you change the name of your directories when you go to CD-ROM, there'll be no way for the Acrobat Search client to find the files it's looking for.

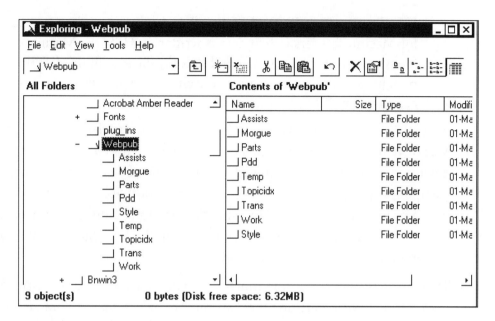

FIGURE 13.2 Directories created to hold files related to Webpub.pdx.

Finishing the CD-ROM Master

Now that you've designed your interface, made your PDF files, created your navigation pages, and maybe even indexed all your PDFs, you're ready to burn the proverbial polycarbonate platter.

ISO or Hybrid?

The first thing you'll need to decide before you burn is whether to make an "ISO" or a "hybrid" disk. This is a choice you make in your CD-ROM recording software (if indeed the software gives you the choice; some don't). In practical terms, the choice of ISO or hyrbid has to do with how the CD-ROM writer machine writes data onto a CD-ROM so that it can be read by users:

- The ISO 9660 format is the international standard for writing data onto a CD-ROM. This method is generally the easiest and least hassle-free for you, the CD-ROM developer.

- Alternatively, you can make a so-called "hybrid" disk that is partitioned into two or more parts. One part is for use with Windows (usually written in ISO 9660 format) and another part is reserved for Macintosh users (when data is written in HFS, the Macintosh file system format). Each user will see only the part of the disk that pertains to him or her—a great convenience, especially if you have any first-time CD-ROM users in the audience.

Hybrid disks have the advantage of being more user-friendly: Each user—Mac or Windows—sees only the files appropriate to him or her. However, the downside of hybrids is that in order to have all the necessary files on each partition, you must put all the data onto the disk twice, in effect creating a separate disk image for the Mac and the Windows side. You also have to remember which files go where: Mac Reader on the HFS partition; Windows Reader on the ISO partition; ditto with installer programs, if any.

There are also limits to how much data you can put onto a hybrid disk. Because you have to partition the disk into two halves, there's a practical limit of about 340 megabytes worth of data per partition. So if you've got 400 megabytes of PDF to publish, you must either make a single ISO disk or make two hybrids. We generally prefer to make ISO disks whenever possible. There are fewer variables in making an ISO than a hybrid, and the work is therefore easier to do right the first time.

With an ISO layout, the Mac and Windows versions of the Acrobat Reader are placed in different directories. Label these ACROMAC and ACROWIN so your users will know where to go to find the appropriate Reader program if they need it. Remember also to give users plenty of instructions on how to install and use your application, both on electronic file on the disk (a simple text file is *de rigueur*, in case your users need help before they can get the Reader program installed) and on the packaging itself. To summarize:

- Put the Mac and Windows versions of the Acrobat Reader program in separate directories on the ISO disk, labeled ACRO-MAC and ACROWIN; and

- On a hybrid put the Mac version of the Reader into the ACRO-MAC folder on the HFS partition, and the Windows version of the Reader into the ACROWIN directory on the ISO partition.

CD-ROM Installation Scripts

Sooner or later you'll find that the basic installation of an Acrobat-based CD-ROM—Mac and Windows readers, plus PDF files—is not robust enough for your application's needs. You'll want to do some things differently—install Plug-ins, for example, or copy an initialization file to the user's drive, or set up your application one way for a Windows user, and another way for a Mac user. Any number of things can drive you to the recognition that, just like a regular software program, your CD-ROM needs an installation routine.

This is not a happy day for you, even though it in some ways marks your arrival among the PDF publishing elite. The fact is that, unlike PDF files, installation scripts are no fun. The reason installation scripts are no fun is that there are a hundred million things that can go wrong with an installation. You have no way to know what a user's machine is, what his or her environment is, how messed up his or her WIN.INI is, what he or she had for breakfast…any of these things can cause an irate user to call you up and complain that your CD-ROM application "doesn't work."

What's more, as soon as you delve into installation scripts, you expose yourself to the differences between computing environments, and the number of things that can go wrong multiplies exponentially. In fact, installation scripts are so tricky that it's become something of a specialty in the computer programming business. Do yourself a favor and find yourself a local specialist who can whip up a good installation script in a day or two. It'll be well worth your while. And once you've got the installation thing wired, the sky's the limit for you and CD-ROM and PDF publishing.

Chapter 14

Distributing PDF via Lotus Notes

When Lotus introduced its Notes software in the early 1990s, nobody quite knew what to make of it. Was it a database? yes, sort of; email? yes, but it's more than that; application development tool? yeah, it does that too. The problem with Notes is that it doesn't fit into any of the traditional software categories. But then, it kind of fits into them all. . . .

A paradigm-buster it sure was, and it still is to some degree. To understand what Notes is is to do better than the more than four million people who use it. But that's another attraction: You don't have to understand what Notes is in order to "get it." Most people, when shown Notes on the screen, have no problem understanding how they can apply it to their own problems of communicating and managing information in a workgroup. Somebody once called Notes *groupware,* and for better or worse it's the name that seems to have stuck, because Notes really does help workgroups to work together.

At its root, Notes is a document database system. That's the first thing that sets it apart from other databases. The unit of commerce inside of Notes is the document. In a traditional database, we think in terms of records; in Notes, the record is in fact a document. In Notes, users typically work with dozens of different databases, which they organize and access through the Notes Desktop (Figure 14.1).

A Notes document is created out of a number of database *fields* arranged together on a *Form.* When all the fields on a Form are filled in, the document

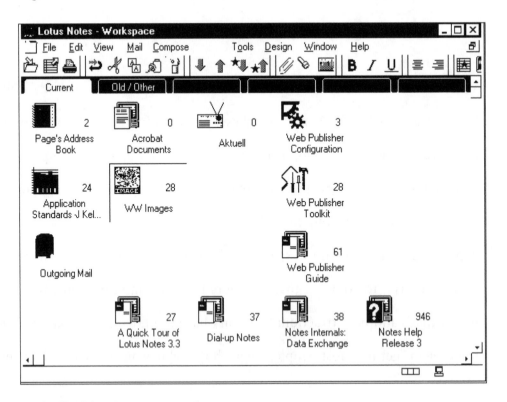

FIGURE 14.1 The Notes Desktop.

is complete and is added to the Notes database (Figure 14.2). Then, to appreciate what's in all those documents, there are *Views* that show the contents of a few fields from many different documents in a column layout that looks something like a spreadsheet. To get a good View, you pick and choose items from the data on various Forms, and write formulas so that it all displays properly (Figure 14.3). There you have the core of what's going on in Notes: Forms and Views.

Notes is very good at some things and very poor at others. For example, it's great as an information organizer, as a repository for data in all kinds of electronic formats, as a secure information delivery environment, and as a structured way to grant or restrict access to information by various methods. In a sense, prior

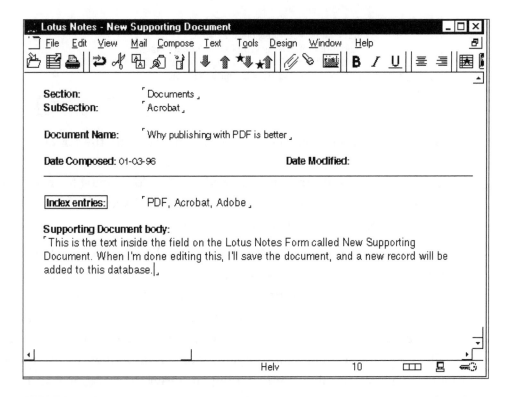

FIGURE 14.2 On a Notes Form, fields are designated by corner brackets. This is a small, simple Form.

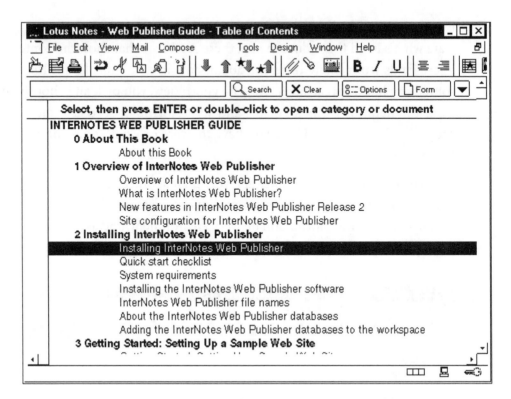

FIGURE 14.3 In a View, each document is a new row on the screen.

to Notes, most PC software was conceived as a tool for helping to create information. Notes marks the first time the organizational issues of information and content have been addressed in business PC software.

If there was ever a piece of software expressly designed for control freaks, Lotus Notes is it. Inside every Notes database, inside each Notes server—indeed, embedded in the very fabric of Notes itself—is the notion of *access control*. What this means is that if you're out of favor with the data czar you can forget about even sneaking a glance at that Notes database. This gives endless pleasure to hierarchical organizations, even though Notes has been touted as a key technology for flattening top-heavy organizational structures.

But while you can argue with Notes' methods, you can't argue with its purpose, which is to provide an environment for the development and distribution of electronic documents. Notes is designed for that—and it does that very well. But it's obviously not been designed as an environment for making documents that look good. In that sense, Notes is really more of a document *database* than it is a *document* database.

Luckily, PDF picks up where Notes leaves off. And Acrobat software tools have nothing to do with communication, access control, and databases. Notes and PDF are therefore perfect partners. In this chapter, we'll look at how, using Notes and PDF together, you can create complete communicating document database applications that deliver fully formatted documents to users on multiple computing platforms. It's the perfect solution for many corporate communications applications. And as we'll see, Notes also presents some intriguing possibilities for publishing PDF over the World Wide Web.

Notes Market Overview

As of early 1996, more than 8,000 companies and 4.5 million people worldwide were using Lotus Notes. Traditionally, Notes has been a "big company" product: Most of Notes' early users were large organizations, whose information-management problems were big enough to justify the development of new applications. It also helped to be a large organization if you were to be able to afford Notes' initial software licensing price: $62,000 for 500 users.

In addition to skewing toward the large organization, Notes' market niche has also favored financial, governmental, and "professional" organizations (consulting firms, law firms, etc.). These kinds of organizations share a rather rigidly defined business structure—or if not rigid, then at least explicitly defined. This is good for Notes, because since common procedures are so well defined, it's easy for programmers to set up parallel processes inside Notes. Gradually, Notes has been moving downmarket, with development tools and user interface design that are more and more appropriate to medium-size and even small organizations, and with pricing to match.

The current version of Notes, release 4, has both client and server modules, like previous versions of Notes. The R4 server software costs only $495 for single-processor machines, and $2,295 for symmetric multiprocessor (SMP) versions for Windows NT. Notes supports an array of operating systems, including OS/2 Warp, Apple Mac OS, UNIX platforms including IBM AIX, Sun Solaris, HP-UX, and SCO OpenServer, and Microsoft Windows and Windows NT. Notes is also available as a NetWare Loadable Module (NLM) for the Novell LAN server environment.

On the client side, there are three different versions of Notes R4 available:

1. Notes Mail license, a new Notes client specifically designed as a messaging client, at $55;

2. Notes Desktop, which is an access module that permits users to use Notes databases but not do any application development, at $69; and

3. The full Lotus Notes client, which permits both database navigation and application development, at $225.

As you can see, Notes pricing has dramatically dropped. But its functionality has also expanded in a remarkable way. Release 4 appears to be much closer to what today's market really wants: The Notes server software for R4 comes with the Internotes Web Publisher software, which automatically turns Notes databases into Web sites (see below), and the Notes clients integrate Web browsing capabilities. Adding this to the other capabilities inherent in Notes R4, you've got a truly formidable information management environment.

One of Notes' strong points has always been how it can be used to collect and distribute information not only within an organization, but also between an organization and its customers and working partners. Notes therefore sits squarely in the middle of a radical shift in our computing habits: the shift from internal corporate computing and networking to intercorporate computing and networking. The Internet is one of the motors of this evolution; Notes is one of the gears in that motor. But rather than get too far into the details of Notes, we'll assume that if you're reading this chapter you already know what you need to about Notes (if you don't, you can find out everything you need to at the Lotus Web site, http://www.lotus.com).

Notes' Support for PDF

Notes and PDF are great partners. As mentioned earlier, Notes is good at what Acrobat and the PDF file format don't or can't provide; and Acrobat and PDF give Notes what it doesn't have—the ability to produce good-looking, highly functional electronic documents.

In order to leverage the best of both worlds, it's necessary to delve into some issues of *information design*—namely, how do you construct your electronic information resource so that it meets its intended purpose? Stated in another way, how do you make Notes databases that will maximize the impact of the PDF files they contain?

AcroNotes Database Design

Unlike traditional Notes database designs, in which Notes documents themselves are the default document format, building a Notes database for delivering PDFs calls very little on Notes' document-editing functions. Rather, we are looking at Notes as the container and PDF files as the content. Therefore, the Notes database will be used primarily to *structure* the PDFs—provide classifications, sortings, and groupings for accessing a number of PDFs of the same type—and to provide *communications* capabilities through which to deliver the PDFs to the target audience, provide feedback from the users, and, if you like, permit the audience to discuss among themselves via email.

In terms of the database structure, Notes can provide a real advantage to publishers with a very large set of documents. By publishing in Notes, you can chop your files up into manageable chunks that are more usable for your audience. Other than the full-text search capabilities that are part of Acrobat

Search, there are no other ways that are native to Acrobat for providing this kind of organization. Notes' database capabilities can therefore be built into an Acrobat document management application.

In terms of communications, Notes can be viewed as an alternative to the Internet. What you're looking for is a way to distribute PDF files efficiently

Here are a few principles that will help to guide your Notes database development:

- PDF publishing applications will generally make use of Broadcast or Reference database types. Broadcast applications are best for applications that are based on a periodical publishing model; Reference databases, as their name implies, will be more useful for publishing PDF archives or other data sets that aren't being continually updated.

- When designing your Forms, many of the traditional Notes database design techniques don't apply. This is because your Forms will not display the contents of the documents themselves, but only classification information that can later be used for constructing Views or full-text indexes.

- PDF files, as we'll see later, will occupy only one field on your Forms. Because Notes is blind to the content of each PDF (unless you're using Notes/FX, see below), you'll have to provide information about each PDF in the appropriate fields on your Form. Therefore, you'll probably want to include a PDF_Title field, and perhaps a field that will contain an abstract of what's inside the PDF.

- Views will work in much the same way as in traditional Notes databases, with the proviso that they'll need to be designed to display in a useful manner the contents of the special fields you've placed on your Forms.

Here are some tips that will help your AcroNotes (Notobat?) database take advantage of the communications capabilities that are built into Notes:

- As publisher, you set the replication schedule with your audience's servers. Of course, you'll want to create a replication schedule that's in line with your publishing frequency. If you're distributing to a professional audience that is scattered all over the country, and are using dial-up connections, set the replication time for each customer in such a way that your own server doesn't get bombarded with replication requests.

- Beyond replication, which will be a part of all PDF/Notes publishing projects, there are a number of optional communications functions. One of these is to create a feedback forum to collect information from your audience. The forum can be private, to give you feedback on how you're doing, to get new product ideas, and so forth, or it can be public, so that users can all view and comment on each others' suggestions. This second idea can be implemented with a simple Notes Discussion Database.

- It would be more fun to create a sophisticated automatic publishing application using Notes, a database publisher application, and either Acrobat PDFWriter or Distiller. First, use Notes to create or collect a bunch of data over the network. Periodically, when it's time to publish, export the Notes data to a standard database-readable format such as WK1 (the Lotus 1-2-3 spreadsheet format), structured text, or tabular text. Next, set up a publishing template in your database publisher application and import the Notes data so that the finished pages look good. Now, publish all your data through the database publisher, print the results to PostScript, and Distill. Now you've got a good-looking PDF file made up entirely of data received through Notes. Bring the PDF back into Notes as *This Week's Report*, and make a Notes macro or two to automate the process. And there you have it: a little automatic PDF/Notes database publishing process. Sit back and let your audience create your publication for you.

to your audience. And if you happen to be a big global banking company where there's Notes on every desktop, Notes is the perfect way to distribute, for example, your company newsletter in PDF format. For the professional publisher, Notes also provides an electronic link onto millions of affluent user desktops.

Once you have your application designed, there's a question of how to bring PDF files into the Notes database. There are three ways of integrating PDF and Notes: as file attachments, as embedded OLE objects, and through Notes Field Exchange (Notes F/X).

PDF Attachments

The easiest method of integrating PDF into Notes—and for publishers the most versatile—is by using the Edit-Insert-File Attachment command. This brings up a dialog box that lets you navigate to your PDF and then select it (Figure 14.4). Note that the field into which you attach a PDF must be a field of type Rich Text.

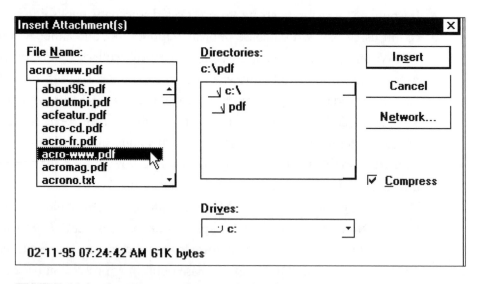

FIGURE 14.4 The File Attachment dialog box.

When you add a new PDF attachment to a Notes Form, Notes will display a PDF icon on the Form, along with the name of the PDF file that's attached (Figure 14.5).

Behind the scenes, Notes makes a copy of the attached file, and stores the file inside the database you're building. So, if you're composing a new document from your own workstation, and you pull a PDF file from your own hard disk, Notes will bring a copy of that file onto the Notes server. Likewise, when you replicate the database to your customers, the attachments will go along for the ride (as long as you have not selected "Truncate long documents and remove attachments" in the Database Information—Replication Settings section). (See Figure 14.6.)

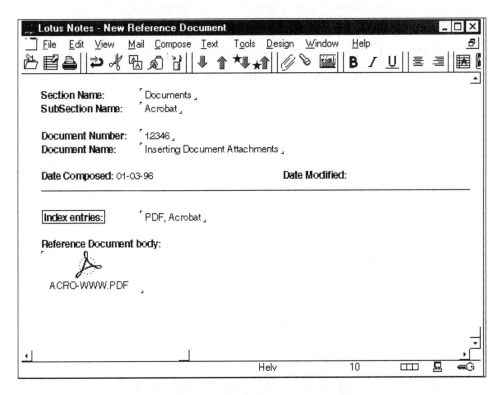

FIGURE 14.5 A PDF document embedded on a Form.

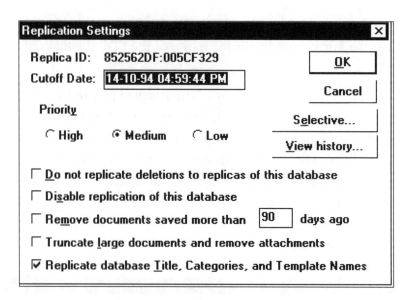

FIGURE 14.6 Be sure the "Truncate long documents" box is not checked in Database Information—Replication Settings.

Once you've attached a PDF, a user will need to double-click on the PDF icon in order to access the attached PDF. This brings up the File Attachment Information dialog box (Figure 14.7). Users may then Detach the PDF file to their local disk (making your Notes application a sort of PDF delivery mechanism), or Launch the file, which activates the local Acrobat viewer application (Reader or Exchange) and opens the file.

You can attach any kind of binary file to your Notes Form, not just PDF files. In fact, it may be a good idea to attach a copy of the Acrobat Reader applications for Macintosh and Windows on one of the Forms, so that new users in your audience can access and download a copy of Acrobat directly from their Notes environment.

Embedding PDF Objects with OLE

The second main method of integrating PDF into Notes is by using linking and embedding technology. The most common of these in the Notes environment

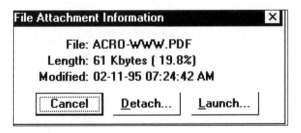

FIGURE 14.7 Users can either detach a PDF attachment to their local disk, or launch their Acrobat viewer application.

is Microsoft's Object Linking and Embedding (OLE) specification, common to Windows, OS/2, and Macintosh systems. But since Notes is a multiplatform environment, it also supports Dynamic Data Exchange (DDE), used only by Windows and OS/2 systems; and Link, Embed, and Launch-to-edit (LEL), OLE's equivalent in the UNIX world.

Linking and embedding are distinct technologies, which makes it rather odd that somebody chose to create a single name for them, as is the case with OLE. Here, however, is the distinction for our purposes:

- *Linking* lets you embed a pointer to a PDF document into your Notes document. The function is identical to the hyperlink in a Web application: "This" document contains a link to "that" document. If "that" document changes, "this" document still has a link to it—the contents of the destination file have simply changed. This makes linking great for structured publishing applications where, for example, you might want to create a link from one document, *This Week's Sales Report*, to another, called *Last Month's Results*. The function is the same; the contents of *This Week* and *Last Month* simply change over time.

- Unlike linking, *embedding* actually takes a copy of the source file and embeds it inside the Notes application. This new "object" becomes separated from the source document: Changes made to the embedded object will not be reflected in the source document. Remember this if you are developing an editorial development process around PDF and Notes: If you want a number of users to be able to access and modify the same PDF document, linking is the solution for you. In terms of information distribution, embedding a PDF file can be useful, as it permits you to embed only part of a PDF document, and to set up so that the Acrobat viewer application is automatically launched when a user opens the Notes document that contains the embedded PDF. This is done in Design-Forms-Form Attibutes-Object Activation (Figure 14.8).

In practice, it will be difficult to use linking for publishing PDF files to an audience that goes beyond the department or small enterprise. The reason is that with a Link, Notes stores the exact network path to the linked object. In order to work properly, all users on the Notes network must have the same network setup, such that they all see, for example, drive T: as the same resource. Since these network drive mappings change as soon as you move network domains, linking remains a technique for local-domain PDF publishing. OLE, on the other hand, can be very useful for building advanced PDF publishing applications.

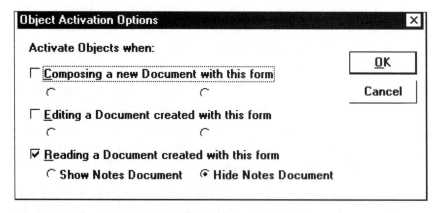

FIGURE 14.8 You can instruct Notes to automatically open PDF files whenever a user opens a form on which a PDF is embedded.

Notes F/X

Another Notes technique for integating PDF is called Notes Field Exchange, or Notes F/X. F/X is a special case of the general class of linking and embedding technologies. In essence, F/X lets you automatically populate the fields in a Notes Form, based on the contents of PDF files that you add to your database. Thus, if you are building PDF files that include fields such as Subject, Author, Title, Date Created, and so forth (see File-Document Info-General in Acrobat), Notes F/X can "see" the entries for those fields and extract that information for the fields in your Notes Form (Figure 14.9).

The process for setting up field exchange is rather cumbersome, but it's worth investing a little time up front when you're creating your PDF database, so that Notes and Acrobat can automatically do the work for you whenever you add a new PDF.

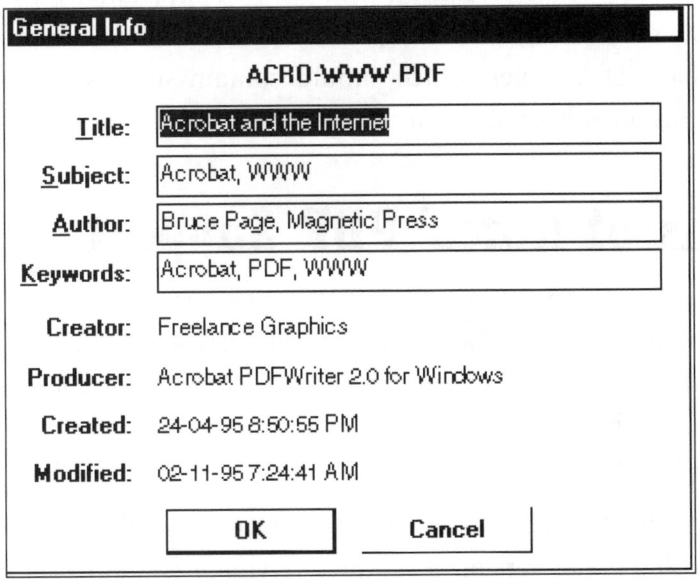

FIGURE 14.9 Information fields in a PDF. Using Notes F/X, you can take the information from these fields and automatically use it to populate Notes Forms.

Here's the process in brief:

1. Identify the fields in your PDFs that you want to use as sorting keys in Notes. Standard fields are Title, Author, Subject, Keywords, and Created and Modified Dates.

2. Create a new Form in your Notes database with a number of fields that have exactly the same names as the fields in your PDFs. Select for each field the data type that is appropriate for the incoming data, for example, Text or Time.

3. Embed PDF files into Notes using Edit-Paste Special-Embed.

4. Notes will extract the field information from the embedded PDF, and store the field values in the appropriate fields on your Notes Form. You may then create Views that slice and dice this information in the most useful way for your audience.

For more details on Notes F/X, consult your Notes manual, the Notes *Application Developer's Reference,* or the Notes on-line Help database. Look also on Adobe's Acrobat CD Sampler, which should contain some sample Notes databases that are already set up to accept PDFs using the F/X technology.

Limitations of Notes' PDF Support

Using Notes as a container and carrier for PDF files has a lot of advantages, as we have seen. But there are also some disadvantages where the PDF-Notes linkage is less than perfect and where therefore the AcroNotes publisher must either reduce his or her expectation for overall functionality, or devise clever and sometimes tedious workarounds.

Here are a few of the limitations we've found in terms of PDF-Notes integration (at least using Notes version 3.3; Notes version 4 is a different animal entirely, which may in fact have addressed some of these issues):

- *Different link syntaxes.* Notes sees the world in terms of Notes Servers, Notes Databases, and Documents Within Notes Databases.

There is a nifty feature in Notes, called Doclink, that permits you to insert a link from any Notes document to any other Notes document (or rather the reverse, as the way you construct a Doclink is to first go to the destination document, then go to Edit-Make Doclink, then return to the source document and go to Edit-Paste). In any case, there is no way to create a Notes Doclink from within a PDF file, which would permit you to make PDF-to-PDF links inside your AcroNotes application. Nor is there a way within Notes to create a link to a PDF document—only to the Notes document containing the PDF, via the Doclink feature.

- *Indexes.* This is a tricky one. Lotus Notes and Acrobat Search have both implemented the same full-text search engine—Verity's Topic engine. So when you create a full-text index of a Notes database, you're creating a Topic index; ditto for Acrobat Search. However, if you try to index an AcroNotes database like the one we've been developing here, you'll index only the contents of the descriptive summary fields—not the contents of the PDFs. If you want to index the PDF file contents too, you've got to extract the text from the PDF, then place the text in another field in your Notes Form, and then index that. If you're going to be doing a lot of this, Software Partners (call (415) 428-0160) makes a nifty plug-in for Acrobat Exchange called Re:mark. One of the things that Re:mark lets you do is to save an entire PDF file as RTF—in fact, it offers you a choice of saving as RTF version 1.0, which Lotus Notes likes, or as RTF version 1.3, which most word processors like. It's a worthy addition to your AcroNotes publishing arsenal.

- *Access.* On the client side, even if you were to go through all the trouble of creating indexes of PDF files using this laborious method, you'll be able to access those indexes only through the Lotus Notes client. If you're within an Acrobat viewer, your Acrobat Search button won't let you attach Lotus Notes indexes—only indexes you've created with Acrobat Catalog.

We hope that some of these incompatibilities are addressed in Notes version 4, because PDF and Notes together are really a hot combination—and V4 could make it even better. Watch the Acropolis web site (http://www.acropolis.com/acropolis) for details.

Web Publishing Using Notes, PDF, and Lotus InterNotes Web Publisher

We mentioned at the top of this chapter that Notes presents some interesting options for Web publishers. Indeed it does, in the form of the InterNotes Web Publisher (IWP) software that, from Notes version 4 on out, is bundled with each copy of the Notes Server software. InterNotes Web Publisher is a conversion tool that converts Notes documents into HTML documents. In fact, you can convert an entire Notes database, or set of databases, into HTML and automatically publish information to the Web. IWP is a very powerful tool indeed.

InterNotes retains the basic Notes architecture of Forms and Views. A Notes document based on a Form will be converted to an HTML document; a Notes View will also be converted to an HTML document with hyperlinks to each of the displayed documents. Further, Notes Doclinks are also converted to HTML links, meaning that once you have a functioning Notes application, you are *very* close to being able to put that same application onto the Web. InterNotes also offers the possibility of creating interactive Web applications, essentially turning any Web-connected user with a forms-compatible browser into a remote Notes client. You can also search Notes full-text indexes over the Web.

Basically, then, Lotus Notes together with InterNotes Web Publisher is like an information publishing kit in a box. You can virtually automatically develop, manage, and publish information to the Web once you've done your database design and set up your Web server. There's only one problem: Notes documents are ugly, even when InterNotes has turned them into HTML. You don't want to publish ugly documents. That's why you've chosen to electronically publish using PDF.

Here again, your choice of PDF positions you to use only the best of what Notes and InterNotes Web Publisher have to offer. Because PDF is a Web-compatible format, there's no need for InterNotes to *convert* your PDFs to HTML or to anything else. All it's got to do is make them available to Web-connected users.

This is exactly what happens when you include PDF files as File Attachments inside your Notes databases. For every attached file, InterNotes will "publish" a link to that file and transfer the attached file to your Web server's directory. Then when users come in over the Web, they'll see your Notes documents as Web pages, and the Acrobat attachments as PDF icons. Click on the icon and download the PDF file. And if the user has Acrobat set up as a helper application, or is using Netscape 2.0/Acrobat Amber, the PDF will automatically display. In essence, InterNotes preserves attachments to a Notes database and makes them attachments to Web pages.

In order to leverage InterNotes most effectively as a PDF Web publishing tool, you'll want to set up an AcroNotes database that makes the most of the brilliant but rather clumsy InterNotes publishing environment. Here are some hints:

- Set up an additional field in your AcroNotes Forms where the document author can put in the file size of the attached PDF. If you're really slick, have Notes automatically compute the value. This is so that Web-attached users will know in advance whether they're downloading a 15-Kilobyte PDF or a 2.5-Megabyte PDF. Of course, if you're publishing linearized PDF that conforms to the Amber spec, and publishing to the Web from a byteserver CGI, and if your users are coming in via Netscape 2/Amber environments, this won't matter. But that's a lot of *ifs.* As a kindness to those who haven't upgraded to the latest in Web access technology, include the PDF file size in a field next to the PDF.

- Be sure you've installed an Acrobat application on your Notes authoring workstations, and on the InterNotes server machine. This will register PDF as an Acrobat file type in the OLE registry, which will permit Notes to find and embed an Acrobat document icon to the file attachments. Otherwise, you'll get a bland "generic-document" icon that will carry along to the Web when InterNotes publishes each document.

- Register application/pdf as a mime-type on your Web server. This will permit it to know that for any document it's serving that has a .pdf file extension, it has to do with an Acrobat file. This is important for certain client/server operations that the Web server negotiates with the Web client software (i.e., Netscape Navigator, Mosaic, etc.).

- Provide links on your Web pages so that users can go and download the appropriate Netscape and/or Amber viewers.

That wraps up our look at distributing PDF files using Lotus Notes. Notes is indeed a capable tool for delivering PDF to internal corporate audiences, to external Notes users, and even to the Web via InterNotes Web Publisher. Expect more and better integration between Notes and Acrobat as Notes version 4—and Acrobat—take greater hold in the marketplace over the coming months and years.

Appendix A

Configuring Your Web Browser to View PDF Files

Most Web browsers are available for free downloading off the browser maker's Web home page. Of course, you need to start out with a browser to get to the site with the browser you want to download. Most computers and online services come bundled with Web browsing software, so once you locate a browser on your system (or copy one from someone else) you can download a different one of your choice. Because Netscape Communications Corporation has worked closely with Adobe in the development of the Acrobat Amber technology, and their Navigator 2.0 was the first browser to support Amber, we have a bias toward using Netscape Navigator. But any browser that is able to launch a helper application can view PDF files, if you show it how. Whichever browser you choose, make sure the Acrobat Reader or Acrobat Exchange is installed on the same local system as the browser software.

The following instructions are based on our own tests configuring Netscape 2.0 to launch Acrobat as an inline viewer, and on instructions printed in Adobe's *Adobe Acrobat on the World Wide Web* guide (1995), which is downloadable off Adobe's Web site in PDF. As upgrades to the various browsers improve their support for Acrobat and integrating helper applications these instructions may become out of date. Check the help files for your browser for the most up-to-date instructions.

Setting Up Netscape Navigator 2.0 to Display PDF Files Inline

Macintosh

1. Download Netscape Navigator 2.0 (or whatever the most recent beta version is) from http://www.netscape.com, and install it on your system.

2. Download the Acrobat Amber Reader for Mac, beta or final release, from Adobe's Web site, and install it on your system.

3. In the Amber Reader, specify Netscape Navigator 2.0 as the browser for the Weblink Plug-in to call up, in Weblink Preferences (under the Edit menu).

4. In the Netscape Navigator 2.0 folder, make sure the PDF Viewer Plug-in is installed in the Netscape Plug-ins folder.

5. When you click on a link to a PDF document in Netscape, the PDF should render within the Netscape browser window. If the PDF document you are downloading has been optimized with Amber Exchange, it will download one page at a time as you

select them. You can use the Acrobat toolbar to navigate the pages of the PDF, or the Netscape toolbar to navigate between Web documents.

Windows

1. Download Netscape Navigator 2.0 (or whatever the most recent beta version is) from http://www.netscape.com, and install it on your system.

2. Download the Acrobat Amber Reader for your version of Windows, beta or final release, from Adobe's Web site, and install it on your system.

3. In the Amber Reader, specify Netscape Navigator 2.0 as the browser for the Weblink Plug-in to call up, in Weblink Preferences (under the Edit menu).

4. When the Amber Reader installs, it should automatically locate the Netscape PDF Viewer in the Netscape Plug-ins directory. If the Amber installer cannot locate the Netscape Plug-ins directory, you will get the installer message, "Warning! Setup couldn't install Netscape Plug-in (NPPDF32.DLL). Failed to locate Netscape Plug-ins directory." In this event, find the Netscape Plug-in NPPDF32.DLL in the [drive]:\Acroweb directory. Then copy \Acroweb\NPPDF32.DLL to \Netscape\Program\Plug-ins.

5. Once Amber locates the Netscape Plug-in for PDF viewing, you should be able to view PDF documents inside the Netscape browser window. If the PDF file you downloaded has been optimized with Amber Exchange, Netscape will display the pages one at a time as you request them. You can use the Acrobat toolbar inside the Netscape window to navigate the PDF, and the Netscape browser toolbar to navigate between Web documents.

Setting Up Mosaic for Macintosh to Recognize PDF Files

1. Download Mosaic from the Spyglass site, at http://www. spyglass.com, and install it.

2. In Mosaic, select Preferences under the Options menu.

3. Click the Apps icon, then click Helper Applications. The Helper Configuration dialog box appears.

4. Check the left-hand scroll box to see if .PDF is one of the file-extension-to-file-types listed. If not, click Add Document Type under the right-hand scroll box.

5. Type "application/pdf" in the New Document Type dialog box, then click OK.

6. You should see application/pdf added as a file type added to the right scroll box in the Helper Configuration box. Select it from the list, and click the Set Application button.

7. You will be prompted to locate and select the Acrobat Exchange or Reader on your system.

8. The Pick a File Type dialog box will appear. Choose the PDF document icon. Select the Launch Automatically option, and click OK.

9. Back in the Helper Configuration dialog box, click the Add Extension button under the left-hand scroll box. Type ".PDF" in Extension box, and choose application/pdf from the MIME Type pull-down menu.

10. To put the changes into effect, quit out of Mosaic and start it up again.

Setting Up Mosaic for Windows (Win Mosaic) to Recognize PDF Files

1. Download Mosaic for Windows from the Spyglass site at http://www.spyglass.com.

2. Using a text editor like the Notepad, open the mosaic.ini file.

3. In the [Viewers] section, add TYPE#: "application/pdf" application/pdf="c:\acroread\acroread.exe %Is" or whatever the correct path and file name are for your version of Acrobat on your system.

4. In the [Suffixes] section, add application/pdf=.pdf.

5. Save the mosaic.ini file, and then restart Mosaic.

Setting Up WinWeb to Recognize PDF Files

1. Open the winweb.ini file using a text editor like the Notepad.

2. Add the following lines to the [Launch] section: ENTRY# =application/pdf,winvoke wingo.inv c:\acroread\acroread.exe %ls" (replace acroread\acroread.exe with acroexch\acroexch.exe if you want the browser to launch Exchange).

3. In the [Extensions] section, add ENTRY# =.pdf,application/pdf,binary.

4. Save the winweb.ini file and restart WinWeb.

Setting Up MacWeb to Recognize PDF Files

1. In MacWeb, select Helpers under the Edit menu. Click New.

2. In the MIME Type text field, type "application/pdf."

3. Deselect the Don't Launch button, and click Select Application.

4. You will be prompted to locate the Acrobat Reader or Exchange on your system. Click Open when you locate the one you want to be launched by the browser.

5. In the Choose a File Type dialog box, find PDF and select it. Click OK.

6. Select Suffixes under the Edit menu. Click New.

7. In the Suffix text box, type "pdf." Choose application/pdf from the MIME Type pull-down menu. Click OK.

8. Quit and restart MacWeb.

Setting Up X Mosaic to Recognize PDF Files

1. Open the .mailcap file and add application/pdf; acroread %s if you want the browser to launch Acrobat Reader, or application/pdf; acroexch %s if you want to launch Acrobat Exchange.

2. Save the .mailcap file and restart X Mosaic.

Setting Up Quarterdeck Mosaic to Recognize PDF Files

1. Start Quarterdeck Mosaic, and select Preferences from the Tools menu.

2. Click the Data Engine tab, then click New.

3. In the MIME Type/SybType text field, type "application/pdf."

4. Type "pdf" in the file name Extensions text field.

5. Type "Acrobat PDF file" in the Comment text box.

6. Click the External Viewer Application option, and click Browse.

7. Find and select the Acrobat Reader or Acrobat Exchange, and click OK.

8. Click OK in the Create New MIME Type dialog box, and click OK at the bottom of the Preferences [Data Engine] dialog box.

9. Restart Quarterdeck Mosaic.

Setting Up Spry AIR Mosaic to Recognize PDF Files

1. Open AIR Mosaic, and choose Configuration under the Options menu.

2. Click Viewers, and click Add New Type in the External Viewers Configuration box.

3. Type "application/pdf" in the New Document Type dialog box, and click OK.

4. Type ".pdf" in the Extensions text box, and click Browse.

5. Find and select Acrobat Reader or Exchange, and click OK.

6. Click Close in the External Viewers Configuration dialog box, and click OK in the Configuration dialog box.

7. Restart AIR Mosaic.

Navigating PDF Documents with Reader and Exchange

Navigating PDF documents is virtually the same whether you are using the Reader or Exchange, except you can't add navigational features of your own using the Reader. In Exchange, you can enhance the navigational functionality of someone else's document by adding Bookmarks and links.

Using the Toolbar Buttons

The following toolbar functions are duplicated in the View and Tools menus, with keyboard shortcuts listed next to the choices. Starting from the left, and skipping nonnavigational tools, this is what the navigational buttons in the toolbar do:

1. *Full page view.* Click here when you want to see just the page, without Bookmarks or thumbnails.

2. *Bookmark view.* Click here to view the Bookmark window. To extend the width of the Bookmark window, place your pointer over the right border of the window and drag it as far to the right as you want.

3. *Thumbnail view.* Click here to see the thumbnail window. To extend the width of the window and view thumbnails in horizontal rows, drag the right border of the window to the right.

4. *Hand tool.* Click here when you want to browse a document, and to change back to browse mode after you have selected the text selection tool or another special-purpose tool.

5. *Magnifying glass: maximize.* Click here to blow up a certain portion of a page. You can either use it to draw a box around the area you want magnified, or just click on a spot on the page. Clicking with it once will magnify to 200 percent and clicking again will double the magnification until you hit the maximum 800 percent.

6. *Magnifying glass: minimize.* Click this tool to decrease the magnification of a page from 100 percent, or from a greater magnification that you set with the "plus" magnifying tool. It minimizes in increments of 200 percent.

7. *Text selection tool.* Click here to select text from the document and copy it to the clipboard (using the Copy command under the Edit menu). The text selection tool is not able to select individual columns, but will select all the text in a horizontal range.

8. *Back to Beginning Arrow.* This tool, symbolized by an arrow pointing left and a vertical line, will jump to the first page of the document when you click on it.

9. *Back One Page Arrow.* Click on this arrow pointing left to go back one consecutive page in the document.

10. *Forward One Page Arrow.* Click on this arrow pointing right to go forward one consecutive page in the document.

11. *Forward to End Arrow.* Click here to jump to the last page of the document.

12. *Back to Previous View Arrow.* These double arrows pointing left will jump to the previous page you were looking at when clicked on.

13. *Next Link Forward Arrow.* After you've clicked on the backward double arrows, click on the forward arrows to go back where you were.

14. *Actual Page Size.* Click here to view the current page at 100 percent.

15. *Fit Page Size.* Click here to view the entire page on the screen.

16. *Fit Width Size.* Click here to view the width of the whole page.

There are some additional navigational functions along the bottom bar of the Acrobat screen.

17. *Page number.* Double-click where it says "1 of 20" or whichever page you are on, and the Go to Page window will pop up. There you can enter a page number to jump to. You can also use the scroll bar on the right side of the screen to go to a specific page. Just drag the box up and down, and a little window will tell you what page you are going to.

18. *Magnification.* Where the magnification percentage is displayed, click once and hold the mouse down while the magnification pull-up menu appears. Scroll to the desired magnification, and release the mouse button. To enter in a specific percentage number, choose "Other."

To Follow Links

You can tell your pointer is over a link because the regular hand tool changes to a pointing finger hand. To follow a link, just click once with the pointing hand. To follow a Weblink, click once when the hand turns to a pointing hand with the letter W on it. Acrobat will launch your browser and connection software, and attempt to take you to the destination site.

To Follow Articles

If you are browsing a multicolumn document, you can tell if it has been threaded by the author if the hand tool changes to a hand with an arrow on it. To follow an article that has been threaded, click once, and the article will be magnified to a readable view. When you are finished reading the selection, click again at the bottom of the screen, and you will automatically be taken to the next portion of the article. When you come to the end of an article, clicking with the hand will bring you back to the beginning of the article.

To View a Document in Full-Screen Mode

To view a document without any of the Acrobat screen showing, select Full Screen from the View menu. Navigate the document by using the forward and back arrow keys on your keyboard, or by clicking on links within the document. To exit Full-Screen mode, press the Escape key.

Appendix C

Searching in Reader and Exchange

Although navigating PDF documents is basically the same in Reader and Exchange, searching is very different between the two products. Searching in the Reader is limited to the slow Find tool (unless a CD-ROM has been loaded with Search for CD-ROMs), while Exchange is equipped with the full-text Verity search engine to search on indexes created with Acrobat Catalog.

Searching with the Find Tool in Reader

1. Select the Find tool in the toolbar, represented by a pair of binoculars (or select Find under the Tools menu, or hit Control/Command-F).

2. In the Find box, enter in the word or words you want to locate in the document.

3. Check Match Whole Word Only if you do not want to search on word stems of the words you entered.

4. Check Match Case if you want your search to be sensitive to upper- or lowercase you entered.

5. Check Find Backwards if you want to search on the portion of the document behind the current page you are on.

6. Click OK. The Find tool will page through the document and highlight words that match your query. Choose Find Again under the Tools menu if you want to continue searching under the same query.

Searching with Search in Exchange

The Search tool will work only if the document you are viewing has been indexed by the publisher with Acrobat Catalog. If there is no index available for the document, you must use the Find tool to search through the document.

1. Select the Search tool in the toolbar, represented by a pair of binoculars with a page behind it (or select Search under the Tools menu).

2. In the Search window, enter in text that you want to search on.

3. In the Options area, check boxes that apply to your query. Check word stemming if you want to search on parts of the words you entered. Check Sounds Like if you want to do a phonetic search

on the text you entered (if you are not sure of the spelling, for example). Check Thesaurus if you want to search on words that have similar meanings to the words you entered. Check Match Case if you want your search to be case-sensitive. Check Proximity if you entered an AND Boolean term in your search, so that the search will find the two words if they are within 100 words of each other in the document.

4. At the bottom of the Search window, the name of the index about to be searched is displayed. If this is not the right index for the document, click on the Index button to select another one. In the Index Selection box, click Add. You will be asked to locate a .PDX index file on your system. Once you find it, click OK, and click Info in the Index Selection box to find out which kinds of searches are allowed with the index. If you cannot locate a .PDX file for your document, it either doesn't exist or was not successfully loaded with the PDF file. Click OK in the Index Selection box.

5. Click Search in the Search box. The search engine will quickly call up the first page on which one of your search terms appears. To go to the next hit, click the icon in the toolbar that has a forward arrow and a page, two to the right of the Search button.

6. To perform a different search, click the Search tool and press Clear to clear the last query.

For information on customizing your search techniques and results, refer to the Acrobat Exchange online Help guide.

Appendix D

Installing Plug-ins in Acrobat Exchange

Plug-ins like Weblink and Movie will be automatically installed with your copy of Acrobat Exchange, residing in a Plug-in folder or directory in the Exchange root folder or directory. To add a new Plug-in that you have purchased from a third-party vendor or downloaded from Adobe's site, just drag the Plug-ins file into the Plug-ins folder. Acrobat Exchange will launch the Plug-in the next time it starts up. To remove a Plug-in, drag it out of the Plug-ins folder.

To get information about the Plug-ins loaded with your copy of Exchange, go to the Help menu, About Plug-ins in Windows, or About Plug-ins under the Apple menu on a Macintosh.

Some Plug-ins will add a new tool to the toolbar, and clicking on it will launch that Plug-in's tool. Also, check the Preferences menu under Edit for options regarding individual Plug-ins.

Appendix E

Web Site URLs for Companies and Products Mentioned in This Book

Acropolis WWW Site and Magazine
http://www.acropolis.com/acropolis

Adobe Systems Inc.
http://www.adobe.com

Apple Computers, Inc.
http://www.apple.com

Architext Software Inc.
http://www.architext.com

Cascade Systems
http://www.cascadenet.com

Cathedral of St. John the Divine
http://plaza.interport.net/cathedral

CERN
http://www.cern.ch/

Citibank
http://www.citibank.com

CMP Publications, Inc.
http://techweb.cmp.com/techweb

Copyright FAQ
http://www.cis.ohio-state.edu/hypertext/faq/usenet/
Copyright-FAQ/top.html

Dial-A-Book Online Bookstore
http://www.psi.com/DownloadBookstore/index.html

Dynamic PDF
http://www.best.com/~dglazer/adobe/

Emerge, Inc. and the PDF Zone
http://www.emrg.com

"Fair Use in the Electronic Age: Serving the Public Interest"
http://arl.cni.org/scomm/copyright/users.html

First Virtual Holdings, Inc.
http://www.fv.com

Fortune Magazine's Fortune 500
http://www.pathfinder.com/

France Telecom
http://www.francetelecom.com

HoTMetaL from SoftQuad
http://www.sq.com

Htmlchek
http://uts.cc.utexas.edu/churchh/htmlchek.html

InContext's Spider
http://www.incontext.com

"Intellectual Property and the National Information Infrastructure"
http://www.uspto.gov/niiip.html

J.P. Morgan
http://www.jpmorgan.com

Lotus InterNotes Web Publisher
http://www.lotus.com/inotes/

Magnetic Press, Inc.
http://www.acropolis.com/acropolis/mpihome.html

McGraw-Hill
http://www.mcgraw-hill.com

Moët
http://www.moet.com

Morbidity and Mortality Weekly Report
http://www.cdc.gov/epo/mmwr/mmwr.html

NCSA
http://www.ncsa.uiuc.edu

Netscape Communications Corp.
http://www.netscape.com

New York TimesFax
http://www.nytimesfax.com

Online HTML Validation Service
http://www.halsoft.com/html-val-svc

Open Market, Inc.
http://www.openmarket.com

PBS Online
http://www.pbs.org

PCWorld Online
http://www.pcworld.com/currentissue/toc.html

Quarterdeck
http://www.qdeck.com

Software Partners, Inc.
http://www.buckaroo.com

Spyglass, Inc.
http://www.spyglass.com

Stephen Nigel Joshua Parkins' C.V.
http://www.pow.com/culinarycreativity/face.html

Tandem Computers
http://www.tandem.com/

Tangent Design
http://www.tangentdesign.com

Time Magazine
http://www.pathfinder.com/time

Verity, Inc.
http://www.verity.com

Vertec Solutions, Inc.
http://www.vertec.com

Weblint
http://www.khoros.umn.edu/staff/ncilb/weblint.html

WebSite Server
http://www.ora.com/gnn/bus/ora/news/c.website.html

WebSTAR Server
http://www.biap.com

Wharton School of the University of Pennsylvania
http://www.upenn.wharton.edu

W3 Organization
http://www.w3.org

XMAN
http://www.xman.com

Yahoo! Internet Directory
http://www.yahoo.com

Zeon Corporation
http://www.zeon.com.tw

Appendix F

About the Software

Introduction to the PDF Version on CD-ROM

Welcome to the *Web Publishing with Adobe Acrobat and PDF* CD-ROM. This CD-ROM is intended as a digital companion to your paper copy, which you can use to perform full-text searches, to navigate quickly with hyperlinks, and visit the Web sites mentioned with a click of the mouse. Whether you use the CD while you read the book or as a reference later on, we think it will convince you that PDF often performs better than paper.

The CD-ROM reproduces, in PDF, the exact desktop publishing files that were used to produce the print version of the book.* We have enhanced those files to enrich your experience of the book, replacing the black and white screen shots with full color shots. We used Acrobat Exchange 2.1 to create a fully-featured PDF version of the book's contents. This includes Bookmark links for jumping from chapter to chapter, artide threads for browsing the text at the right magnification for your screen, and inter-document links for jumping from the Table of Contents to the corresponding sections in the book. We have also taken advantage of the Acrobat Weblink feature: Click on any Web address (URL) mentioned in the text, or on any screen shot of a Web page, and your Web browser software will automatically launch and take you to that site.

To learn how to navigate this CD-ROM using those tools, refer to Appendix B, "Navigating PDF Documents with Reader and Exchange," or refer to the Help file in your version of Acrobat Reader or Exchange. For help using the Acrobat Search tool, refer to Appendix C, "Searching in Reader and Exchange."

Software Included on the CD-ROM

This CD-ROM will install Acrobat Reader with Search 2.1 on your hard drive. unless our installation program detects that you have a recent version of Acrobat that can display the PDF files. It will also install a set of license-free Adobe Acrobat Plug-ins that you can install and use with your version of Acrobat Exchange (most of them will not work with the Acrobat Reader).

The free Plug-ins on this disc will increase your authoring power in Acrobat Exchange. The installers for them, and the "readme" files that explain what they do, are located in the Plug-ins directory on your CD-ROM. To activate them, go into the right directory for your platform, Mac or Windows, and drag them into the Plug-ins folder in your Acrobat Exchange folder. Be sure to read the text files that accompany each Plug-in for important information on functionality and compatibility issues.

The PDF documents on this disc are encrypted and protected by the Magnetic Press Inc. Keychain TM document security system. Once you have installed the book onto your hard disk, you will be able to open these files in the usual fashion, without having to enter a password. However, should you move the files to another computer, you will not be able to open them without running the installation program on that machine. If the setup.exe program still does not install the proper software, please call Magnetic Press Inc. at (212) 219-2831.

We hope you enjoy using the Web Publishing with Acrobat CD-ROM.

Magnetic Press CD-ROM Production Team: Sanford Bingham, Sam Dushkin, Diana Holm, Barry Kaplan, Art Murphy, and Paul Sussan.

Thank you's: Angela Murphy and Mike Green at Wiley, Andrea Mulligan at Benchmark Productions.

User Assistance and Information

The software accompanying this book is being provided as is without warranty or support of any kind. Should you require basic installation assistance, or if your media is defective, please call our product support number at (212) 850-6194 weekdays between 9 AM and 4 PM Eastern Standard Time. Or, we can be reached via e-mail at: **wprtusw@wiley.com**.

To place additional orders or to request information about other Wiley products, please call (800) 879-4539.

Notes

*Any discrepancies between the PDF version and the print version are due to design changes made after the production of this CD-ROM.

Index

CUSTOMER NOTE